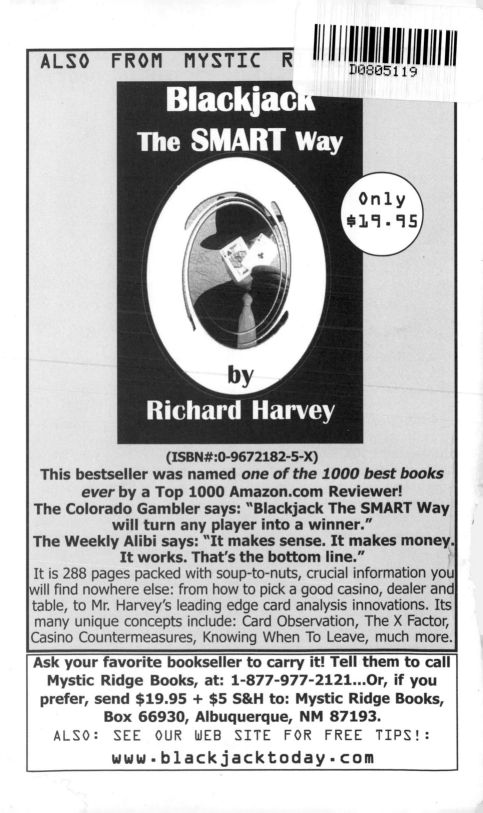

Cutting Edge Blackjack

by

Richard Harvey

MYSTIC RIDGE BOOKS

ALBUQUERQUE, NEW MEXICO

MYSTIC RIDGE BOOKS
P.O. BOX 66930
ALBUQUERQUE, NM 87193-6930
(505) 899-2121
Find us on the World Wide Web at:
http://www.blackjacktoday.com
MYSTIC RIDGE BOOKS is a division of Mystic Ridge Productions, Inc.

First Edition Printed March 2002. Second Printing July 2002.
Second Edition Printed July 2003.

Library of Congress Catalog Card No. PENDING

ISBN: 0-9672182-7-6

PRINTED AND BOUND IN THE UNITED STATES OF AMERICA.

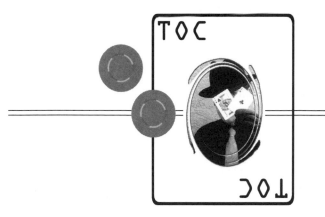

Contents

Table of Contents   e

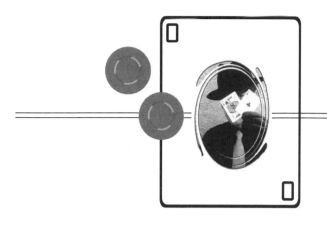

Author's Note: What Makes This Book Different

J anuary 1, 2001 went by without so much as a whimper. Although it was a very historic day, it did not become the huge media event the same date a year before did. However, it was the REAL start of the New Millennium.

So, the question arises: why didn't the world celebrate it with huge New Millennium parties? *Because the world was fooled into thinking that the New Millennium had begun the year before!* It was a case of mass delusion.

Why do I mention this? Because there are similar widely held misunderstandings in the blackjack world that are deluding many players into adopting strategies that don't work well. Yet, these myths crumble to dust under closer scrutiny, just like the New Millennium misconception above.

Part of the reason for the longevity of these myths is the blackjack world's tendency to cling to what is old and familiar. Think about it: isn't it sobering when you realize that *the great majority of books written about blackjack since 1961 were based upon just ONE researcher's study, now well more than 30 years old?*

Challenging Some Assumptions of the Past

I need to start by addressing blackjack's biggest myth, because, to appreciate how much on the cutting edge *Cutting Edge Blackjack* is, you have to understand why this is wrong. Blackjack's biggest myth is:

The good computer studies of the 1960s and early 70s were the equivalent of the Ten Commandments -- handed down from On High, perfect in every way, never to be questioned. They were infallible and complete, and could not be improved upon.

This is patently wrongheaded and naive. But, to some, it's *heresy* to suggest that there's anything new to be discovered.

I anticipate some resistance to what I am about to tell you: those excellent studies of the past -- though they were on the cutting edge for their time -- contained some flawed basic assumptions.

Let's Not Shut Out New Ideas

This reminds me of the story (unbelievable, but true) of the man who ran the United States Patent Office at the turn of the 20th Century, who actually *shut down the Office because he believed that everything that could possibly be invented had already been invented!*

While today we view this as close-mindedness, a similar mindset has existed among blackjack experts for decades. Yet, in other fields of research, such as mathematics and science, new ideas are welcomed with open arms.

My Research Began With A New Premise

The point is, in Chapter 1, I will need to address the defects of the past -- they must be identified and corrected in order to get beyond them. This is, after all, how progress is made. Once that is done, I will present what I consider to be a more modern and effective approach to blackjack. That is my goal.

Now, how did I go about correcting the mistakes of the past? This bears an explanation.

When I was planning my most recent computer studies, I asked myself: "What can I do that might move blackjack thinking *forward*, and provide some *new* insights into how to approach the game and win more consistently?" After all, why would I want to write yet another blackjack book, in such a glutted market, if I had nothing *new* to say?

The answer came to me. *Prior computer studies were based entirely on computer-generated information!* The men behind the early computer studies were not active, expert blackjack players. **They didn't realize the importance of shuffling cards and then dealing those cards as casino dealers do, in conducting their research!** Because of this oversight -- as you will see in Chapter 1 -- *some of their conclusions were off the mark.*

So, in order to produce the most accurate results possible, I designed *my* computer research with a major twist: *it would start with the actual shuffling of cards (with exacting, real-world casino shuffling techniques) and the casino-style dealing of hands and collection of spent cards. Only then would I let the computer take over and analyze the results. The final data would then reflect real-world casino realities.*

The results have been both startling and powerful.

What Is A Cutting Edge Approach?

What do I mean by a *cutting edge* approach to blackjack? And how will we move beyond the misconceptions of the past, to come up with a better way of playing the game?

Having come from a Bridge background many years ago, I always felt that the designers of blackjack's first modern strategy avoided the obvious. What you should do in any complex card game is to look at the cards that have been dealt (factoring in everything that had been played in prior rounds since the last shuffle), analyze those cards, and make an intelligent move based upon what your analysis tells you about the probability of what cards will be dealt next. This is the most accurate way of going about things.

So, this, indeed, will be a governing principle behind all of the many new insights and methods that you will read about here. This approach will give you the ability to react to the card realities *of the moment*. You will learn to read the cards, discern what they are telling you, and make precise moves that will greatly increase your win rate.

Let's Talk About The Benefits To YOU

Cutting Edge Blackjack is a treasure trove of leading edge information that will force you to rethink everything. Its benefits to you are many.

To start with, it will give you a complete understanding of *card behavior*. I will explain how the cards (which are really just numbers) tend to combine with each other, and what this tells you about each hand you're dealt, as well as the dealer's prospects of winning or losing.

You will learn about the predictabilities and probabilities that will greatly improve your game and *give you a much greater edge on the house*. You will be among the first to find out about my latest discoveries, such as repeating card phenomena and the Low Up Card Stiffs Effect -- discoveries that you can take to the bank. Your win rate will vastly improve as you absorb the many innovations that have come from my research -- the Strategic Card Analysis method, Real-time Card Strategy, and The Circle of 13. Your betting will become more accurate with your use of two new concepts: Win/Loss Margin Units and Player Progress Patterns.

In addition, I will show you how shuffling affects your game, and how to follow the cards you want to follow, from one shuffle to the next; how the placing of the cut card affects the cards you will receive; how the number of players at the table affects not only your game, but your chances of winning; and how to respond to changes in the number of betting spots being played.

Another benefit of *Cutting Edge Blackjack* is that it will give you scientific new safeguards to protect your bankroll, on the occasional losing day (as I warned you in *Blackjack The SMART Way*, you cannot and will not win every time -- no one can or should promise you that). My newest methods and discoveries will alert you promptly, and get you out of the casino with very minimal losses, when the cards are bad. So, you should never leave a big loser ever again.

And there's much, much more.

Other Commonly Held Assumptions Questioned

There are other commonly believed assumptions I am going to dispel in *Cutting Edge Blackjack*. Here are some of them:

❶ *That there's one, perfect Basic Strategy that is all a player needs to become a big winner and a great player.* This assumption is responsible for many players becoming consistent losers.

❷ *That card counting is the only way to approach the game and win big.* This assumption is tightly held by some diehards who, when questioned, will admit (if they've done the math) that card counting doesn't give players a huge extra advantage. In fact, *one well-respected book is on record as saying that if the player paid attention to every card played, the player would have twice the advantage a card counter would.* That's kind of the idea, with my invention, Strategic Card Analysis, which rides the wave of the future.

❸ *That a player can never figure out what the dealer's hole card is.* I proved this was possible in my previous book, *Blackjack The SMART Way.* In this book, you'll be given many more tools, to make your hole card prediction skills that much more accurate.

❹ *A related myth is that you should always assume the hole card to be a 10.* You'll see how *wrong* this is!

❺ *That a player can never figure out what the face-down cards are in 1- and 2-deck games, so why bother?* With my breakthrough innovations, presented in two chapters, "How To Count Cards At 1- & 2-Deck Tables" and "How To Do Advanced Card Analysis At 1- & 2-Deck Tables," you will find that you CAN determine, with regularity, what those face-down cards are -- and play a much better game. Indeed, these chapters represent historic firsts, as far as I know. I am not aware of anyone else who has solved this riddle, with any degree of accuracy.

Questions This Book Will Answer For You

Actually, this book has so much to offer, it would be hard to express the depth of its offerings here. Now, for the first time, for instance, you will get answers to some of the questions that have puzzled you for years, such as:

❶ *Why does it seem sometimes as if I cannot win?*

❷ *Do the number of decks in the game affect my ability to win?*

❸ *Does the number of players at the table affect my game?*

❹ *Do fluctuations in the number of betting spots being played hurt me?*

❺ *Should I play the dealer head-on for the best results?*

❻ *Should I ever play more than one betting spot?*

❼ *Should I play at 1-deck tables, if I only get one round between shuffles?*

❽ *How often should the dealer bust? Get Blackjacks? Score 20s and 21s? Beat me?*

❾ *How do I know whether or not I should hit my stiffs of 14, 15 and 16?*

❿ *Where should I put the cut card? Can I really follow the progress of the cards through the shuffle?*

And that's just a small portion of the questions this book will answer for you.

A Word of Advice

You will find it easier to get up to speed if you've already read my first book *Blackjack The SMART Way*. It gives you a foundation for my unique approach to the game. *Cutting Edge Blackjack* goes beyond the concepts I introduced in *Blackjack The SMART Way*, and is not aimed at beginners. While *Blackjack The SMART Way* was written in a way that players at all levels could understand, *Cutting Edge Blackjack* starts at a higher level.

Cutting Edge Blackjack is for players who crave the latest blackjack knowledge and methods, and are eager and willing to do a bit of studying and practicing to become a better player, and bigger winner. If you are one of those players who loves the game and who seeks answers to the game's mysteries, you will find this book very valuable.

A Word About Multi-Deck Games

By the way, there's one issue regarding blackjack games of more than 2 decks I need to address here. While you will see in convincing detail why 1- and 2-deck games offer you a much greater chance of winning, and the opportunity for a higher win rate, this does not mean that people who play in casinos that offer only 6- and 8-deck games cannot benefit greatly from this book.

No book is going to make those 6- and 8-deck games more winnable than they are by design. If you play those games, you are accepting handicaps. Just as a surgeon cannot do as good a job in a wartime M.A.S.H. unit as he'd be able to do in a peacetime hospital situation, a blackjack player cannot do as well against multi-deck games as against the 1- and 2-deck pitch games (and I will make the reasons clear, with a wealth of mathematical information).

That being said, let me point out that *the same principles that govern pitch games govern their larger cousins, too.* Yet, the fact that I'm being honest about your lesser chances against the 6- and 8-deck games apparently confuses some people. So I want to make this crystal clear: *this book will make you a much smarter blackjack player, no matter what blackjack variant you play!*

Actually, as some of you already know, I began my blackjack career in Atlantic City, where 6-deck tables are the norm, and I did very, very well there. So, I know firsthand what it takes to win against the multi-deck games; that knowledge is included in this book.

Not only that -- *at my seminars in New York and elsewhere on the East Coast, I do multi-deck as well as pitch game demonstrations, and players who have taken those seminars have seen that my system is very effective in all situations.*

In fact, you will especially find this book helpful if you play the 6- and 8-deck games, because you will learn in vivid detail the mathematical challenges you're up against -- and you will not find much of this information in any other book.

I Put My Money On The Line

Another thing that makes *Cutting Edge Blackjack* different is the fact that I am not just a researcher and theoretician -- I am also an active blackjack player, who puts his money where his mouth is. I use the methods I describe in this book, and with great success.

More important -- my system has also brought great success to the many thousands who have read my books and taken my seminars. I know it's worked very well for others because a significant number of readers and seminar-goers have told me so -- in person, in letters, in calls to the publisher, and in email messages. (You can read a small portion of their feedback on the Mystic Ridge Books web site at **www.blackjacktoday.com.** Be sure to surf that site regularly, by the way, for free monthly blackjack tips!)

Regarding The Examples In This Book

Just as many authors and strategy chart designers before me have done, I've decided that it would be wisest to limit the examples in this book mostly to data that came from research on one specific blackjack variant, and, in this book, that will be the 1-deck game. This makes things easiest in terms of graphic card demonstrations; it also makes things clearer. Multi-deck game examples would have required more space to present, and would have muddied the waters. Cards would have had to have been identified as to which decks they had come from, in explaining repeating phenomenon, for example. Moreover, everything stems from the card relationships found in the 1-deck game, anyway.

So, understand that the results you will read about pertain to *all* blackjack games (plus, I will relate my results to *all* of blackjack's various legitimate variants). To have presented the results of hundreds and hundreds of charts on every game variant would have turned this book into a cumbersome multi-volume encyclopedia. And to what end? *The discoveries revealed to you in Cutting Edge Blackjack hold true no matter what game you're playing.*

How The Card Runs Were Conducted

Now, for your information, the casino rules that were followed for the card runs in my computer studies were those that I have always encouraged players to seek out when choosing a casino at which to play:

Dealers stood on all 17s; late surrender was available; splitting was allowed up to three times, except for Aces (only one split was granted); doubling was permitted after splitting; and, there were no restrictions on doubling.

The virtual players followed the Basic Strategy recommendations you'll find at the end of this chapter. No Insurance or Even Money was taken.

Shuffling was done to exacting casino standards, using this method: one riffle was followed by one stripping and two more riffles (see Chapter 5, regarding shuffling practices, if you're not familiar with these terms). The cut card was placed roughly in the middle of the cards, as most players do. One card was burned before dealing after a shuffle. Players were given exactly 60% penetration before the cards were reshuffled, and the cards were replaced with new decks after approximately two hours of action. Different player combinations -- from a solitary player situation, up to seven players maximum --were tested for any possible differences in results.

Three Caveats

Three final things:

First, we're moving forward into the future in *Cutting Edge Blackjack*, and so, for space and other reasons, I will not be repeating any of the material I presented in *Blackjack The SMART Way*.

Second: please don't use the techniques in this book unless you are certain you are playing at an honest casino, against an honest dealer. (If you don't know how to determine that, Chapter 11 of Blackjack The SMART Way, on Casino Countermeasures & Dirty Tricks, contains a wealth of information.)

This should go without saying -- no matter what system you use -- but I want to make this clear now, because I will not be talking about this issue in *Cutting Edge Blackjack,* which is purely a book about advanced playing techniques. Your choice of casinos is crucial to your success. Since much of the large scale proliferation of casinos in recent years has occurred in areas without governmental oversight or regulation, today's blackjack players especially need to be on guard for any practices that might make winning difficult, if not impossible.

Third, as you might have surmised, this is *not* a card-counting-driven system. This goes *beyond* that old approach. For those who can handle the extra work load, you will find see areas where card counting might still come in handy, as an auxiliary tool (my All-Inclusive Counting System, first introduced in *Blackjack The SMART Way*, will be especially useful in uncovering the identity of the face-down cards at 1- and 2-deck games, as you will see in Chapter 10). But by no means is card counting the be-all and end-all of this system, which should especially please those who have found card counting to be of marginal help to them, or have found it too difficult.

Cutting Edge Blackjack represents the wave of the *future*, which should produce even greater rewards for you than the methods of the past.

OK. Let's get going!

I thank you for choosing *Cutting Edge Blackjack*. I think you will find this book an exciting journey of many discoveries and rewards!

Basic Strategy
Used For Card Runs
HARD HANDS

	2	3	4	5	6	7	8	9	10	A
4-8	H	H	H	H	H	H	H	H	H	H
9	H	D	D	D	D	D	H	H	H	H
10	D	D	D	D	D	D	D	H	H	H
11	D	D	D	D	D	D	D	D	H	H
12	H	H	S	S	S	H	H	H	H	H
13	S	S	S	S	S	H	H	H	H	H
14	S	S	S	S	S	H	H	H	H	Sur/H*
15	S	S	S	S	S	H	H	H	Sur/H*	Sur/H*
16	S	S	S	S	S	H	H	Sur/H*	Sur/H*	Sur/H*
17+	S	S	S	S	S	S	S	S	S	S
BJ	S	S	S	S	S	S	S	S	S	S

Basic Strategy
Used For Card Runs

HARD HANDS:
AFTER TAKING A HIT CARD

	2	3	4	5	6	7	8	9	10	A
4-8	H	H	H	H	H	H	H	H	H	H
9	H	H	H	H	H	H	H	H	H	H
10	H	H	H	H	H	H	H	H	H	H
11	H	H	H	H	H	H	H	H	H	H
12	H	H	S	S	S	H	H	H	H	H
13	S	S	S	S	S	H	H	H	H	H
14	S	S	S	S	S	H	H	H	H	H
15	S	S	S	S	S	H	H	H	H	H
16	S	S	S	S	S	H	H	H	H	H
17+	S	S	S	S	S	S	S	S	S	S

Basic Strategy
Used For Card Runs

SOFT HANDS

	2	3	4	5	6	7	8	9	10	A
Ace-2 to Ace-5	H	H	D	D	D	H	H	H	H	H
Ace-6	H	D	D	D	D	H	H	H	H	H
Ace-7	S	D	D	D	D	S	S	H	H	S
Ace-8	S	S	S	S	S	S	S	S	S	S
Ace-9	S	S	S	S	S	S	S	S	S	S
BJ	S	S	S	S	S	S	S	S	S	S
Ace-Ace	Sp	Sp	Sp	Sp	Sp	Sp	Sp	Sp	Sp	Sp

Basic Strategy
Used For Card Runs

LIKE PAIRS/SPLITTING

	2	3	4	5	6	7	8	9	10	A
2-2	Sp	Sp	Sp	Sp	Sp	Sp	H	H	H	H
3-3	H	Sp	Sp	Sp	Sp	Sp	H	H	H	H
4-4	H	H	H	H	H	H	H	H	H	H
5-5	D	D	D	D	D	D	D	H	H	H
6-6	H	Sp	Sp	Sp	Sp	Sp	H	H	H	H
7-7	Sp	Sp	Sp	Sp	Sp	Sp	H	H	H	H
8-8	Sp	Sp	Sp	Sp	Sp	Sp	Sp	Sp	Sp	Sp
9-9	Sp	Sp	Sp	Sp	Sp	S	Sp	Sp	S	S
10-10	S	S	S	S	S	S	S	S	S	S
A-A	Sp	Sp	Sp	Sp	Sp	Sp	Sp	Sp	Sp	Sp

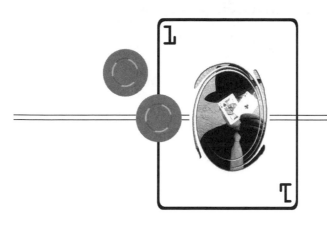

A House of Cards:
Why You Need
A New Approach

Many players have told me they had experienced frustration when they used the blackjack methods devised in the early 1960s.

Admittedly, casino *countermeasures* are partly to blame, and I enumerated them in *Blackjack The SMART Way*. These include: the dealing of just a portion of the cards before the next shuffle; the institution of multi-deck games; and the requirement that certain player cards be placed face-down, out of view, at pitch game tables (a problem whose historic solution you'll find in this book).

But there is another, more startling reason for the relative ineffectiveness of the old methods. In some ways the pioneering computer studies of the mid-20th Century were built upon a house of cards. This is because:

❶ *There are reasons to question some of the pre-research presumptions blackjack's first great researchers made before they even began their experiments.* These were the precepts upon which everything would rest, and some of these were shaky.

❷ The *way* in which the research was done was problematical. *The use of computers to simulate input data, for instance, is questionable.*

❸ Once the studies were over, *researchers often disregarded what their numbers were telling them, in seeking an impossibly simple solution to a complex problem.*

All of this led to a certain percentage of flawed conclusions, whose revelations throw into question some of the pillars of truth that support the very foundations of modern blackjack thinking.

After reading this chapter, I think you'll agree that it speaks to the need for a better understanding of card behavior, as well as improvements in the way the game is played -- issues that will be addressed in this book.

Problem #1: The Use of Random Number Generators

One of the first mistakes made by blackjack's original computer wizards was their pre-research decision to use *random number generators* to the exclusion of cards. In fact, *the use of these devices in the computer studies of the 1960s provides one major cause for concern about the validity of their conclusions.*

Random number generators are gadgets that spew out numbers randomly. They were inside the computers used by the first modern blackjack researchers, to churn out *simulated* blackjack rounds.

Why were these inventions used? Because *computers cannot handle or shuffle cards, like real casino dealers do, and the researchers had no desire to use real cards.*

I do believe the men who designed those bold and ambitious early blackjack experiments did their best to do their subject justice. Unbeknownst to them, however, their reliance upon their computer's random number generator to facilitate their production and examination of many lifetimes' worth of simulated blackjack rounds *clouded their vision of how the game really works, and left them with flawed results.*

Why Is It So Important To Use Actual Cards?

Those who performed the initial computer studies did not recognize that there is such a thing as card behavior! Therefore, they did not study the significant ways in which casino dealer shuffling, dealing and card collection impact the game, in the rearrangement of the cards. Nor did they realize that the "cards" in their runs did not reflect reality.

They simply had their computer assign cards to each hand at random, using their computers' random number generators, which is a far different procedure than what occurs in a casino, and produces far different results.

Why does this matter?

It *matters*, because, *with the standardized shuffling, dealing and card collection done by casino dealers, the cards do NOT play out in a random fashion. And so the early blackjack researchers could not possibly discover the numerous NON-random phenomena that are a part of the game. Furthermore, it is these phenomena that make blackjack* so *winnable; they provide players with tremendous advantages.*

(By the way, there have been one or two studies before mine that have agreed with my conclusion that standardized casino dealer shuffling does not randomize the cards. Because the purpose of those prior studies was purely to see how much shuffling it would take to radically alter the sequence of the cards, they did not go on to create a system that might *take advantage* of shuffling's Achilles heel.)

In Chapter 5 (How Shuffling Affects Your Game), for instance, you will learn that *standardized casino dealer shuffling actually produces a number of different kinds of repeating phenomena, which give players the ability to predict, to a good extent, what the future holds -- in both general and specific ways -- from shuffle to shuffle.* That's a *major* player benefit that cannot be discovered in random computer simulations!

Some Other Missed Discoveries

But there were other consequences of the researchers' use of random number generators, some of which are listed below:

❶   *They could not and did not discover that there are crucial aspects of the game that are predictable, with reference to both current and future round action. So, they could not and did not design systems that would allow players to benefit from this.* (You will come to understand that blackjack has *many* predictable elements, including: the composition of the dealer's and players' hands from shuffle to shuffle; card patterns that recur from shuffle to shuffle; what hit cards are coming your way; and the probable identity of the dealer's hole card! And these are just a few examples.)

❷   *Their betting schemes were based upon a surreal, random world, unreflective of reality, in which a player would never know what card would come next, let alone what cards would likely be dealt after a shuffle.* Therefore, the methods they created could not take advantage of the factors listed in ❶ above.

❸   *They did not realize that a smart player can actually follow the approximate location of certain cards from shuffle-to-shuffle. This ability -- only possible in the nonrandom world of cards -- provides terrific opportunities in the way of betting and the intelligent cutting of the cards (as you will see later on).*

Problem #2: Betting On Collective Results

Another mistake blackjack's early computer researchers made was in assuming they could arrive at a simple card strategy by applying generalizations (based upon millions of simulated rounds of action) to each *specific* card situation.

To understand the point I'm making, you need to understand that:

❶   *The probability of what is likely to occur in a given round of action is very different than the probability of what will occur in 8 million combined rounds of action.*

❷   *When you make a bet, you cannot bet on the collective results of 8 million rounds of blackjack. Your bet rides on the results of one particular round.*

Yet this is exactly what their generalized card strategy taught you to do: to make card decisions *as if you were betting on the collective results of millions of rounds,* in spite of the fact that *the vast number of those rounds have nothing in common with the realities you face at any given moment.*

This approach requires you to deny what your eyes are seeing. *They were unable to see the trees for the forest.*

Problem #3: The All-Powerful Up Card Misconception

Here's another way the researchers made a wrong turn: they concluded that *the up card was the only determining factor as to how each round would wind up, for every player at the table.* So, they divided their results *by what up card was present during each round.* They then decided that you could simply take note of what up card you were against and your point total, and the rest was cut-and-dried.

They did not take into account the differing realities each player experienced during each appearance of the up card, nor the specific cards that factored into each round's final results (which also included cards dealt in *prior* rounds, since the last shuffle).

They did not seem to be aware that *the cards that were dealt to you and your fellow players immediately prior to your turn might be a bigger determinant in making your decision than what the dealer's up card is.* They did not seem to realize that *your decision might go in any of a number of ways, depending on what cards had been dealt in the current round as well as prior rounds, up to the last shuffle.*

Let's take a look at a couple of examples, which illustrate how wrong this kind of thinking is. Illustration 1-1, on the following page, gives you an idea of what I'm talking about -- of how a player, with a particular point total versus one specific up card, might NOT want to make the same move each time that situation arises. In card situations A and B, the player marked "Your Hand" has 10 points and the dealer shows an up card of 7. However, in Example A, you'd be wise to play it safe and simply take hit cards, and, in B, you'd be smart to double. (The reasons for this will become clear later in the book.)

You wouldn't have known the correct move had you followed the more inaccurate approach of decades past, where you were told that all you

Illustration 1-1

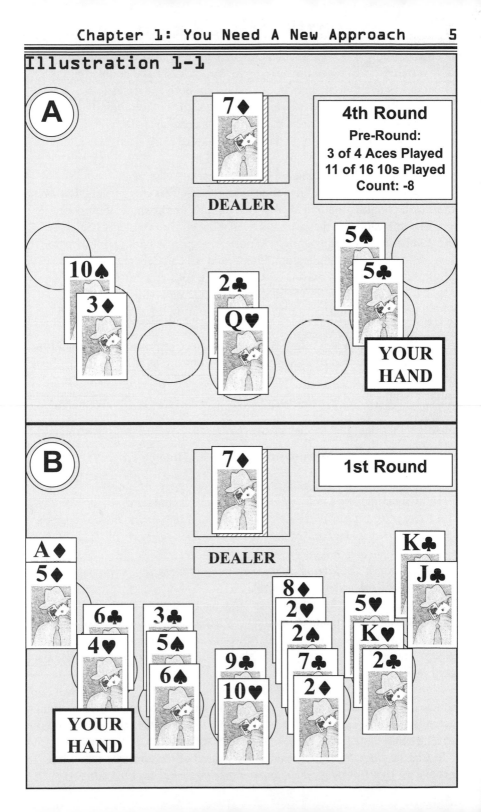

needed to know was what the dealer's up card was, and what your total was, to ascertain how to make the best move. You would have doubled in both situations (since that method would have seen both examples as being the same), and you would have lost in example A. (The "Your Hand" player in example A doubled, and drew a 3; the dealer drew to an 18, with a hole card of 6 and a hit card of 5. If you had had Advanced Card Analysis skills, which you will learn in this book, you could have *foreseen* this result.)

(Note: those willing to engage in card counting were given a bit more information in Old School handbooks than Basic Strategy players, but even their card counting methods had shortcomings; unlike mine, their counting systems left out cards that are vital to making card strategy decisions, and the numbers from card counting do not carry specific enough information to be considered precise indicators. Plus -- and we can debate why this is so until the cows come home -- I've rarely met a card counter who could tell me, for instance, when they would NOT double on a 10 versus a 7. I've found that, for a majority of players, card counting hasn't been the panacea it was promised to be.)

OK, so what have we so far? Betting on collective results rather than the facts of a specific round...Using the dealer's up card as the sole determinant of your strategy...If this Old School way were applied to baseball, the pitcher would adopt one strategy for each *team*, pitching the same way to each hitter, based upon his *team's* batting stats and averaged-out hitter profile rather than that of the specific batter. Boy, would that backfire!

Problem #4: Ignoring The Hole Card

...Which brings me to a related point. The designers of the strategy still used by most players *totally ignored the dealer's hole card; they did not realize that its identity is predictable, with good regularity. In so doing, they completely overlooked one of the most empowering aspects of the game!*

It is the hole card that, more than anything else, determines how strong the dealer's up card is. Judging an up card without factoring in the dealer's hole card will often steer you wrong.

With the dealer's stronger up cards, this handicapped thinking leads you to adopt a kind of a vigilante approach -- assuming the worst, you come in with guns drawn, ready to "fire" whether the up card is "armed" or not. In other words, you will, on occasion, foolishly risk busting in cases where the hole card makes the dealer vulnerable to busting.

With the dealer's weaker up cards, this shortsighted practice lulls you into a state of relaxed optimism in a good number of situations where you should actually be more vigilant. This means you will sometimes wrongly stand on stiffs when the hole card almost guarantees the dealer a winning score.

In *Cutting Edge Blackjack*, you'll see that all of the up cards can either behave as tigers or pussy cats, *depending upon what the hole card is.*

Problem #5: The Fast Fix -- The Use of Constants

THIS brings me to what might be the biggest factor leading players down the wrong path today: the notion of the *fast fix*.

This notion led blackjack's pioneering researchers astray – before they conducted any research. Their thinking went something like this: after our computers have produced millions of rounds of blackjack action, *we could then just add everything up and come up with an easily-remembered set of numbers that could be applied to every round of action! All players would have to do would be to memorize those numbers, and then every hand would be a piece of cake!*

But the indiscriminate application of mythological numbers that magically remained the same over time (similar to the science world's *constants*), for every conceivable card situation, ignored reality.

The authors of these computer studies suggested that, with their amazing numbers, you could reliably predict how each dealer up card would behave in the course of every round, or every hour, or every six hours, for that matter, because (they believed) those numbers would pertain to every situation, and *never change. Unfortunately, they were wrong!* Your reality is always in flux, and because of not one, but *many* factors -- as you will learn in detail, in the many chapters that lie ahead.

As a result, we need to reevaluate all of the factors we were told hold constant, which -- as it turns out -- are *variables* :

❶ *Dealer bust rates.* (Did you know, for instance, that the dealer sometimes busts *less* with an up card of 2 than with a 7?)

❷ *Player bust rates.* (Did you know that there are times when you are more prone to busting than at others?)

❸ *Up card score profiles.* (This is the percentage of times each dealer up card reaches scores of 17, 18, 19, 20 and 21 over time.)

❹ *Player score profiles.* (The percentage of times you reach scores of 17, 18, 19, 20 and 21.)

❺ *Dealer winning and losing rates.* (These are more dependent upon how strong the dealer's score profile is than how high or low the dealer's bust rate is at any point in time!)

❻ *Player winning and losing rates.* (Did you know this depends not only on the "personality" of the decks being used, but also the "personality" of the individual betting spots?)

❼ *The percentage of dealer Blackjacks.*

❽ *The percentage of player Blackjacks.*

❾ *Up Card Ranking.* (Did you realize that sometimes the dealer's 5 is your best card, and at other times, the 4, etc.?)

These factors, long considered constants, all figured into the equations that created the mathematical logic behind blackjack's original Basic Strategy recommendations.

But -- wait a minute! How can Basic Strategy be highly *accurate* if it is based upon numbers that we now know are constantly *changing with the card flow?* The answer is: it *cannot.* And so what *relevance* can it have if the numbers used to craft it are, in a sense, fiction? The answer is that *it is really only good in providing beginners with an entry-level approach to the game.* It, unfortunately, has *very little relevance* to the many varied card situations you will find yourself facing.

Problem #6: Ignoring The Evidence

Actually, there is reason to suspect that there was evidence early on, contradicting the faulty assumptions I've pointed out, but it was ignored. The proof of this lies in the claims of one early proponent of the use of constants. He wrote -- in defense of his system -- that others were coming up with numbers that conflicted with his, because they had not examined as many rounds of action. He went on to assert that *a researcher would have to run 8 million rounds of blackjack action, if that researcher wanted to arrive at the "correct" numbers, as he purportedly did.*

This, to me, is not only a case of *faulty logic; it's an admission that his numbers were not the way to go.* If it took *8 million rounds* of action to arrive at his supposed *constants* (up card bust figures, etc.), then these are not constants. When a scientist calls something a constant, it is a number that stays the *same,* under *all* conditions. The speed of light is a constant. It doesn't *vary,* no matter how many trips you take, or how large your space vehicle is. Similarly, if this author's "constants" are valid, this should be readily apparent in the results from *any* number of rounds; but, by his own admission, it's *not.*

Furthermore -- let's take a bite from a reality sandwich! *It's an absolute impossibility for you to even come close to playing 8 million rounds!* To even *hope* to accomplish that many rounds, you'd have to devote your entire life to the task. You'd have to start in your late teens or early 20s, and then – during the course of a long life — perform like a robot and ignore every human need and desire for a life beyond the blackjack table. Even then (assuming you'd be able to earn a living during this period and meet your expenses), you'd be very old (or *dead*) before you completed this Herculean task. I mean, let's be real!

Chart 1-2 on the next page makes this painfully obvious. It shows you how long it would take to complete 8 million rounds, depending on how many hours per day and days per week you play. For example (referring to the column entitled "Years Per 8M"), if you were to play *3 hours a day, 365 days a year, it would take you more than 120 years! If you played twice that*

Chart 1-2
How Long To Play 8M Hands

HOURS/DAY	# DAYS/WEEK	YEARS PER 8M
1	1	2564
1	2	1282
1	3	855
1	4	641
1	5	513
1	6	427
1	7	366
2	1	1282
2	2	641
2	3	427
2	4	321
2	5	256
2	6	214
2	7	183
3	1	855
3	2	427
3	3	285
3	4	214
3	5	171
3	6	142
3	7	122
4	1	641
4	2	321
4	3	214
4	4	160
4	5	128
4	6	107
4	7	92
5	1	513
5	2	256
5	3	171
5	4	128
5	5	103
5	6	85
5	7	73
6	1	427
6	2	214
6	3	142
6	4	107
6	5	85
6	6	71
6	7	61

much -- 6 hours a day, every day of the year -- it would take you more than 61 years!

It's very simple. *You cannot cash in on profits you are projected to achieve in 8 million rounds if you cannot play anywhere near that amount of rounds. Moreover, it's risky to use a strategy based upon this misconception. Severe monetary losses can occur in a matter of hours or days if players are unaware of the game's changeability, and fail to react to it.*

Problem #7: The Myth of Card Balance

Incredible as it may seem, it appears that the creators of blackjack's mid-20th Century game plans were *aware* to some extent that the Basic Strategy method they developed had its flaws. How can I say this?

They issued a *warning* with their Basic Strategies *that they applied to balanced card situations only. That is, they would be correct only if the number of low cards that remained undealt equalled the number of unplayed high cards. This rarely occurs, and even then, only for a fleeting moment in the course of a round. In fact, a balanced situation can only occur, by the way, when an even number of cards have been played! Think about it! So, half the time, balance is mathematically impossible to achieve!*

But something else is inherently wrong. Their definition of a state of balance was conditioned upon the presumption that all cards could be thrown together into two groups -- low and high -- and that each of the cards in these groups had no differences with regard to how they affect the game's outcome! This is another faulty idea (as you will see later in this book). True balance can only be achieved if each of the cards is equal in number (with the exception of the 10s, which, in a truly balanced state, would be four times as numerous as any other card). And that doesn't happen very often!!

Yet, this shortcoming in the way of a *confession* went unnoticed by most players; and, *the few players who DID pick up on it did not understand that it revealed a major problem.*

(Speaking of which, I had a very lively email debate recently with some-one who *had* noticed the warning, and yet he defended this "balanced card" logic by arguing that the cards *are* balanced, *right after a shuffle.* Well, this may be true, but then the cards are *dealt.* I mean, yes, that's a condition that exists *before* the game is played, but not frequently *during.*)

Therefore The Need For A Better System

So, as you can see, there are some serious flaws in the Old School ap-proach to the game. It was great for its day, when it represented the first systematic plan for blackjack, but it is time to rectify the misunderstandings of the past and move forward.

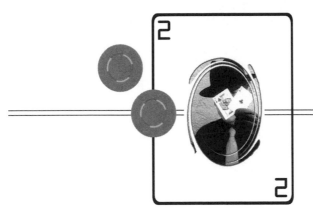

Penetration
And How It Affects
Your Game

P enctration is often defined as *the percentage of cards that will be dealt to the players following the shuffle, based upon where the dealer places the cut card.* For example, if the dealer places the cut card in the middle of the cards, so that roughly half the cards will be dealt, most would say that you are getting 50% penetration. If the dealer places the cut card so that players will be dealt only about 30% of the cards, this is commonly referred to as 30% penetration. (Whether you define penetration in this way after reading the following chapter is doubtful. There, I'll introduce you to a more modern, more accurate way to measure this. For now, it's sufficient that you understand the origin of this idea, and what it means to you.)

The Origin Of The Term Penetration

This term popped up in the early 1960s, when casinos first instituted restrictions on the number of cards that would be dealt to players, in an attempt to hurt the new breed of player, the card counter. The game, for centuries, had been played with one deck, and most, if not all of the cards were dealt before being reshuffled. When the new restrictions were put in place, players then had to contend with cut cards (sometimes called re-shuffle cards) that dealers would put in place after a player had cut the deck; once reached, the dealer would reshuffle after the round in which the card cut came up. Hence, the need for a term to describe the percent of the total number of cards that would be dealt.

Penetration Varies With The Casino

Cut card placement is set by casino policy. Some casinos are very stingy with the number of cards they want you to be dealt; others are quite generous. Dealers must place the cut card roughly where they've been told to by their bosses.

As a smart player, you should therefore understand that the issue of penetration is something you should consider in choosing a casino. If their policy is to deal less than 50% of the cards between shuffles, take your business elsewhere.

Why Penetration Might Vary *Within* A Casino

Penetration is also a factor that can, on occasion, make some games *within* a casino undesirable, while others there are OK. This is when cut card placement varies from table to table *within* the casino, dependent upon the number of decks in the game. I've seen clubs, for example, where the 1-deck penetration was a paltry 30%, and yet the 2-deck penetration was more reasonable -- about 55%. Given that choice, you should *avoid* the 1-deck tables, and play at the 2-deck tables.

You'll often get lower penetration at a casino's 1- and 2-deck tables than at their 6- or 8-deck tables. Many casinos, understanding the greater winning potential for players at the 1- and 2-deck tables, restrict the number of cards dealt at those tables to make it harder for players to take advantage of a certain predictability as the cards near completion.

It's not unusual, for example, to find a penetration level of 66% to 75% at 6- and 8-deck games. Penetration at 4-deck tables -- if you can find them -- might be a tiny bit less. At 1- and 2-deck tables, however, you'll occasionally experience severe limitations; some casinos, for example, require dealers to shuffle up after just one round, or after a certain number of *hands* have been dealt (for instance, they might only deal to 6 betting spots before reshuffling). Why players continue to play under those circumstances beats me. You cannot play a good game that way.

Penetration Might Vary With The Dealer

Dealers, by the way, do sometimes have discretion as to when to reshuffle. This is especially true at the small minority of casinos that don't use reshuffle cards. There, they let the dealers decide when to reshuffle the cards. I suppose that, at those casinos, penetration would have to refer to the true number of cards that are dealt between shuffles.

This can have good and bad results for the player. I've seen good dealers at these places deal out practically *every* card (often as the result of generous player tips; you might want to join the others in this practice, by the way, if it has this benefit). I've also seen good dealers shuffle up early, to shuffle away *bad* cards that were killing the players. Then again, I've seen bad dealers at casinos that don't use cut cards, who shuffled up when the cards started benefitting the players.

At your typical casino, however, which uses reshuffle cards, you might also find dealer fluctuations. I've seen nice dealers ignore the cut card and shuffle up early to help the players when the cards went bad. I've also seen not-so-nice dealers move up the reshuffle card to lessen the penetration in later rounds when players are winning regularly.

I point this out so you are aware that: 1) dealers, at some casinos, have a certain degree of control over penetration; and, 2) part of your job as a discriminating player is to seek out the dealers who, with discretion, exercise it on the players' behalf, and avoid the dealers who don't.

Why Penetration Is Such An Important Issue

Penetration is an important concept -- one to which you should pay attention, avoiding the casinos and dealers who are stingy in this regard.

Why does this make a difference? The more cards you see, the more predictable the action becomes, as you will learn in later chapters.

For now, just understand that: *the more cards that are dealt, the more you will know about the cards that remain undealt, and therefore the more it is to your advantage.*

Also, a good general rule to follow is: never play if the penetration is less than 50%. And, if all things are equal, play at the casinos that give you the best penetration.

In the next chapter, you'll learn that the dealer's cut card is only one factor that determines how many cards players will be dealt between shuffles. While that chapter is primarily about how the number of players affects the game, it will also introduce you to a new concept, which I have named: *true penetration.*

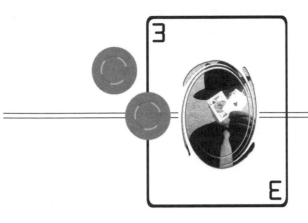

How The Number of Players Affects Your Bottom Line

(Including New Revelations About Why You Should *Not* Play Head-On Versus The Dealer)

It's amazing, but few players pay any attention to the number of players who are at the table. Yet there are numerous reasons why you *need* to do so – *before* you sit down, and *while* you're playing.

Right now you're undoubtedly ignoring this factor, because you're unaware of how it affects your ability to win. What you are about to find is that *blackjack is almost a different game, per each variation in the number of players involved.*

Hold on tight. You are about to get a complete picture of this overlooked but absolutely fundamental aspect of blackjack, from every aspect that concerns you. Then, I will give you practical advice on how to apply what you've learned.

Astonishing Discoveries

I imagine many of you are wondering: is this such a big deal? I might not have thought so a year ago. But even I was astounded by some of the discoveries you will read about here.

It was the fact that my computer data pointed to a surprisingly momentous conclusion that led me to write this chapter, which is:

Your very ability to win is apparently governed, in part, by how many betting spots are being played!

This is because, not unlike the effect of the moon's gravity on the Earth's tides, players' cards seem to hold some sway over the dealer's final results. The more players, the greater the potential influence. I am not aware of anyone having noticed this before, but the data certainly suggests it is real. I'd like to refer to this phenomenon from now on as *Player Card Gravity* (or *PCG*, for short).

In other words, my research results show that *the dealer's likelihood of winning and, conversely, busting (and therefore your chances of winning) vary with the number of betting spots in the mix. Plus, that can be said as well about all of the underlying numbers that form the basis for player strategy recommendations!* And here's the kicker: there is a direct, linear correlation here. According to the evidence I've accumulated, *your winning potential goes UP with every extra betting spot that is occupied at the table.*

(This conclusion, by the way, accentuates the futility of taking a Basic Strategy approach to blackjack. For one thing, it suggests that the Basic Strategy folks should really carry around cards for *every* possible player combination. Because, *if the defining numbers are different per the amount of players at the table, then your strategy needs to be customized to fit each player combination.*)

How This Chapter Is Organized

But, I'm getting ahead of myself!

Let me begin by explaining how I'd like to tackle this issue. First, I'll provide you with the *indisputable* reasons why tables with a maximum number of players are best. Then, I'll move on to admittedly more controversial territory, and share some of my exciting research results with you.

Another "Gospel Truth" Unravels

Now, some of you already realize that I have, indirectly, just challenged one of the game's Gospel Truths: that playing one spot, head-on versus the dealer offers you the best game, with the highest winning potential. You're right. Because, in fact, that's a misconception, and I think it's high time that we put it to rest, especially because it has sent some down the path to their own ruin.

> **FACTOID 3-1:**
> Your winning potential is determined, in part, by the number of betting spots being played. The *higher* the number, the better.

After all, how do proponents of this myth defend it? Their main assertion is that you will *see more cards* that way than you would if there were others at the table. (If you see more cards, you will have a better handle on predicting what cards are due at any one time.) Let's see if that holds true, as we examine this matter more closely.

(Before we look at this, however, I want to take a moment for a reality check. *People who say that you see more cards if you play the dealer head-on have not tried this practice very often. Because, the fact the of the matter is, most dealers are instructed to give players far less penetration in that situation. Dealers usually shuffle up on solitary players after they've gotten no more than 30% to 40% penetration.* But -- I tell you what: in this chapter, we are going to *ignore* this reality for argument's sake, and *pretend* for the time being that dealers place the reshuffle card in the same place for solitary players as they do for other players. That way, the results of this inquiry will be even more stark.)

Before we go further, though, I have to introduce a new concept of mine: *true penetration.*

True Penetration

I define true penetration as: *the actual number of cards that are dealt between shuffles.* You may not be aware of this, but true penetration is *not* determined by where the dealer places the cut card. It is ordained by *the total number of betting spots that are being played.*

Said in a different way: *the number of players in the mix predetermines the number of cards that will be dealt between shuffles, which directly impacts on your ability to win.* And, as you will see, *true penetration tends to increase with the number of players.* (If this is true, I think you'll agree that we've identified the first reason why it's true that *the higher the number of players at your table, the better.* Plus, it would scotch the misunderstanding that going *solo* is your best bet.)

How True Penetration Varies With The Number of Players

You're probably asking yourself: why would true penetration generally go *up* with the number of betting spots that have been taken?

It's easy. Think of it: when the reshuffle card is reached, the action does not immediately cease. Depending on the number of players at the table, a certain number of cards must *still be dealt,* to complete the round. *The more players at the table, the more cards that are usually required to do so.* I call this the *Post-Marker-Dealing Phenomenon.* (See charts on following pages.)

Now -- I don't expect you to take my word for it. Here's the *proof:*

In my computer card runs, the virtual dealers were programmed to place the reshuffle card *exactly* 60% into the cards, because this is a pretty good

CHART 3-1:

How the Number of Betting Spots Affects The Total Number of Cards That Will Be Dealt Between Shuffles

(NOTE: Numbers in white boxes include dealer cards.)

# BETTING SPOTS BEING PLAYED	AVG. # CARDS DEALT PER ROUND	AVG. # CARDS DEALT BETWEEN SHUFFLES	AVG. # CARDS BEYOND RESHUFFLE MARKER	AVG. # ROUNDS DEALT BETWEEN SHUFFLES	AVERAGE TRUE PENETRATION
1	6	32*	1	6*	62%*
2	8	33	2	4	63%
3	11	35	4	3	67%
4	13	39	8	3	76%
5	16	36	5	2	70%
6	19	39	8	2	75%
7	22	43*	12	2*	83%*

* Unless casino imposes greater limits with these player situations.

CHART 3-2:

Average Extra Cards Dealt (Beyond 60% Reshuffle Card Placement) Per # of Players: *The Post-Marker-Dealing Phenomenon*

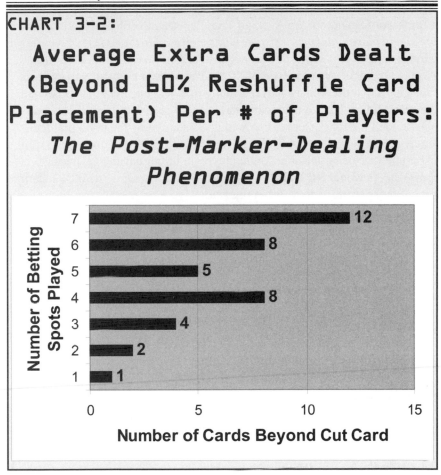

approximation of the average placement at most casinos. Unlike the practice at real casinos, though, there was absolutely no variation in this practice from round to round -- the reshuffle marker was placed in the *same* location every time (for example, with 1-deck games, the marker was placed after the *31st* card). Obviously, real dealers will never be so precise. But, by keeping the marker placement constant, I could then conclude with certainty that *any change in the average true penetration that was documented per each player combination was purely the result of the total number of betting spots that were in play* -- because that was the only variable.

You will find the results of this study in Chart 3-1. (This chart reflects numbers from my 1-deck runs. It speaks volumes, by the way, about the wisdom of playing at 1-deck tables, where true penetration reaches its height, making the prediction of coming cards after the first round that much easier. To avoid tedium, we will not go into charts for all deck combinations -- the principles are the same, even though the results are most significant at tables with the fewest decks.) The facts couldn't be more clear.

Look, for instance, at the Average True Penetration column. Notice that *the single player, playing one spot, will receive on average just 2% more cards once the 60% reshuffle point is reached.* In fact, if you look at the Average Number of Cards Beyond Reshuffle Marker column, you can see this means that the solitary player usually gets just *one paltry card* beyond the reshuffle card! If you compare that to the true penetration levels other player combinations achieve, you will understand why the myth that the single player sees the most cards is absolutely false. (And, once again: this experiment actually gave the single player an unfair advantage, because most dealers would NOT likely put the reshuffle marker at the 60% location for solitary players as they did in my studies!)

This reality is one of the things that makes playing at a table with 4 to 7 players so advantageous. By having 13 to 22 cards available to analyze per round, including a good number of hit cards that lead up to your turn, trends can often be detected that enable you to predict what cards are coming next. In other words, you might very well be able to figure out what your hit card will be, and perhaps the dealer's hole card, as well (you'll see how this works, in Chapter 12, on "Strategic Card Analysis & Your Real-time Card Strategy").

There are a number of other interesting facts in Chart 3-1, on page 18. *Look at how high the true penetration gets with 7 players at the table: on average, 83%!* Understand, too, that this was the *average* -- there were, of course, times during my card runs where that average was exceeded. My data shows, for instance, that *true penetration at 7-player tables will go above 90% approximately 16% of the time!* (Incredibly enough, on very rare occasions, *100%* of the cards were needed to complete the second round at these tables! This was the only player total that produced that result.)

Granted, as the chart also shows you, you'll only get two rounds at 7-player tables between shuffles. But, *you will see practically all the cards! This is the way blackjack was meant to be played!* (By the way -- some casinos restrict 7-player tables to just one round of action. My response to that is: if it hurts your game, don't play there!) Of course, some of you are thinking: no, I don't get to *see* all the cards, because players have to place some of their cards facedown on the table, out of view. Yes, but now, for the first time in blackjack history, you *can* identify what they are with good success, with new methods I've invented! (See the chapters on "How To Count Cards At 1- & 2-Deck Tables" and "How To Do Advanced Card Analysis At 1- & 2-Deck Tables.") Enough said.

Now, in *contrast* with the figures associated with the 7-player tables, which I've just discussed, the MAXIMUM true penetration achieved by the single player was 67%, which translated into just 4 cards past the reshuffle card. And that was only achieved on rare occasion.

For your information, the highest true penetration levels reached by the rest of the player totals was: 67% with 2 players; 81% with 3 players (11 cards past the reshuffle point); 90% with 4 players (16 cards past the shuffle point); 94% with 5 players (18 cards past the shuffle point); and 98% with 6 players (20 cards past the shuffle point, AND 51 cards into the deck!).

So, I've proved my point. The numbers speak for themselves -- *the more players, the more cards you tend to see.*

A Quirk At The 4-Player Tables

I say *tend* to see, because we're talking about averages. Plus, as you might have noticed, the average true penetration level for 4 players is actually *higher* than that for 5 players! That's right. *The true penetration seen by 4 players is roughly on a par with what 6 players get.* This is not a statistical abnormality. It is due to a true and *unusual* phenomenon.

The reason for this blip becomes evident when you examine the 4- and 5-player card runs. Looking at where the reshuffle card appears, you will see that, with 5 players, the card often appears toward the end of the second round. With 4 players, however, the reshuffle card usually appears at the very start of the third round. So, as a result, as Chart 3-1 on page 18 shows you, 4 players get an average of 3 rounds between shuffles, while 5 players get an average of just 2 rounds. It's the two less betting spots in the first two rounds of action that prevents the coming of the reshuffle card, enabling the 4 players to squeeze out, on average, one more round than 5 players would. With 4 players averaging 3 rounds between shuffles, that means 15 player and dealer spots are being played between shuffles (if you take into account the fact that 5 hands -- those of the 4 players and one dealer -- are being played per round). In contrast, with 5 players averaging 2 rounds between shuffles, that amounts to only 12 player and dealer hands being played per shuffle. There are three less hands being played per shuffle at the 1-deck tables with 5 players.

A similar phenomenon results in 4- and 6-player true penetration being essentially the same. However -- there are other advantages to playing at tables with 5 or 6 players that outweigh this anomaly in favor of the 4-player table.

The Number of Cards Per Round

Another factor you should consider is: *you and your fellow players will be dealt, collectively, more cards per round, on average, the higher the number of betting spots that are taken* (see Chart 3-3 on the next page). *This goes up consistently, with each additional player.*

This is another reason why the player who goes head-on with the dealer, playing one betting spot, is at a disadvantage. Look at how few cards they get on average per round! Just six! That's not enough cards to enable that player to do a good analysis of what cards are likely to come. Whereas, at

CHART 3-3:

Average Number of Cards That Will Be Dealt Per Round (Per Number of Players)

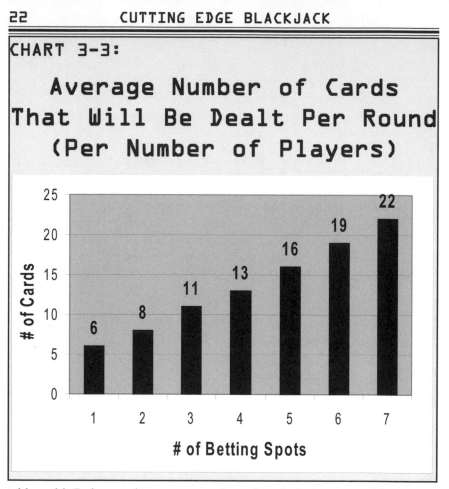

tables with 7 players, the average number of cards dealt per round is an amazing 22 cards! That's nearly half a deck of cards!

So, here you have it: the assertion that the solitary player sees more cards is absolutely false. But let's not stop there. The details make this even more apparent:

With 7 betting spots played, you'll see 20 or more cards per round a whopping 79% of the time. You can draw great conclusions by having that many cards to analyze. Furthermore, you'll see 23 or more cards 36% of the time; 26 or more cards (half a deck) more than 6% of the time; and, on a rare occasion, you'll even see a high of 29 cards!!!

With 6 betting spots played, you'll see 20 or more cards per round a healthy 48% of the time; 23 or more cards 7% of the time; and, on occasion, you'll see a high of 25 cards.

With 5 betting spots played, you'll see 13 or more cards per round a whopping 97% of the time; 20 or more cards per round 6 % of the time; and, on occasion, you'll see a high of 21 cards.

With 4 betting spots played, you'll see 13 or more cards per round 66% of the time; and, 1% of the time, you'll see a high of 18 cards.

With 3 betting spots played, you'll see 13 or more cards per round only 15% of the time; and, about a half percent of the time, you'll reach a high of 15 cards.

With 2 betting spots played, you'll see a high of 10 or more cards per round just 9% of the time, and you will never see more.

With 1 player, you'll see a high of 9 or more cards per round less than 2% of the time, and you will never see more.

With this data, how can anybody argue that you see more cards by playing one spot, head-on with the dealer??? That idea should seem ridiculous to you by now.

But, there's a bigger point to be made here. The data indisputably proves: *the more players, the better*, from the standpoint of *seeing more cards* -- not only *per round*, but also *between shuffles*. If you see more cards, you have more information when it's your turn, so you can play a better game and win more. It's that simple. (If you find yourself in a debate about this in the future, just tell the person who isn't aware of the facts to read this chapter!)

This is precisely why, in *Blackjack The SMART Way,* I warned you against playing at tables with less than 4 players. The numbers we've been discussing are not very favorable -- and there are other factors to take into account as well, as you'll soon recognize.

The Low Up Card Stiffs Effect

The next phenomenon I'd like to talk about is one I discovered only recently, and I haven't read about it elsewhere. I've decided to call it the *Low Up Card Stiffs Effect.*

Here's what it is: *if you analyze the hands of players who decide to stand on stiffs versus the dealer's lower up cards (the 2s through the 6s), you come up with an amazing result: low cards predominate. It's as though low cards are drawn to those hands by a vacuum. This tends to produce higher dealer bust rates.* (I will explain this in a moment.) It certainly provides another vital clue into why the game's fundamentals change with each variation in the number of betting spots.

Let's back up for a moment, and see what this is all about. In Chart 3-4, on the top of the next page, you'll see that *player stiffs (versus low dealer up cards) contain nearly 175% as many 2s, 3s, 4s, 5s and 6s as they do 9s and 10s. That's close to double the amount. (The 7s also outnumber the 8s.) The 2s through the 6s were overrepresented to the tune of 38%. The 9s and 10s were nearly 10% under-represented.*

(I separated the 7s from the rest of the low cards, because my studies show that, of all the cards, the 7s seem to have no effect on whether or not the dealer busts. The 7s were equally represented in the dealer hands that busted and the dealer hands that attained acceptable scores.)

CHART 3-4:

The Card Makeup of Player Stiffs
(vs. Low Dealer Up Cards)

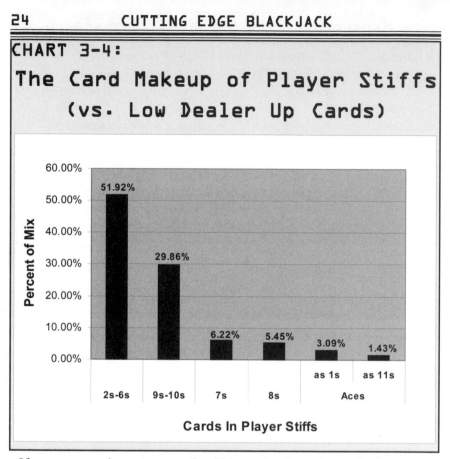

If you are a card counter, you should immediately understand what the numbers above mean: those player stiffs are forcing the count toward the positive side. For those of you not familiar with card counting: *by players' tendencies (because of Basic Strategy recommendations) to stand on stiff totals versus the dealer's lower up cards, an imbalance is created. The composition of these player stiffs make it that much more likely that high cards will be dealt when the dealer's turn arrives; therefore, the dealer is more likely to bust in these situations, when drawing stiffs.* (The ability of the players' stiffs to influence things in favor of higher dealer busting depends upon whether or not the Low Up Card Stiffs Effect is countered by the hands of players that tend to contain a high card majority -- hands that draw to scores of 17 through 21 or bust.)

Here's what I'm saying in a nutshell:

Low Up Card Stiffs Effect = Low Card Imbalance = Higher Dealer Bust Rate = Higher Player Win Rate

But there's a catch, which gives you another reason to sit at tables with a maximum number of players: *the strength of the Low Up Card Stiffs Effect is greatest with a maximum number of players.*

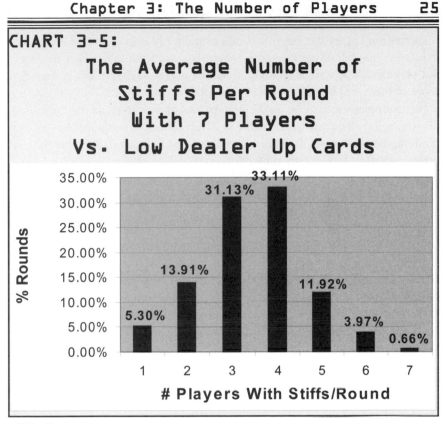

CHART 3-5:

The Average Number of Stiffs Per Round With 7 Players Vs. Low Dealer Up Cards

Why?

The answer's in Chart 3-5 above. *Nearly 50% of the time at 7-player tables when the dealer has a low up card, four or more players (more than half of them) will have stiffs upon which they'll stand. And, more than 80% of the time, there will be three or more players standing on stiffs.* ***These numbers mean that stiffs will usually come in significant enough numbers to produce the Low Up Card Stiffs Effect.***

Conversely, with a lower number of players, these numbers go down, thus lessening the Effect incrementally until, with 1- and 2-player situations, it is virtually nonexistent.

Now, I need to get more specific here. *All stiffs don't create the Low Up Card Stiffs Effect.* The two types of stiffs that do are: 1) those either with two low cards; or, 2) those with three or more cards -- hands that are overloaded with low cards. Plus, there is a third type of stiff that often contributes to the Effect (even though these might not contain more low cards than high cards): those that contain one or more Aces. By eating up Aces -- cards that might help the dealer attain an acceptable score -- these stiffs also help raise the dealer's bust rate. However, *there is a type of stiff that does NOT factor into the Low Up Card Stiffs Effect: those with one low and one high card.*

The reason I point this out is this makes it doubly important that there be a maximum number of betting spots being played at your table. This ensures not only that there will be a good number of player stiffs, but that at least *some* of them will be of the variety that produces the Effect.

The example in Chart 3-6 on the next page -- drawn from my card runs -- illustrates how the Low Up Card Stiffs Effect works. It was chosen at random; there are more dramatic examples to be found, I'm sure, but this is pretty typical of how the Effect works.

Here you see that, of the seven betting spots taken, four have stiffs that players stood on (they're marked with arrows). Of those, three contribute to the Low Up Card Stiffs Effect (the 3rd Baseman's low card-high card hand is of the type that is neutral, and, therefore, has no influence on what is to come). The dealer in this case had a stiff of 14 points. With three players' stiffs sucking up a surplus of 6 low cards and one Ace -- the cards that would have been of greatest value to the dealer -- the dealer then went on to bust.

The Low Up Card Stiffs Effect turned the tide. The stiffs had enough of a presence and influence to create a situation that made it probable that the dealer would bust.

There's No Cause-And-Effect If You Play Solo

In contrast, the Low Up Card Stiffs Effect is practically *nonexistent* at tables with solitary players who take just one betting spot. I would love to see someone attempt to prove that one hand has a tremendous effect on the very next hand. That's not how things work.

Take a look at Chart 3-7 page 28, showing the average number of cards that are taken, per hand, over time. (This includes both player and dealer hands.) *More than 80% of the time, hands contain no more than two or three cards.* In fact, *hands contain just two cards roughly half the time!*

Where am I going with this?

If the average hand usually contains just two cards, and, sometimes, three, there is no way that a solitary player's hand of that size would likely swing what the dealer gets next. (Nor could that player use those two or three cards to predict what the dealer's hit card would be to good effect, I might add.)

This becomes even more obvious when you consider the *order* in which the cards are placed on the table. The dealer's second card (which, at most casinos is the dealer's hole card) is dealt immediately after the solitary player gets his or her second card. That means, of the two or three cards the player takes on average, *only the third would come directly before the dealer's hit cards.* So, if the player takes just two cards, the *hole card* precedes the dealer's extra hit cards, and therefore the player's cards don't really factor into the dealer's eventual score. And, even if the player *does*

CHART 3-6:

An Example Of The Stiffs Effect

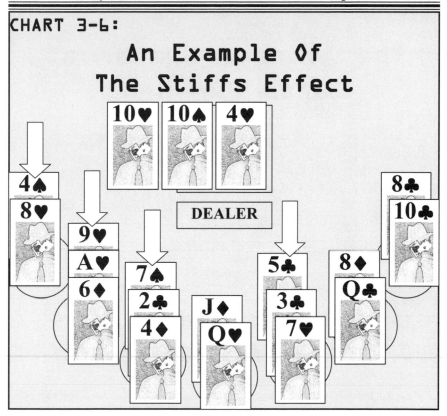

take a third card, one card won't greatly influence the dealer's result, either.

Busting, Gains & Winning Rates Vary

...And there are four additional phenomena I've uncovered that also seem to argue in favor of playing at full tables, or playing a maximum number of betting spots:

First: *dealer busting rates appear to vary per the number of betting spots being taken!* In fact, my preliminary findings suggest that *the dealer's overall bust rate is about 10% less when just one betting spot is being played than when 7 spots are being taken!* Even 2- and 3-betting spot situations won't help you change this bleak reality very much.

Second: *the greater the number of betting spots taken, the higher the overall player gains seem to be* (gains being the amount of money a player takes from the table -- this takes into account not only how many hands players won or lost, but also the extra income that comes from Blackjacks, loss savings from surrendering, and gains or losses from doubling). *The data, in fact, suggest that a solitary player playing just one betting spot can expect to accumulate losses over time; in contrast, players at tables with 6 or 7 players are likely to achieve net winnings.*

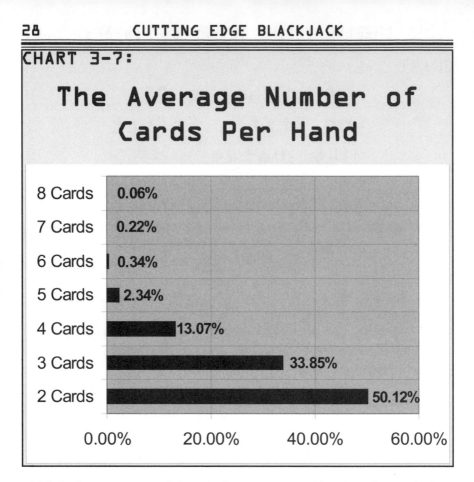

CHART 3-7:

The Average Number of Cards Per Hand

Third: *player win rates* (vis a vis the percentage of hands a player wins) *also seem to increase with the number of betting spots.* In fact, *the data speak strongly in favor of playing in 6- and 7-player situations.* (I might add that the 7-player tables did significantly better than the 6-player tables.)

And, fourth: an analysis of dealer cards-per-hand averages confirmed what the first three phenomena I've mentioned indicated. For example, the dealer, facing a solitary player playing one betting spot, drew 2-card hands 38.16% of the time, and 3-card hands 42.07% of the time. On the other hand, at a 7-player table, those averages were: 30.56% for 2-card dealer hands, and 48.89% for 3-card hands. The high 1-player 2-card hand figure reveals that the dealer achieved better results than in the 7-player situation. *It's a signal that the dealer busted less, by drawing more initial high cards to make an immediate winning score* (a corollary to this is that *the dealer obviously pulled fewer stiffs when facing a solitary player who took just one betting spot, and therefore had a lower risk of busting, than when the dealer went up against a packed table*). The more 2-card hands, the stronger the dealer.

All of the numbers surrounding the four phenomena listed above are rather dramatic.

For The Very Stubborn

Of course, there are some players who will stubbornly continue to play head-on against the dealer, no matter what the facts are. If this includes you, you undoubtedly have one more question for me at this point, which is: "So...what if I go one-on-one with the dealer, but, taking heed of what you've taught me here, I play four or more betting spots?

The answer is: that, too, presents its problems.

Casinos often require that you put five or more times the minimum bet down for each betting spot you take, if you play more than two hands. Are you ready to do so? This factor alone takes the average player out of the running.

But, let's say that money is no obstacle. There are still these drawbacks:

❶ the increased scrutiny you'll get, which might result in your facing countermeasures such as early shuffling up, or, perhaps in your being barred

❷ the possibility that *you might only be allowed to look at just one hand at a time* (if you play multiple hands), and therefore lose most of the advantages of playing more than one spot (if other players were playing those hands, you'd have a very good idea of what their cards were -- as you will learn in the chapters on "How To Count Cards At 1- & 2-Deck Tables" and "How To Do Advanced Card Analysis At 1- & 2-Deck Tables")

❸ the increased probability that a card mechanic will be brought in to face you (a card mechanic being something of a magician, who can sometimes influence the course of events)

❹ the greatly sped up pace you'll likely face (a common practice that, while not a major consideration, is certainly detrimental to your game)

And, along these lines, I might add this word for those high rollers and whales who ask for their own private table: boy are *you* asking for trouble! The advice above goes *double* for you!

Going head-on against the dealer is, in many ways, being too *flamboyant*. And that comes with pitfalls. Ask the late Ken Uston. Uston, a great player of his time, sometimes flaunted his prowess by playing all the betting spots at not just one, but two or three tables at a time. He drew adoring crowds, and won a lot of money in those multi-table feats.

But he ultimately paid the price for it. These showy displays earned him unwanted attention from casino personnel, which hurt his ability to get a good game. One Strip casino dealer -- who approached me at one of my Las Vegas book events -- told me, boastfully: "Ya know how I handled Uston? I shuffled up on him after every round!" Worse yet, Uston was eventually barred from every casino in Las Vegas.

You don't want this to happen to you. It pays to be discreet.

How Table Variants Affect Your Game

Now, you won't find much written about this, but there are times you'll encounter tables that are not standard, 7-player tables.

This often leads to confusion. At a book event in El Paso, Texas, for instance, someone, very concerned, got up and asked me: "Our local casino has tables with 10 betting spots. What do we do? It makes things much *tougher*, doesn't it?"

I had to explain to him the reasons that you are now aware of, why, the more betting spots, the better. Therefore, those 10-player tables are actually a *benefit* to the player -- especially if you're sitting in or near the 3rd Baseman's seat! (Think of all the cards those players get to see per round!)

I'm really amazed, though, that no one has asked me about those mysterious 6-seat tables that have cropped up in Vegas and elsewhere.

Are they not aware that, the fewer the number of betting spots, the fewer cards they'll see? *The 6-seat tables restrict the maximum true penetration levels you'll get and the average number of cards you'll see per round to levels below those you'd get at a 7-player table.* More important, as you've seen, *the 6-player-maximum tables also cut down on your likelihood of winning!*

I have to believe that the designers of those tables were aware of what I am telling you, because, otherwise, why would casinos want tables that limit the number of players they can accommodate???

And...One Final Factor: Round Speed

Before I wrap things up, there's one more bug I'd like to put in your ear: the number of betting spots also affects the number of rounds you will see per hour. This is not only because of the obvious, which is: the more players who need to take turns, the longer each round will take. It is also because of other variables, including the relative speed of each dealer, and the amount of time each player takes, in making up his or her mind. Plus, with more players, and, therefore less rounds between shuffles (see Chart 3-1, page 18), the more *shuffling* the dealer will have to do per hour, which is additional down time.

This factor is apart from the extra velocity with which dealers deliver the cards to the solitary player. What I'm talking about here is the fact that there are variations in the normal pace of the game (even if the dealer speed holds the same).

This, too, favors the higher multiple player tables. The slower the round, the more time you have to think, and make the correct decisions. This may seem like a minor issue, but it's really not. You'll realize later on in this book how many things you need to keep track of; at that time, you'll appreciate the point I'm making here: the more time you have, the better you'll play.

So...What Should You Do With This Information?

At this time, you should appreciate the fact that *one of the critical choices you must make is: how many betting spots should be in play before you are willing to put your money on the line?*

Here is some advice, in conclusion:

❶ *Do not sit down to play at tables where less than 3 betting spots are being played* -- unless you don't mind playing multiple betting spots to make up the deficit. You want there to be a *minimum* of 4 spots (including yours) in play before you put your money down.

❷ Better yet -- when entering a casino, try to locate tables where 5 or 6 betting spots arc already taken.

❸ Once you've settled down at a table, if the number of betting spots being played dips below the number you have now decided is wise (either 4, if you're the average player, or, perhaps 6, or 7, if you're an especially discriminating player), either leave the table, or make what I call *placemaker bets* -- that means placing additional bets to bring the table total up to what you feel is necessary for a maximum win rate.

❹ Beware of changes in the number of betting spots *while you play*. This happens when players leave or if they vary the number of bets they're making. It's desirable that the total remains the *same,* because your realities then stay *constant,* and (as you'll find out later), a certain *predictability* results. You have two choices in this regard. First, you can be proactive and make placemaker bets to keep the number of betting spots *steady*. Or, second, you might instead decide to play only at tables where betting spot fluctuations are minimal, either because of casino policy (at "No Mid-Point Entry" tables, for example, new players are prevented from entering between shuffles), or because there's a stability in the number of players and a constancy in their betting habits.

❺ If the cards are bad, and you want to attempt to make them better, your only hope of doing so through changing the number of betting spots is to *increase* the number you've taken, to bring the table to a maximum number played (unless this condition already exists). In other words -- raising the number of spots taken to 6 or 7 might indeed raise your winning rate, now that you understand how the number of betting spots affects your probability of coming out a winner. Similarly, it should be painfully obvious to you now that doing the opposite -- *lowering* the number of betting spots to try to change the card flow for the better -- is actually helping to make them *worse*. The lower number of betting spots, the lower your chances of winning, as you've seen.

The only reason I don't urge everyone to seek out 6 or 7 player tables, or make placemaker bets to bring the number to that level, is because, for some, this is financially impractical. That's why I leave the door open to your playing in 4 and 5 player situations. If money is no object, though, you now know what you should do.

(A few words of clarification: finding a crowded table is always preferable to taking extra betting positions from the start -- for that, you usually want to see some action, put your toe in the water, so to speak, and make sure it's a good time to do so. There will be more on that topic in the chapters on "Gains Stages, Betting Spot Discoveries & More Precise Betting" and "Auxiliary Betting Indicators.")

What's Next?

In the next chapter, you'll get a look at blackjack's mathematical underpinnings as well as an introduction to the concept of probability, through my creation, *The Circle of 13*.

You will also find out how to make greater use of the information in this chapter, from a different angle. You will see how your *thinking* needs to adjust with every variation in the number of betting spots being played.

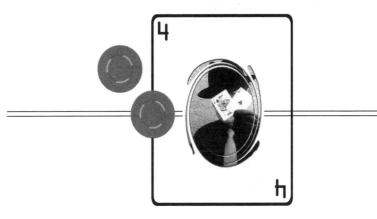

The Circle Of 13

What's Your
Question?

Herein May Lie
Your Answer!

T he number 13 is at the very heart of the game of blackjack, no matter how many cards are involved.

The game's lowest common denominators are the 13 different cards. Although they are associated together in four suits, all mathematical relationships in blackjack go back to these basic building blocks.

Understand, too, that cards are just *numbers*, and so simple math rules the game.

To get this very important concept across, I've invented a simple learning device I call *The Circle of 13*. The Circle of 13 will make you aware of the mathematical forces that rule the game; it will also be a valuable tool of which you can avail yourself in getting in touch with certain probabilities, in making card decisions. Plus -- it's a lot easier to think in terms of 13 rather than in terms of 52, 104 or other multi-deck multiples. You'll see how empowering this learning tool can be when we play some Circle of 13 games at the end of this chapter.

Why A *Circle?*

Now...why do I call my invention the *Circle* of 13?

First, because blackjack *revolves* around 13 cards. No matter how many decks are in play, the principles governing blackjack's predictability go back to its 13 basic building blocks, and the *proportion* in which each type of card appears (which always remains the same).

Second, because the Ace ties the relationship of the cards together in a neat circle, by its dual nature (its ability to be either be a 1-point or an 11-point card). The Ace is comfortable next to the 2 and the 10, because, like a chameleon, it can act like a low or a high card, in differing circumstances.

Circle of 13 Proportions and Imbalances

The Circle of 13 opens the doors to many crucial discoveries. We can use it to determine mathematical probabilities that will enable us to estimate, on the fly, what the dealer's hole card is likely to be, and what your hit cards are likely to be, in order to make smart moves. We can use it to understand the differing behavior of the dealer's various up cards. But let's start by using it to reveal to us the underlying card proportions that lead to certain mathematical realities a blackjack player must understand.

You'll notice, looking at the Circle (on the first page of this chapter), that two anomalies or imbalances have been built into the game (beyond those created by the fact that each suit contains an odd number of cards). They were created when the game's designers decided to make the Jack, Queen and King no more important or valuable than the "pip," the card sporting the number 10, and when they decided that the Ace would have a dual nature. If the Ace had been assigned just one, permanent value -- as either a low or a high card -- I think players would have a better handle on how this 13th card throws things off.

Let's see what effect these imbalances have on the game. You'd be surprised at how many players are not aware of these basic numbers, so it bears mentioning, especially because it is important to what comes later.

Looking again at The Circle of 13 diagram on page 33, you will see that four of the cards are 10-pointers. By dividing 4 by 13, you will find that those 10-pointers make up 30.77%, or nearly 31% of the cards -- which is a little less than one-third of each deck. That means that your *probability* of getting a 10-point card right after a shuffle is about 31%. That means, all things being equal, you would reasonably expect that about one of every three cards that was dealt would be a 10-pointer. We must definitely take this ratio into account when debating the wisdom of making any move. (By the way, I'll refer to all the 10-pointers from now on simply as 10s.)

Exposing Blackjack Misconceptions

With this information, we can use the Circle of 13 to expose a widely held *misconception* that has arisen from the fact that Circle of 13 is weighted in favor of the 10s. I'm referring particularly to what has seemed to become accepted as the Gospel Truth regarding the dealer's hole card, and this is how that Gospel Truth goes: you should always assume the dealer's hole card to be a 10. Sound familiar? This mistaken thinking has caused countless players to make mathematically illogical card strategy decisions, and, therefore, lose a lot of money.

Why is this thinking wrong? Looking at the Circle of 13, answer this question: how many of the cards are NOT 10s? *Nine of 13 cards! So, overall you have a much greater chance of NOT getting a 10 than you do of getting a 10. You will get a card that is NOT a 10 more than 69% of the time!*

So, the first major lesson I want you to take away from this chapter is: *you should NOT assume the dealer's hole card is likely to be a 10. If you've been among the many who have based their strategy on the assumption that the dealer's hole card is LIKELY to be a 10, you've been correct 31% of the time, and WRONG 69% of the time!*

In fact, when I show you (in the "What's Your Up Card IQ?" chapter) what scores the dealer's up cards tend to arrive at, you'll see how wrong this common misconception is. Like the sun's gravity attracts the planets, the imbalance involving the 10s does tend to draw each up card's average score one way or another; but its influence is not so great that you can simply add a 10 to each up card to figure out what score the dealer is likely to reach.

And yet, time after time, players I meet at my book signing events will state confidently: "you should *always* assume the hole card to be a 10!" That's what they've been taught.

When I explain to them how *wrong* that thinking is, they respond: "Well then, what SHOULD I assume the hole card to be?"

Intelligent question. That's one of many things you'll learn in this book. I will introduce you to a new method I've devised, in Chapter 9, which you will use to obtain the answer.

Another warning with regard to misconceptions that have arisen from the Circle of 13's imbalance of 10s: *if you're thinking of splitting or doubling, don't assume you're likely to get a 10.* This is another conclusion we can draw from the fact that the 10s, although overrepresented in the mix, are still in the minority. So, perhaps you will want to exercise greater caution before launching into doubling or splitting moves that require 10s to make them successful. (We'll discuss this in detail in Chapter 12.)

The Second Circle Imbalance

OK. So that's the first inequality that's been built into the game -- the imbalance due to the fact that four of the 13 basic building blocks are 10s. Now, let's talk about the second such condition: that is, the one caused by the Ace's ability to be either a 1- or an 11-point card. Without the Ace, six of the Circle of 13 cards (the cards that make up each suit) are low cards (the 2s through the 7s), and six are high cards (the 8s through the four different 10s). With the Ace weighing in as the 13th card, the scales will tip one way or another, depending on whether it acts as a low card or high card.

Here's one thing you should remember: if the Ace comes as one of the dealer's or player's first two cards, it will act as an 11-point card more times than not. However, if the Ace arrives after the dealer's or player's first two cards, it usually becomes a 1-point card.

How does this affect your game? One way is that, you should remember that if you need to take a hit card, an Ace, which could seem terribly good when it's part of your first two cards, might, in fact, only push you one step closer to busting. It might be undesirable in that situation. (If, however, you are doubling on a hand of 10 points the Ace of course is highly desirable.) So, it has a good/bad quality, of which you must remind yourself when figuring out whether it's smart to take a hit card or double.

This imbalance can also either tip the scales in favor of the dealer, or help lead to the dealer's busting -- depending on what the dealer's first two cards are. If the dealer has a 16, for instance, all of a sudden the Circle of 13, for all intents and purposes, contains 7 low cards -- the Ace would then cause the dealer to reach a score rather than bust, which, if you've stood on a stiff, would not be so good.

These are some of the reasons why you are going to want to keep track of how many Aces have been played. We'll talk about this in a moment; and, in greater detail, in Chapter 12, on "Strategic Card Analysis & Your Real-time Card Strategy."

The Concept of Balance Vis a Vis Probability

Now that we've spoken about imbalances that occur *within* the Circle of 13, let's talk about those that occur within the greater whole, the decks of cards in the game, as the game progresses. Such situations speak volumes about the types of cards that are likely to be dealt next; you must learn to read these imbalances and translate them into expressions of mathematical probability. Don't panic -- by the end of this book, this will become second nature to you. Let's start by seeing how you can use the Circle of 13 to spot and react to the imbalances that arise after each shuffle.

This application of The Circle of 13 is akin to cooking by recipe. For example -- in cooking by recipe, you must keep the prescribed proportion of each ingredient the same, no matter how many people you are cooking for. In other words, if your recipe requires that water make up 50% of the contents, no matter how many you will be cooking for -- 2, 5, 10, 20 people, or whatever -- you will have to adjust the amount of water you add to the ingredients to bring it to the 50% level. If, in the process of cooking, you find that one ingredient's proportion in relation to the other ingredients is less than it should be, you could say that the resulting food would be "off," or unbalanced, and you'd need to add MORE of the ingredients that were lacking to return it to its proper balance.

One difference is that, in blackjack, our "recipe" is represented by The Circle of 13, and any imbalance that develops in the course of play (through the disproportionate appearance of certain "ingredients" -- types of cards) will eventually be self-correcting. If everyone at the table has been "served" more than their "share" of low cards than the cards' proportions in the Circle would indicate, for instance, you would be correct in assuming that you would probably be "served" more than your "share" of HIGH cards in future rounds (and the reverse is true, of course). That's because the Circle of 13's "ingredients" consist of an equal number of low cards and high cards (not counting the Aces); so, if more low than high cards have been dealt, you know there's a surplus of high cards amongst the cards that remain.

This analogy deviates from the realities of cooking in another important way, though: in the modern game of blackjack, where the dealer shuffles up before all of the cards are dealt, things might NOT return to a balanced state (a balanced state being where the number of low cards played equals the number of high cards played). But, during the course of play, what is certain is that the tendency for the cards to right themselves to reflect their Circle of 13 proportions is an inevitable force. You can really profit from understanding this mathematical truth.

(Of course, *this truth becomes hard to utilize if you jump into the action between rounds, without any idea of what cards were already dealt before you sat down. That gives you a good reason NOT join a table in mid-action,*

UNLESS, of course, you have observed all of the cards after the shuffle, before choosing to join the table.)

So, now you see that the cards, based upon the composition of The Circle of 13, can be either *in* balance or *out of* balance. We will say the cards are *in balance* when each of them -- the Aces through the 10s -- have been dealt roughly in the same proportion they represent in the Circle. The cards are *out of* balance, or *unbalanced,* when individual cards or groups of cards are either under-represented or overrepresented among the cards dealt, based upon their Circle of 13 proportions. *From this we can obtain basic probabilities of certain cards being dealt: whatever has been overplayed is less likely to come with the cards the dealer deals next; whatever has been underplayed is more likely to come with the next cards.*

Circle of 13 Numbers

Now, to make this concept work to your benefit, you need a general reference, to figure out: 1) whether conditions are balanced or not, and, if not, which cards have been overrepresented and which cards have been under-represented; and, 2) how likely you are to get the card or cards you need to arrive at an acceptable score. Hence, the chart on the next page, which contains what I call the Circle of 13 Numbers. Please familiarize yourself with this chart -- these are numbers you should have at your fingertips in making card decisions.

One basic conclusion we can reach -- looking at the chart on the next page -- is that when the cards are *balanced*, each of the non-10s (the Aces through the 9s), which each account for 1 of 13 cards, will appear about 8% of the time, and the 10s will appear nearly 31% of the time. Said in terms of probabilities, this means that, in a balanced situation, you'll have an 8% likelihood of getting any one of the non-10s, (or, since non-10s account for 9 of 13 cards, you'd have a 69% probability overall of getting any one of the non-10s), and a 31% probability or likelihood of getting a 10.

Another way can use the Circle of 13 Numbers is to figure out how to handle each particular hand you get. You especially would want to know if you are likely to get what you might need, in considering any particular move -- doubling, splitting, hitting, surrendering, or standing. Now, understand this: *you always want your probability of getting what you want to be greater than 50%, and sometimes much more, before deciding that a particular move is wise, or that you are likely to do well with it.* So, that's where the percentages represented by the Circle of 13 Numbers come in.

For instance -- you might have an Ace and a 2. What's you're chance of getting one hit card that will give you a good score? You're thinking of doubling. First, use the Circle of 13 on page 33 (actually, you should be able to do this in your head by now) to determine which cards would help you. OK, they're the 4, 5, 6, 7 and 8. That's five cards. Now, look at the chart

CHART 4-1:

Circle of 13 Numbers

C13 #	%
1/13	7.69%
2/13	15.38%
3/13	23.08%
4/13	30.77%
5/13	38.46%
6/13	46.15%
7/13	53.85%
8/13	61.54%
9/13	69.23%
10/13	76.92%
11/13	84.62%

containing the Circle of 13 Numbers. Five of 13 gives you a percentage, or probability, of about 38%. Said in a different way, if you double on your Ace-2, you'll have a 62% chance of *not* drawing to an acceptable score. (Actually, an acceptable score might be even more difficult to achieve. If you're facing the dealer's up card of 7, for instance, you'd want to know that you'd reach a score of at least 18 points; 17 would give you, at best, a push in that situation. But -- I'm getting ahead of myself. You'll learn how to do this kind of fine tuning in later chapters.) So, your answer is: you definitely don't want to double here, if you're facing anything but the dealer's weakest up cards!

(In an unbalanced situation, by the way, the Circle of 13 Numbers can be used, but you'll want to factor in whether the particular cards you need have been under- or overplayed. If they've been underplayed, then the percentage represented by the Circle of 13 Number would go up by a certain extent, depending on how underplayed. If they've been overplayed, then you need to exercise some caution, because the Circle of 13 Number would have to be reduced to reflect the relative paucity of whatever cards you need that had been overplayed.)

How The Number of Players Affects Things

Now, one real important way we want to apply the Circle of 13 Numbers is in preparing ourselves for every variation in realities caused by the various numbers of betting spots that might be in use. We want to be armed with this information *before* sitting down to play, and we need to exercise it *during* the course of play. Don't forget to adjust your point of reference with this regard, with any change in the number of betting spots that are being taken. These types of changes occur practically every time you play.

Why do you need to do this? Because, as you saw in the last chapter, *depending on the number of betting spots being played, there will be a different number of cards showing on the table after the first two cards are dealt, and a different average number of cards played during each round.* (See page 18, Chapter 3.)

You already know these numbers -- and you should commit them to memory. Once you do that, you need to remember: 1) how many of each type of card should normally appear on the table, with each variation in the number of betting spots played (in a balanced card situation); and 2) knowing this -- if you've determined that the cards are out of balance, you then need to know how *far* out of balance each card or card group might be.

You can't answer the two questions above if you don't know beforehand what numbers to expect of each card in a balanced situation. And, if you can't answer the questions, you won't be able to come to important conclusions to make intelligent decisions about how to play your hand. And when I say *beforehand*, I mean that you should know these numbers *before* arriving at the casino.

To give you a point of reference to make it easier for you to answer these questions, I've used the Circle of 13 proportions to create Chart 4-2, on the following page. This chart tells you what to expect in card composition, per number of betting spots played. For each number of betting spots, I've given you numbers corresponding to two situations: 1) the total number of cards that are on the table right after the first two cards are dealt; and, 2) the average number of cards dealt per round, which would roughly correspond to how many cards might have been played by the time it's your turn -- if you're smart, and you're sitting in or very close to the 3rd Baseman's seat. (The latter are numbers to which you were introduced in the previous chapter -- you'll find them in the column titled "Cards Dealt," in the rows that refer to "Avg. Per Round.")

A word of explanation: the fractions, in the column representing the likelihood of your seeing any one of the non-10s on the table (in the column called "Probability for Each Non-10"), is simply a reminder that: a) with numbers below 1, there's no guarantee any one of them will be represented; and b) with numbers above 1, that means don't be surprised if one or more of the non-10s appears twice among the cards dealt -- they'd still be within a balanced scenario.

Tips In Remembering Key Information

One fascinating fact that makes committing this chart to memory easy is that: *the number of 10s dealt during any round -- if the cards are balanced -- should be equal to the number of betting spots being played at the table!* (If that's not the case, the 10s are probably out of balance.) (To clear up any confusion: I'm talking about the total number of cards played per round on average. Once again, a player sitting in or close to the 3rd Baseman's seat might expect to see nearly this many cards.) You can use this information before your turn, and after the round is over, to check on how balanced things are. For example -- if there are five players at your table, and eight 10s have appeared before your turn, you would know (because, in a balanced state, there would only be as many 10s as players, or five in this case) that the 10s have been *overplayed* and you're not terribly likely to get one if you need one to make your hand. For the same reason, you would know that the 10s are likely to show up in below-normal numbers in the next round.

Now, we can make a simple change to this rule to help the players whose turns come *before* anyone has taken any hit cards; in that situation, *the number of 10s dealt with the first two cards -- if the cards are balanced -- should, on average, be equal to the number of betting spots being played minus 1! If that's not the case, the cards are probably out of balance.*

Now, as I mentioned before, I don't recommend you play at a table with less than at least 4 betting spots being played (including yours), so this will

CHART 4-2:

Circle of 13 Re: # of Players

# Players	Cards Dealt (2-Tiered)	#10s	# Non-10s Overall	Probability for Each Non-10	# Low or High Cards
1: First 2	4	1	3	Miniscule	2 each
1: Avg. Per Round	6	2	4	Less than .5	3 each
2: First 2	6	2	4	Less than .5	3 each
2: Avg. Per Round	8	2	6	.62	4 each
3: First 2	8	2	6	.62	4 each
3: Avg. Per Round	11	3	8	.85	5 each (assumes 1 Ace)
4: First 2	10	3	7	.77	9 total: 4 or 5 each (assumes 1 Ace)
4: Avg. Per Round	13	4	9	1	6 each (assumes 1 Ace)
5: First 2	12	4	8	.92	11 total: 5 or 6 each (assumes 1 Ace)
5: Avg. Per Round	16	5	11	1.23	15 total: 7 or 8 each (assumes 1 Ace)
6: First 2	14	4	10	1	13 total: 6 or 7 each (assumes 1 Ace)
6: Avg. Per Round	19	6	13	1.46	9 each (assumes 1 Ace)
7: First 2	16	5	11	1.23	15 total: 7 or 8 each (assumes 1 Ace)
7: Avg. Per Round	22	7	15	1.69	10 each (assumes 2 Aces)

cut down on what you need to remember from the chart, too. Along these lines, here's a trick to remembering the average number of cards you'll get per round at all table situations you'll encounter: at a table with four betting spots in play, the average number is 13, the same number as in one of the suits. The number goes up exactly 3 for each player that's added! So, if you're at a table where six spots are being played, you can expect to see 13+3+3 = 19 cards per round. This is an important consideration, of course, especially for card counters and for those who play at multiple deck tables (you'll see why later) -- you need to keep track of roughly how many cards have been played, and the method I've just taught you is super for that.

Getting A Grip On Probability

The reason why you need to determine whether the cards are balanced or not is that this information enables you to get a grip on the probabilities you need to know each round; in that way, you will be able to figure out how the cards are likely to behave. Once you have a handle on the probability of certain important events happening -- such as the dealer getting a good or bad hole card -- you can then make smarter moves and make more money.

Let's have some fun and see how you might do this. I have come up with a simple way of quickly demonstrating the principles we've just discussed. I use only one suit of cards -- I play out rounds with only 13 cards, the same cards found in The Circle of 13. This exercise really seems to get the point across, so let's spend a little time playing hands, as if blackjack only contained 13 cards, and see what we might learn.

Of course, you'll need a more sophisticated approach at the casino than is required when only 13 cards are used, and I will get to that later. My goal here is simply to show you the mathematical forces you can harness to play a great game. I also want to show you the limitations of something we've yet to discuss -- Basic Card Strategy.

Circle of 13 Games

Now, if you were at one of my workshops, I'd have you come up and sit at a table with the others, to play what I call Circle of 13 demonstration games. These are blackjack demonstrations using just one suit of cards. Just to let you know -- I'm using real cards, and what follows are graphical representations of what really happened in these actual card examples. The reason I mention this, is that I won't sugar coat these examples, or manipulate them to give you any false impressions. Blackjack strategy -- whether we're talking Basic Strategy, or card counting strategies, or my methods -- do not enable you to win every hand. Nor does each prediction based on sound mathematical logic lead to 100% accuracy. In this way, I hope to prepare you for the actualities you'll face at the casino. I can't emphasize or repeat this enough: winning at blackjack involves *playing the percentages*. If you

know that making a particular move will work 60% of the time, then, that's
the way to go; I'm sure you understand the flip side of that equation,
however: that, a minority of the time, or 40% in this case, the move won't
work. Nothing works 100% of the time.

OK. Let's have some fun. The dealer has shuffled the 13 cards our Circle
of 13 game contains, and the cards are balanced -- none have been played.

There are three players at this table, including yourself. You are sitting in
the 3rd Baseman's seat. You're smart -- you're there because you want to
see a maximum number of cards before it's your turn. The more cards you
are able to observe, the better you will be at predicting what your hit card
will be. The more you know about that hit card, the smarter you will be in
deciding what move to make. (By the way, while the dealer normally burns
the top card, we won't do so in these examples, so we have enough cards to
play out all of the hands.)

Let's start! The dealer deals these cards:

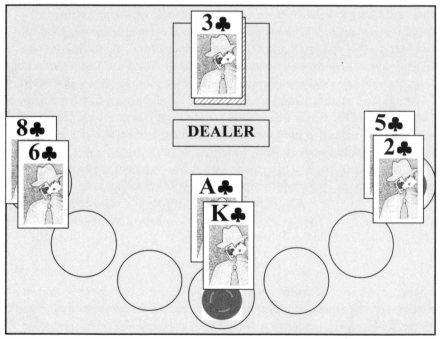

The first thing you want to do is see whether the cards are balanced or not,
and, if not, what that imbalance tells you about the probabilities. Referring
to Chart 4-2 on page 42 (which you should try to memorize before your next
trip to a casino), you'll see that *because three betting spots are in play, 8
cards have been dealt with the first two cards. Of those eight -- if the cards
are balanced -- two of them should be 10s. Also, there should be four low
cards and four high cards, with non-10s accounting for 6 of the cards.* This
is how your mind should work.

Then, you compare this balanced scenario to the reality you're faced with. In the example on page 44, what do you see? Yes, there are four low cards. But there's one Ace (which was not a given with this number of cards), and just two high cards showing; the eighth card is the hole card, hidden from view. So, the face-up cards are unbalanced in favor of two more low cards than high cards. Plus -- while we expected to see two 10s, there's just one.

Figuring Out What The Dealer's Hole Card Is

Now, earlier in this chapter, I promised to teach you how to find the answer to one of the primary questions a player wants answered: *What's the dealer's hole card likely to be?*

Some writers suggest that making this determination is impossible, and others ignore the matter entirely. Yet, as you will see, this mystery indeed can be unraveled. This knowledge will give you a tremendous edge, as you might imagine. (This issue will be covered further in later chapters, as well.)

In answering this question, we especially want to know: what is the probability that the hole card will be a *bad* card for the dealer, one that would make the dealer likely to bust with the next hit card? With the 3 as the up card, this would be a 9 or a 10. These cards would give the dealer a stiff, a total that might then bust with one more card. Anything less would give the dealer a good shot at achieving an acceptable score (which, for the dealer, would be anything from 17 through 21).

We know that, with seven of 13 cards face up on the table, six cards remain unknown to us, one of those being the hole card. Of those, three of those must be 10s, because, of the cards we can observe, only one of the four 10s -- the King -- is represented.

Now, notice that the cards are unbalanced here: four of the six low cards have been dealt, but only two of the six high cards have appeared. Reading the cards in this way tells us that it's much more likely that the hole card will be one of the cards we just mentioned that would be bad for the dealer -- a 9 or one of the 10s -- than a low card.

In fact, with only 13 cards in our game, we can get more specific (take a moment to look at the cards and figure out what's *not* been played)...

Here's what we can conclude: with a 4, 7, 9 and three 10s left unplayed, there's a *66% probability* that the hole card will give the dealer a dangerous stiff total. That's good news for you!

Of course, overall, we can say with certainty that, with 3 of six cards unknown to us being 10s, there is a 50% probability of the hole card being a 10. But, our 8-card analysis should actually be even more precise a predictor. Based on that, I would guess it's likely to be a 10. Our 8-card analysis -- which offers a snapshot of the reality of the moment -- indicates we are short one 10: you should expect two 10s to arrive with every 8 cards, and we see just one.

See how simple math and deduction, working in concert with your under-standing of The Circle of 13, can give you very important answers, in determining probabilities and how you should move?

Let's look at the 1st Baseman's cards. With a 2 and a 5, a total of 7, there's no chance of busting. With a strong likelihood of getting a high card (if we figure the hole card is a 10, then two 10s and one 9 remain among the five cards yet to be dealt -- 60% of the remaining cards, the other two cards or 40% consisting of a 4 and the 7), we know this player will probably score a 16 or 17. Assuming the dealer indeed has a 10, the dealer would have to get one of the remaining high cards to bust. We also know that, if the 1st Baseman does get a high card, four cards would remain, half high and half low, so the dealer will most likely have a 50-50 chance of scoring or busting; the low cards would lead to likely dealer scores of either 17 or 20. I wouldn't double here. I want the probabilities to be above 50% in my favor before I would consider putting twice my money on the line.

OK, so the 1st Baseman just hits this hand. The hit card turns out to be a 7, as we see below:

The probabilities had told us that the hit card was most *likely* to be a high card. In this case, the player's reality reflected the *minority* side of the equation -- we knew 40% of the remaining cards were low cards, and that, over time, they'd make their appearance.

I'm actually glad that happened. That demonstrates something important: *probabilities are NOT certainties*.

We cannot predict events with 100% accuracy. But it's nothing to get upset about. *What matters is that you determine the probabilities within a good degree of accuracy, and then most of the time you'll win in that situation. That's all you need to tip the scales in your favor, and become a consistent winner. This is an important concept to understand.*

(A small number of players who see my Circle of 13 game demonstrations don't seem to understand this. When they see the minority of times when the probabilities fail us, they groan. They're missing the point!)

And, in fact -- nothing is lost here!

Although the 1st Baseman's total of 14 points is nothing to cheer about, the 7 dealt to that player is actually very good news. The probabilities are now greatly in the favor of *everyone* at the table *winning*.

If our assumption that the hole card is a 10 is true, then two 10s and one 9 remain among the four undealt cards, giving the dealer a 75% probability of busting!

OK, so the First Baseman now wisely stands, as do you, the 3rd Baseman. (The 2nd Baseman gets paid off for the Blackjack immediately.) Most of the remaining cards would bust your hand. The dealer displays the hole card (which is one of the 10s as we predicted!) and then takes a hit card:

The dealer busts with the hit card, which -- no surprise to us -- was one of the high cards. *We knew with good assurance what was likely to happen.* The mathematical realities we were able to ferret out told us the dealer was likely to have a high card under the 3, and then was likely to bust with another high card, and that's what happened. *This is the kind of information that will often enable you to make winning moves, and increase not only your winning rate, but your monetary gains as well.*

However, don't forget that if you faced this very same situation hundreds or more times over the course of years, in a minority of cases you would run into times where the dealer's hole card in fact turned out to be that one low card, the 4. In that case, the dealer -- with one 9 and three 10s remaining unplayed -- would stand a 75% chance of drawing to a 17, beating your stiff.

Once again, we play the percentages. Make the move that wins most, understanding that it will lose a minority of times.

OK. Let's continue with our Circle of 13 games! Now that you've got the idea, here are seven card Circle of 13 game situations, with questions for you to anwer. The answers are on page 51, following the examples.

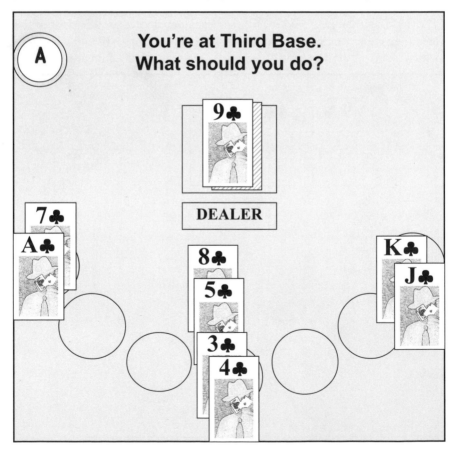

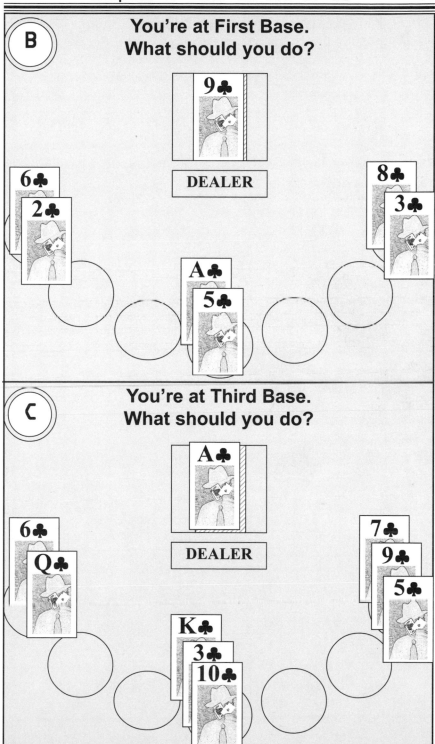

You're at First Base.
What should you do?

9♣

DEALER

6♣
2♣

8♣
3♣

A♣
5♣

You're at Third Base.
What should you do?

A♣

DEALER

6♣
Q♣

7♣
9♣
5♣

K♣
3♣
10♣

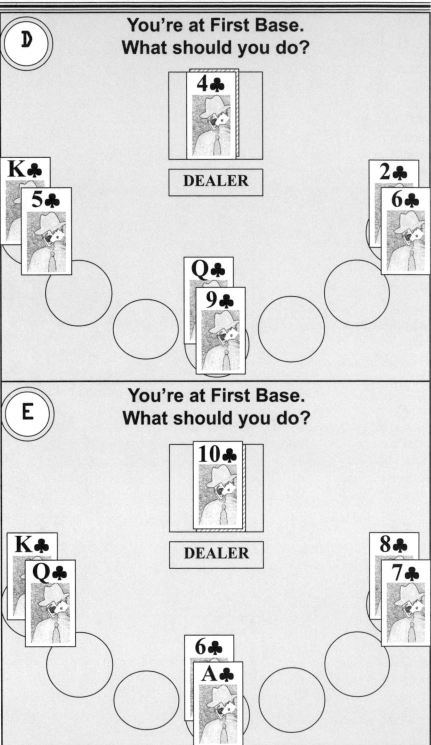

D

You're at First Base.
What should you do?

4♣

DEALER

K♣
5♣

2♣
6♣

Q♣
9♣

E

You're at First Base.
What should you do?

10♣

DEALER

K♣
Q♣

8♣
7♣

6♣
A♣

Circle of 13 Games Answers

Here are the answers to the seven examples. Let's see how well you did!:

Example A: You should hit. It looks unlikely your soft 18 will beat the dealer. Of the four cards unknown are a 2, 6 and two 10s. If the 2 is the hole card, the dealer has a 66% probability of scoring a 21, beating you; if the hole card is one of the 10s, the dealer scores a 19, beating you. Only the 6 as a hole card would make the dealer likely to bust. Also -- since 3 of 4 possible cards, the 2 and the 10s, would either help you or at least not hurt you, you therefore have a 75% shot at beating your odds of losing here. Note how this goes against Basic Strategy recommendations, but is the wisest move. Here's how it played out: you drew the 2, scoring 20 points. The dealer's hole card was a 6; the dealer busted with the hit card, a Queen.

Example B: You should double. Of the 6 unknown cards, FOUR are 10s, giving you a 21, and a fifth, the 7, wouldn't be so bad -- it wouldn't give you a strong total, but you still might win with it. The 10s would give you a 66% probability of winning -- that's enough to double. Here's how it played out: you drew the 10. The next player drew the Queen and King, busting. The next player drew the 4 and 7, achieving a 19. The hole card was a 9, for a dealer score of 19. You won, double. Note: My Basic Strategy warns against doubling with the dealer's 9; however, here, because of the specific card situation, it was a smart move.

Example C: This is a bit tricky, but very instructive regarding cases where the dealer has an Ace as the up card. Let's figure this out: what cards might you receive as hit cards? The 2, 4, 8 and Jack. Half of these, the 8 and Jack, would bust you. Now, we have an advantage here. We *know* the dealer doesn't have the Jack in the hole -- that was ruled out during the dealer's routine Blackjack check. So we know you have a 33.33% likelihood of getting the Jack -- it's definitely one of the three undealt cards. Of the two other undealt cards, you have a 33.33% chance of getting the 8 (the other bust card), and a 66.66% shot at getting the more helpful 2 and 4. But, don't forget: *you'll lose half the time with the 2 or 4 due to the dealer outscoring you.* (If you get the 2, the dealer will have the 4 or 8 in the hole; the 8 would provide the dealer with a higher score than yours. If you get the 4, the dealer will beat you if the hole card is the 2.) Overall, you have a 78% probability of *losing* (33.33% because of the Jack, plus 44.44% in likely losses from the realities presented by the two other mystery cards held by the dealer). So, you should *surrender* if you have that option (or hit if you don't). Here's how it played out: you received the 4, pulling to a 20. But the dealer had the 2 in the hole and drew the 8 as the hit card, beating you with 21 points.

Example D: I would have doubled here -- a somewhat risky move, but the odds are in your favor. If four of the 6 unknown cards -- the 8, two 10s and Ace -- turned out to be the dealer's hole card, the dealer would have a greater risk of busting than of scoring. A bit on the edge, and so, if you chose to hit here, I wouldn't fault you. Here's how it played out: you drew the Ace, for a score of 19. The dealer then drew a 3, for a 17. You won, double.

Example E: You should NOT have surrendered here, even though Basic Strategy recommends it. An advanced player knows that, with a distinct majority of the six unknown cards (66%) -- the 2, 3, 4 and 5 -- being low cards, cards you want, you should go for broke, take a hit. Here's how it played out: you drew the 9 and busted. Nonetheless, it was the smartest move, and, if you'd faced this same situation repeatedly over time, you would have won more that way than you'd have gained by surrendering.

Don't be confused by what happens in situations where you get the short end of the probability stick -- that is, when what is least likely to happen happens, and your move results in a loss. (That being said, there are plenty of know-it-alls who'll tell you that you made a wrong move in those cases. Pay them no mind.) I mentioned how these hands played out to satisfy your curiosity, but *one hand does not a rule make*. This is an important point that bears repeating.

What I'm teaching you is how to play hands so that you're choosing the way that wins *most often*. You will see each situation many times over the course of a lifetime of playing. Play them the right way, and you'll do best. *No* strategy, after all, will enable you to win with any one move all the time (even your Blackjacks will sometimes be negated when the dealer's 10 has an Ace in the hole, or the dealer's Ace has a 10 in the hole and you've chosen not to take Insurance or Even Money).

What I hope you've learned, with the Circle of 13 Games, is the concept that you should determine what your odds of winning are with any move, and then go with the strategy that gives you the best odds. Each move will have its risk of losing -- if you choose the right move, however, that risk will be less than had you gone another way.

As any poker player can tell you, once you decide the odds and make your best move, the rest is up to chance, regarding the particular round you are playing; you will get your share of bad breaks, but that's OK. You'll win in the long run by making the smartest moves that, over time, will cause you to do the best in each situation, over time.

What Do These Games Tell Us?

To clear up any other misconceptions, let's summarize what lessons we can draw from the Circle of 13 Games, and what lessons we cannot. Sometimes I get the feeling that some people, having seen these games at my book events, leave as if they believe they've learned all they need to know to win at blackjack. No -- a 13-card game is a different animal than the one we play (for one thing, it's *much* easier!).

The purpose of these games was to demonstrate to you the principles of probability and predictability; the need and usefulness of paying attention to what cards have been played; the need to think on your feet; and also, how your card strategy should be flexible enough to respond to the card situations at hand -- that you should not be a slave to rigid strategy guidelines, such as you find in Basic Strategy.

You cannot play blackjack exactly as we have in these Circle Games. You need a more sophisticated approach (which is what this book is about)!

Other Questions Answered By The Circle of 13

You've seen how useful the Circle of 13 can be. But, before we move on, I'd like to suggest at least one other use for The Circle of 13, although there are others. Let's look at how the Circle can give you insight into why each of the dealer's different value up cards behaves differently -- why some are strong for the dealer, and some weak. Each of the dealer's different up cards draws to a different average total because of the way its numerical value combines with the numerical values of the other cards.

Let's start with the dealer's Ace, with a view toward figuring out why it is such a strong card for the dealer. Look at The Circle of 13, on page 33, and answer this question: how many of those cards would combine with the dealer's Ace to give the dealer a score of 17 through 21? (These are the scores upon which the dealer would stand at most casinos, with the possible exception of a soft 17 -- the Ace-6).

The answer?: EIGHT of the 13 possible hole cards, would immediately provide the dealer with scores of 17 through 21 points -- the 6 through the four 10s. Put another way, 62% (a significant majority) of the possible hole cards would immediately put the dealer in a strong position. Understand, too, that, if any of the remaining 5 cards were the hole card -- the Ace, 2, 3, 4 and 5 -- the dealer would achieve a certain number of additional acceptable totals, too, with hands of 3 cards and more. *The Circle of 13 in this way gives you some insight into the strength of the dealer's Ace, and why a player would not want to stand on stiffs (totals of 12 through 16) against it.*

Similarly, using The Circle of 13, you see why the dealer's 10 and 9 also lead to strong positions for the dealer:

With the dealer's 10, The Circle of 13 shows you that eight of the possible 13 hole cards would give the dealer an immediate, 2-card hand that's within the range of 17 to 21 points. That's more than 60% of the cards! While we shouldn't really call these "winning" scores, because players might indeed beat, or push (tie) against these totals, they certainly put players in a position of having to hit their stiffs to try to beat the dealer. Any time the player has to do that, he or she risks busting, and that, of course favors the dealer.

With the dealer's 9, seven of the 13 possible hole cards (refer to The Circle of 13) -- the 8, 9, four 10s and Ace -- give the dealer immediate totals of between 17 and 21 points. That's nearly 54% of the cards! And another card

-- the 2 -- would give the dealer's 9 a good start, too, with a total of 11 points -- one that would lead to strong scores with just one more card: eight of the 13 possible hit cards the dealer might then draw (the 6, 7, 8, 9 and four 10s) would lead to totals of 17 to 21 points.

In contrast, let's use The Circle of 13 to understand why the dealer's 6 is such a weak up card.

Go to the chart, and answer the question: how many of these 13 cards would give the dealer a stiff (a hand of between 12 and 16 points that is in danger of busting with one more card) or underscore (a score below 17, on which the dealer could not stand)?

The answers? The 6, 7, 8, 9 and four 10s -- eight of 13 possible hole cards would put the dealer's 6 in a precarious position. Put another way, the dealer's would get into immediate trouble 62% of the time, simply because of the way the 13 possible hole cards combine with the number 6. In addition, the 6 would reach an underscore with the 2 through 5 -- four addtional cards. Some of those underscores will result in the dealer busting as well. Only one card in the Circle of 13 would give the dealer's 6 an acceptable score -- the Ace -- and that's only if the casino allows dealers to stand on soft 17s.

(There will more much more on the dealer's up cards in later chapters.)

You can do this kind of exercise yourself, and get answers to many of your questions, by using the Circle of 13. As you have seen, the cards are just numbers, which combine with each other in ways that can be explained with simple math, through the Circle of 13.

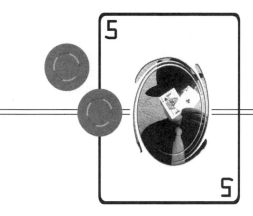

How Shuffling Affects Your Game

The next time you're at the casino, watch what your fellow players are doing while the dealer is shuffling. Most take their eyes off the table. Some chat with the dealer, or amongst themselves. Some even go to the bathroom. *The vast majority pay absolutely no attention to how the dealer is shuffling!* They're unaware of the huge impact it has on their game. (This is especially apparent when the dealer asks them to cut the cards; they don't have a *clue* as to how to do it, or that it can produce beneficial results if done properly.)

Yet, *shuffling is one of the most important aspects of the game, and, in many ways, it holds the key to your success.* You can gain a lot of power *if* you watch how the shuffling is being done *and* understand what's going on.

Why You Should Pay Attention To Shuffling

Standardized casino shuffling predetermines what your next hands will be; where the *good* cards from prior rounds will go, and the *bad*. Master its ins and outs, and you will know:

❶   What cards are likely to return, and *when*.

❷   What your chances of winning are.

❸   Where to place the cut card, if that duty falls to you.

❹   What effect others' placing of the cut card will have on rounds to come.

❺   How to bet.

❻   What up cards are most likely to repeat.

In this chapter, we will solve the mystery of where the cards go during dealer shuffling. Then, you'll learn how to cash in on these revelations.

Dealer Versus Machine Shuffling

As of this writing, most casinos are still using dealers to shuffle the cards. But this could change rapidly, if players don't exercise their power of discrimination -- in a positive sense. So, one thing you should take away with you from this chapter is: *avoid tables where shuffling machines are being used.* If everyone does this, casinos will have to chuck those insidious devices, which take a big bite out of your winning potential.

Why do we want to play at tables where *humans* do the shuffling?

As you will see in detail, dealer shuffling produces a **nonrandom** result. Similarities persist from shuffle to shuffle. Amazingly enough, my studies have shown that, *30 to 60 shuffles after they've first been introduced, the cards have yet to be randomized. Because of this, repeating phenomena are produced (some of which I've newly discovered), which lead to a predictability factor of which smart players can take advantage. In fact, this is one reason blackjack is so winnable.*

The cards don't vary much in their order from one shuffle to another, especially from the standpoint of their proximity to one another. They also tend to keep the same relative order because of the fact that most players cut the cards in the same place: the middle.

The Drawbacks of Shuffling Machines

A threat to this favorable reality are new, computerized shuffling machines that randomize the cards. The intent of these machines is to eliminate the predictability that comes from dealer shuffling.

The older machines are not randomizers and are less damaging to your game. In fact, when one such machine was opened for repairs, I noticed that it was doing just one simple riffle shuffle. It was producing far less reordering than dealer shuffling would do! So playing against this machine might not have been terribly detrimental to your game -- so long as you understood what a riffle shuffle does to the cards (as you soon will).

Some casinos, however, are using the older machines to *continuously* shuffle the cards during play, which leads to a pseudo-randomizing effect that makes it hard for players to keep track of what's coming. Try to avoid these tables.

There are also the Digital 21 games encroaching on the scene, where tables contain videoscreens instead of betting spots. The virtual cards appearing on players' screens are -- at *best* -- randomly chosen by computer, destroying the player advantage that comes with predictable, NON-random cards, and dealer shuffling (one wonders, also, whether those games aren't programmed, as slot machines are, to ensure that players *lose a specific percentage of times*). My advice to you is: *avoid these games*, too.

The Different Types of Dealer Shuffling

Let's start by talking about the various types of shuffles of which you should be aware (see the photos on the following pages). Each one affects the order of the cards differently.

There's: washing, riffling, stripping, and boxing (see photos on pages 58-62). We'll go into each in detail, and then we'll look at: how the cards are affected by the practice of having a player cut the cards after shuffling; how the dealer's placing of the undealt cards in the discards just before the next shuffle affects the cards you will see next; and, how the actual dealing of the cards affects what you get in the future. But first, let me stress that, *no matter how many decks are in the game you're playing, dealer shuffling can be reduced to the basic elements of washing, riffling, stripping and boxing.*

Now, *each casino has its own style of standardized shuffling routine that involves different sequences and patterns of cutting the cards, riffling, stripping (if done) and boxing (if done).* That means the cards wind up in different places at different casinos. The good news, however, is that the results are equally predictable.

You have to do some homework, though, and preferably *before* you play. You should go to your favorite casinos and observe their shuffling method: notice how often they do each type, and in what order. Then, go home and -- taking what you're going to learn in this chapter -- see what effect each casino's method does to the order of the cards. I'll give you a simple way of doing this at the end of the chapter. (It would be a daunting task to list the way each casino in the world does it; I'm not even going to try. Plus, these shuffling methods change from time to time and sometimes vary per dealer. So, it's best if you learn to analyze what's going on, at any particular time.)

Typical Shuffling Styles

Dealer shuffling is done in a sequence of procedures that usually includes at least two types of shuffles: riffling, and stripping. It's not uncommon for casinos to have their dealers do one riffle, one strip, followed by two riffles, for example. We'll call this the **RS2R** from now on. *You'll find this procedure, with subtle variations, at 1- and 2-deck pitch game tables, as well as at multi-deck shoe game tables.* No matter how many decks are in the game, most casinos have dealers shuffle just one deck's worth of cards at any time.

For instance, at one casino that offers 2-deck games, the shuffling procedure goes this way: the dealer takes the undealt cards and places them on top of the cards in the discard tray *(always watch where the undealt cards go vis a vis the discards!).* So, all the cards wind up together in one big 2-deck pile again. Then the dealer cuts the cards in half, so they're roughly in 1-deck

(Continued on page 63)

CHART 5-1:

Washing: In 3 Steps

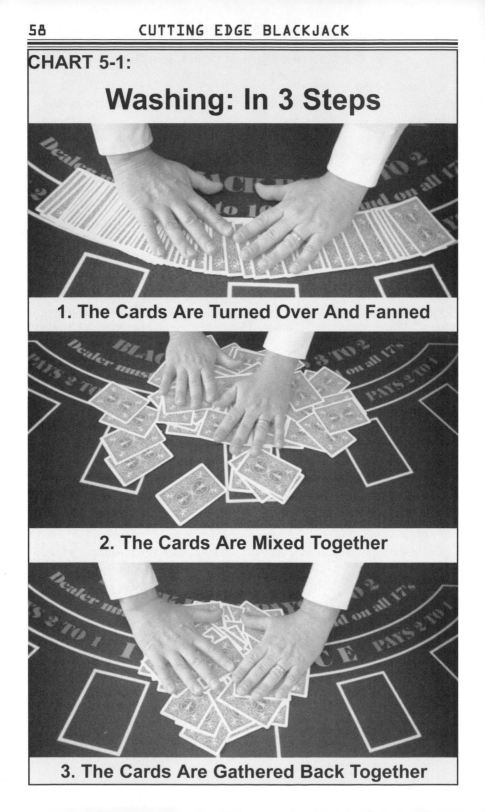

1. The Cards Are Turned Over And Fanned

2. The Cards Are Mixed Together

3. The Cards Are Gathered Back Together

CHART 5-2:

Riffling: In 2 Steps

1. The Dealer Cuts The Cards In Halves

2. The Halves Are Riffled Together

CHART 5-3:

Stripping: In A Variable Number of Steps

The Dealer Progressively...

Moves Clumps of Cards...

**From The Top of The Deck
To A New, Re-Arranged Pile on the Table**

CHART 5-4:

Boxing: In 2 Steps

1. The Dealer Cuts The Cards In Halves

2. The Bottom Half Is Placed On Top

CHART 5-5:

The Final Steps

1. A Player Cuts The Cards With A Plastic Marker

2. The Dealer Moves The Cards Below The Cut Card To The Top, And Then Inserts The Marker Into The Cards To Indicate The Reshuffle Point

piles. The dealer then takes about a half of a deck's worth of cards from the top of each pile, and riffles them together. Then he or she strips them, and does two more quick riffles. The dealer then does the same procedure to the *bottom halves* of the original 1-deck piles that were created from the 2-deck pile of discards and undealt remainders after the last round of action. (By the way, I've noticed that the dealers sometimes get lazy and only riffle the cards *once* after the stripping. That's a player benefit, because less reordering occurs; therefore, the result produces rounds that are that much more similar to what came before the shuffle!)

The procedure described above can be found at many casinos, with slight variations. One casino, for instance, has its dealers place the undealt cards in the *middle* of the discards, and then they do a procedure similar to the above, *and* they also do one boxing procedure. Another casino has its pitch game dealers do a simple riffle-strip-riffle procedure.

(Shuffling at 1-deck games, by the way, is handled in a similar way, except, of course, there are just two deck halves to shuffle together.)

Multi-deck (Shoe Game) Shuffling

Shuffling at multi-deck shoe game tables may seem different, but it's not. It just involves more repetitions of a simple procedure. Dealers shuffle the cards in sequential fashion. They don't shuffle all the cards at once.

It starts with the removal of the undealt cards from the shoe, then the discards from the discard tray. How they combine these cards differs from casino to casino, so watch this carefully.

The dealer then usually creates two more or less equal halves. Then he or she will typically take approximately one deck of cards from the tops of the two large piles, and place them on the table, until there are two rows containing more or less equal stacks. From those new smaller piles, the dealer will probably take half a deck of cards from the tops, and do a shuffling procedure which is frequently a bit *simpler* than what you see at pitch game tables -- such as a riffle/stripping/riffle (or **RSR**) sequence, which creates a new 1-deck pile. Then he or she will take the bottoms of the small 1-deck piles whose tops were just shuffled together, and do the same **RSR** sequence on those cards (which creates a second new 1-deck pile).

Once completed, the 1-deck piles will be riffled together, into a new 2-deck pile. Upon this 2-deck pile will be placed other 2-deck piles created in the same way, until the process is complete, depending on the number of decks in the game.

Because multi-deck shuffling takes more time than with the pitch games, and time is money, most casinos limit their multi-deck shuffling to the simplest of procedures. The simpler the procedure, of course, the less the card order is being changed, which also means the cards will be more predictable later.

Given the fact that multi-deck shuffling is done in 1- and 2-deck blocks of cards, each block of cards getting only the simplest of shuffling procedures, it should not be hard for you to figure out what's occurring in each block during the shuffling process: *it's basically the same thing that's occurring in the 2-deck games*, with secondary subsets of 2-decks' worth of cards not being shuffled further, but simply being stacked together with other similar subsets of cards, until all the cards are shuffled in this 2-deck by 2-deck fashion.

The point is -- it doesn't matter what variation or style the casinos use. Each *type* of shuffling used in any casino's shuffling sequence has its own particular effect on the cards, about which I will teach you. So, no matter what the sequence, you should be able to tell where the cards you want to follow might be.

OK -- let's see exactly where the cards go during each type of shuffle!

What Does Washing Do?

The washing procedure is only done with new cards. This particular type of shuffling is very individual to each dealer. (See photo, page 58.) Some try to do a real good job of mixing the suits together, others are in a hurry and give it the once over, leaving many cards grouped among cards of their suit.

One thing you definitely want to make sure of is that the dealer -- inadvertently or otherwise -- doesn't end up creating clumps of high cards and low cards during the washing phase. The photos on the next page illustrate how this might happen. (For simplicity, the example pictured is that of a 1-deck game; the principle demonstrated operates in the very same way, however, for all the multi-deck variants, as well.)

The top photo shows how the cards are ordered before the process begins (they are pictured face-up here so you can see what's going on; but, of course, they'd be face-down in actuality). Look specifically at the middle of the fanned out cards (in the top two photos). This is how the cards are arranged in the box. The two suits in the middle -- the clubs and the diamonds -- are in reverse order to each other, which creates a grouping of 8 of the deck's 16 10-point cards. *Half of the 10s in each deck are right in the middle!*

Now, if the dealer is careless (see the bottom photo), and does the washing procedure by moving this group of eight 10s in the middle off to one side, keeping them separated and closely associated during the procedure, this could lead to problems. For one thing, it might create a long string of low cards that could devastate players -- those low cards, for instance, would help the dealer's stiffs reach acceptable scores and not bust, while tending to freeze players in their tracks, with stiffs facing low up cards; players would also suffer from the lack of hand-making high cards.

Now, this kind of problem happens only rarely. But it doesn't hurt to be on

CHART 5-6:

Washing Away The Middle 10s

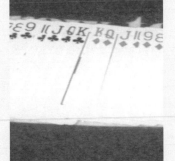

Above: Enlargement of Inset In Top Photo,
Showing The Middle 10s.
Below: The Dealer Shuffling Away These 10s.

the lookout for it -- I've seen it happen from time to time.

However, hasty and sloppy washing jobs are not infrequent. These cause cards to stay pretty much amongst cards of their own suit, with detrimental strings of low cards. (On the other hand, this can sometimes work to your advantage -- if a Jack of Spades is dealt, for instance, you might be able to anticipate the coming of the Queen and King.)

So, if you are playing when new cards are brought in, be on alert for these kinds of problems. If the washing is done poorly, it might be best to move to another table. Once you've absorbed the concept that the cards don't change very much from shuffle to shuffle, then you'll understand that, if the cards start off in a bad order, they'll stay that way for some time.

(By the way -- the radical changes and uncertainties brought about by the introduction of new cards is one reason I *leave immediately* if new cards are brought in after I've achieved a sizeable gain.)

What Does Riffling Do?

Riffling is a much more standardized and predictable procedure than washing. How carefully it is done is often set by casino policy, but it is also sometimes determined by the skill level of the dealer. Actually, I should probably refer to this procedure as *cutting* and riffling, because before the dealer riffles the cards, he or she must divide the cards into approximate halves. (See photo, page 59.)

Now, a real talented dealer, in a casino that wants dealers to riffle real well, will attempt to be exacting about this, alternately placing one card from one of the halves on top of one card from the other half, and so on. Typically, this type of dealer will begin quite slowly and deliberately, and then speed up as soon as much of the lower halves have been carefully knitted together. As the dealer quickens the pace (resulting in the telltale *riffling* sound), the tendency is for *two* cards from one half to occasionally find their way between cards of the other half.

In contrast, a *sloppy* dealer is less likely to join the two halves together card-by-card. Cards from one half are likely to come in groups of three or more before cards from the other half fall. Of course, for players, *the sloppier the dealer, the better.* That's one reason why we love beginners. The more the cards stay together exactly as they were from prior rounds, the more predictable the cards will be following the shuffle.

So, observe the dealer carefully with regard to skill level. That will tell you volumes about how well the cards are being mixed.

For a detailed demonstration, take a look at the chart on the next page. This is a graphic depiction of just one riffling event. The results, of course, would vary somewhat from shuffle to shuffle, and from dealer to dealer. (The cards from one of the halves is shaded to better indicate where the cards wound up. For ease of display, this is a 1-deck example. However, the

CHART 5-7:

The Effects of Riffling

New Order	Original Order	Original Position
1	28	MIDDLE/BOTTOM
2	1	TOP
3	2	TOP
4	29	MIDDLE/BOTTOM
5	3	TOP
6	4	TOP
7	30	MIDDLE/BOTTOM
8	5	TOP
9	6	TOP
10	31	MIDDLE/BOTTOM
11	7	TOP
12	32	MIDDLE/BOTTOM
13	8	TOP
14	9	TOP
15	33	MIDDLE/BOTTOM
16	10	TOP
17	34	MIDDLE/BOTTOM
18	11	TOP
19	35	MIDDLE/BOTTOM
20	12	TOP
21	36	MIDDLE/BOTTOM
22	37	MIDDLE/BOTTOM
23	13	TOP
24	38	MIDDLE/BOTTOM
25	14	MIDDLE/TOP
26	39	MIDDLE/BOTTOM
27	15	MIDDLE/TOP
28	16	MIDDLE/TOP
29	40	BOTTOM
30	17	MIDDLE/TOP
31	41	BOTTOM
32	42	BOTTOM
33	18	MIDDLE/TOP
34	19	MIDDLE/TOP
35	43	BOTTOM
36	44	BOTTOM
37	20	MIDDLE/TOP
38	45	BOTTOM
39	21	MIDDLE/TOP
40	46	BOTTOM
41	22	MIDDLE/TOP
42	47	BOTTOM
43	23	MIDDLE/TOP
44	48	BOTTOM
45	24	MIDDLE/TOP
46	49	BOTTOM
47	25	MIDDLE/TOP
48	50	BOTTOM
49	26	MIDDLE/TOP
50	51	BOTTOM
51	27	MIDDLE/TOP
52	52	BOTTOM

principle and the results, remain the same, now matter how many decks are ultimately involved. The cards are identified by the order in which they were found before the riffling, and then, after.)

Note, first, that the dealer's pre-riffle cutting of the cards into two piles resulted in one "half" being 27 cards, and the other being 25 cards (the evidence of this being that card number 27 is near the bottom, one away from number 26). Sometimes, depending on the skill of the dealer, the cut might be executed with exactly 26 cards in each half, but, more commonly, it will be off a slight bit.

Next, notice that the bottom 16 cards are neatly mixed together -- with one card from each half sandwiched between each other. These would have been riffled together first, as riffling starts with the bottom cards. This, as I described before, is when dealers tend to concentrate the most, slowing down the shuffle to its most controllable speed, before speeding up the riffle to finish it off.

The riffle must have sped up after the first 16 cards were placed on the table, because the dealer became less precise -- witness the occasional groups of two cards that fell together from one half. A very skilled dealer might be able to do a perfect job of intertwining the cards, if pressed to do so, but whether *any* dealer would take the time to be so exact, when under the gun to keep the action going as fast as possible, is questionable.

But, most important -- look at the bigger picture of what a cutting and riffling procedure produces. *The cards that had been the top 13 cards before the riffle are still in the top half; and the 13 cards that were on the bottom before the riffle are still in the bottom half.* What changes most is that the *middle* cards move: *the Middle/Bottom cards* -- the 13 cards that had been directly below the 26th card before the riffle -- *are now in the top half*; whereas, *the Middle/Top cards* -- the 13 cards that had been directly below the 13th card before the riffle -- *are now mostly in the bottom half. This result is predictable in its regularity with each riffle. It is something with which you must get real familiar, so that, at the table, you will see it happening in your mind's eye.*

To see a graphic representation of why every riffle results in the same general movement of the cards, take a moment now to study the charts on pages 70-71. You'll see exactly why the middle cards kind of do a flip flop in order -- the Middle/Tops moving to the bottom half and the Middle/ Bottoms moving to the top. It is the *cutting* procedure that causes this.

What Does Stripping Do?

Stripping is the most *variable* type of shuffling, next to washing. It also produces the most dramatic results (aside from boxing, which you won't see as often). (See photo page 60.)

Stripping comes mainly in two types. *Normal* involves the moving of clumps of 10 or so cards, one after the other, from the top of the pile to a new pile on the table. *Severe* means that the clumps of cards contain roughly half a dozen or less cards each. (Granted, it can be less uniform -- kind of a combination of both normal and severe stripping.) In rare cases, the dealer might simultaneously pull off small groups of cards from both the top and the bottom of the pile of cards in the dealer's hand, with each stripping action.

On page 72, you'll find an illustration of the results of normal stripping. In this case, six clumps of between seven and ten cards were progressively moved from the deck in the dealer's hand to the new, rearranged pile on the table. Once again, this varies greatly from dealer to dealer, as far as how many clumps are created, how uniform the clumps are, and how severe the stripping -- you must pay close attention to how this is being done.

(As in the riffling example, the cards in the stripping example are identified by the order in which they were before the stripping procedure, and then, afterward. Also, the cards from each strip are set apart by shading.)

What is the final result? *The Top cards are moved to the bottom, the Bottom to the top, and the Middle/Top cards exchange positions with the Middle/Bottom cards, in rough fashion. This is typical of all stripping procedures, except the rare cases where both top and bottom cards are stripped together in each clump.*

Now, one thing you are going to do is to *count how many times the dealer strips cards off the top during any stripping procedure.* This is your quick and easy way to determine whether the stripping is normal or severe. If the dealer does seven or more strips with one deck (or a one deck section, during multi-deck sectional shuffling), or 14 or more strips with *two* decks (or a 2-deck section, during multi-deck sectional shuffling), this is *severe* stripping. (See Chart 5-11, page 73.)

Either way, you'll know where the cards wind up. With severe stripping, the very top cards will -- with great certainty -- wind up at or close to the bottom; the cards at the very bottom will wind up at or very close to the top. With normal stripping, the topmost cards will end up higher up in the bottom section, and the cards at the very bottom will wind up lower in the top section. This will be accentuated if the dealer takes even bigger chunks than normal (see Chart 5-12, page 74). There's actually a big benefit to supernormal chunk-style stripping: more cards stay near their original neighboring cards, making the final arrangement of cards after all the shuffling is done that much less random, and, therefore, more predictable. You'd recognize this by there only being about 4 strips done per deck.

A variant you might see on a rare occasion, involves the dealer doing a *reverse* stripping kind of motion -- moving clumps of cards from the bottom,

(Continued on page 76)

CHART 5-8:

Pre-Riffling 1-Deck Card Order (By 13s)

Card Order	Relative Position
1	TOP
2	TOP
3	TOP
4	TOP
5	TOP
6	TOP
7	TOP
8	TOP
9	TOP
10	TOP
11	TOP
12	TOP
13	TOP
14	MIDDLE/TOP
15	MIDDLE/TOP
16	MIDDLE/TOP
17	MIDDLE/TOP
18	MIDDLE/TOP
19	MIDDLE/TOP
20	MIDDLE/TOP
21	MIDDLE/TOP
22	MIDDLE/TOP
23	MIDDLE/TOP
24	MIDDLE/TOP
25	MIDDLE/TOP
26	MIDDLE/TOP
27	MIDDLE/BOTTOM
28	MIDDLE/BOTTOM
29	MIDDLE/BOTTOM
30	MIDDLE/BOTTOM
31	MIDDLE/BOTTOM
32	MIDDLE/BOTTOM
33	MIDDLE/BOTTOM
34	MIDDLE/BOTTOM
35	MIDDLE/BOTTOM
36	MIDDLE/BOTTOM
37	MIDDLE/BOTTOM
38	MIDDLE/BOTTOM
39	MIDDLE/BOTTOM
40	BOTTOM
41	BOTTOM
42	BOTTOM
43	BOTTOM
44	BOTTOM
45	BOTTOM
46	BOTTOM
47	BOTTOM
48	BOTTOM
49	BOTTOM
50	BOTTOM
51	BOTTOM
52	BOTTOM

CHART 5-9:

Graphic Representation
of Riffling
(After Dealer Cutting Procedure)

1	TOP		27	MIDDLE/BOTTOM
2	TOP		28	MIDDLE/BOTTOM
3	TOP		29	MIDDLE/BOTTOM
4	TOP		30	MIDDLE/BOTTOM
5	TOP		31	MIDDLE/BOTTOM
6	TOP		32	MIDDLE/BOTTOM
7	TOP		33	MIDDLE/BOTTOM
8	TOP		34	MIDDLE/BOTTOM
9	TOP		35	MIDDLE/BOTTOM
10	TOP		36	MIDDLE/BOTTOM
11	TOP		37	MIDDLE/BOTTOM
12	TOP		38	MIDDLE/BOTTOM
13	TOP		39	MIDDLE/BOTTOM
14	MIDDLE/TOP		40	BOTTOM
15	MIDDLE/TOP		41	BOTTOM
16	MIDDLE/TOP		42	BOTTOM
17	MIDDLE/TOP		43	BOTTOM
18	MIDDLE/TOP		44	BOTTOM
19	MIDDLE/TOP		45	BOTTOM
20	MIDDLE/TOP		46	BOTTOM
21	MIDDLE/TOP		47	BOTTOM
22	MIDDLE/TOP		48	BOTTOM
23	MIDDLE/TOP		49	BOTTOM
24	MIDDLE/TOP		50	BOTTOM
25	MIDDLE/TOP		51	BOTTOM
26	MIDDLE/TOP		52	BOTTOM

This had been the top half before the dealer cut.

This had been the bottom half before the dealer cut.

CHART 5-10:

The Effects of Stripping (Normal)

New Order	Original Order	Original Position
1	45	BOTTOM
2	46	BOTTOM
3	47	BOTTOM
4	48	BOTTOM
5	49	BOTTOM
6	50	BOTTOM
7	51	BOTTOM
8	52	BOTTOM
9	38	MIDDLE/BOTTOM
10	39	MIDDLE/BOTTOM
11	40	BOTTOM
12	41	BOTTOM
13	42	BOTTOM
14	43	BOTTOM
15	44	BOTTOM
16	28	MIDDLE/BOTTOM
17	29	MIDDLE/BOTTOM
18	30	MIDDLE/BOTTOM
19	31	MIDDLE/BOTTOM
20	32	MIDDLE/BOTTOM
21	33	MIDDLE/BOTTOM
22	34	MIDDLE/BOTTOM
23	35	MIDDLE/BOTTOM
24	36	MIDDLE/BOTTOM
25	37	MIDDLE/BOTTOM
26	19	MIDDLE/TOP
27	20	MIDDLE/TOP
28	21	MIDDLE/TOP
29	22	MIDDLE/TOP
30	23	MIDDLE/TOP
31	24	MIDDLE/TOP
32	25	MIDDLE/TOP
33	26	MIDDLE/TOP
34	27	MIDDLE/BOTTOM
35	11	TOP
36	12	TOP
37	13	TOP
38	14	MIDDLE/TOP
39	15	MIDDLE/TOP
40	16	MIDDLE/TOP
41	17	MIDDLE/TOP
42	18	MIDDLE/TOP
43	1	TOP
44	2	TOP
45	3	TOP
46	4	TOP
47	5	TOP
48	6	TOP
49	7	TOP
50	8	TOP
51	9	TOP
52	10	TOP

CHART 5-11:

The Effects of Stripping (Severe -- done perfectly to dramatize)

New Order	Original Order	Original Position
1	46	BOTTOM
2	47	BOTTOM
3	48	BOTTOM
4	49	BOTTOM
5	50	BOTTOM
6	51	BOTTOM
7	52	BOTTOM
8	40	BOTTOM
9	41	BOTTOM
10	42	BOTTOM
11	43	BOTTOM
12	44	BOTTOM
13	45	BOTTOM
14	33	MIDDLE/BOTTOM
15	34	MIDDLE/BOTTOM
16	35	MIDDLE/BOTTOM
17	36	MIDDLE/BOTTOM
18	37	MIDDLE/BOTTOM
19	38	MIDDLE/BOTTOM
20	39	MIDDLE/BOTTOM
21	27	MIDDLE/BOTTOM
22	28	MIDDLE/BOTTOM
23	29	MIDDLE/BOTTOM
24	30	MIDDLE/BOTTOM
25	31	MIDDLE/BOTTOM
26	32	MIDDLE/BOTTOM
27	20	MIDDLE/TOP
28	21	MIDDLE/TOP
29	22	MIDDLE/TOP
30	23	MIDDLE/TOP
31	24	MIDDLE/TOP
32	25	MIDDLE/TOP
33	26	MIDDLE/TOP
34	14	MIDDLE/TOP
35	15	MIDDLE/TOP
36	16	MIDDLE/TOP
37	17	MIDDLE/TOP
38	18	MIDDLE/TOP
39	19	MIDDLE/TOP
40	7	TOP
41	8	TOP
42	9	TOP
43	10	TOP
44	11	TOP
45	12	TOP
46	13	TOP
47	1	TOP
48	2	TOP
49	3	TOP
50	4	TOP
51	5	TOP
52	6	TOP

CHART 5-12:

The Effects of Stripping (Chunks -- done perfectly to dramatize)

New Order	Original Order	Original Position
1	40	BOTTOM
2	41	BOTTOM
3	42	BOTTOM
4	43	BOTTOM
5	44	BOTTOM
6	45	BOTTOM
7	46	BOTTOM
8	47	BOTTOM
9	48	BOTTOM
10	49	BOTTOM
11	50	BOTTOM
12	51	BOTTOM
13	52	BOTTOM
14	27	MIDDLE/BOTTOM
15	28	MIDDLE/BOTTOM
16	29	MIDDLE/BOTTOM
17	30	MIDDLE/BOTTOM
18	31	MIDDLE/BOTTOM
19	32	MIDDLE/BOTTOM
20	33	MIDDLE/BOTTOM
21	34	MIDDLE/BOTTOM
22	35	MIDDLE/BOTTOM
23	36	MIDDLE/BOTTOM
24	37	MIDDLE/BOTTOM
25	38	MIDDLE/BOTTOM
26	39	MIDDLE/BOTTOM
27	14	MIDDLE/TOP
28	15	MIDDLE/TOP
29	16	MIDDLE/TOP
30	17	MIDDLE/TOP
31	18	MIDDLE/TOP
32	19	MIDDLE/TOP
33	20	MIDDLE/TOP
34	21	MIDDLE/TOP
35	22	MIDDLE/TOP
36	23	MIDDLE/TOP
37	24	MIDDLE/TOP
38	25	MIDDLE/TOP
39	26	MIDDLE/TOP
40	1	TOP
41	2	TOP
42	3	TOP
43	4	TOP
44	5	TOP
45	6	TOP
46	7	TOP
47	8	TOP
48	9	TOP
49	10	TOP
50	11	TOP
51	12	TOP
52	13	TOP

CHART 5-13:

The Effects of Boxing (If Done Perfectly)

New Order	Original Order	Original Position
1	27	MIDDLE/BOTTOM
2	28	MIDDLE/BOTTOM
3	29	MIDDLE/BOTTOM
4	30	MIDDLE/BOTTOM
5	31	MIDDLE/BOTTOM
6	32	MIDDLE/BOTTOM
7	33	MIDDLE/BOTTOM
8	34	MIDDLE/BOTTOM
9	35	MIDDLE/BOTTOM
10	36	MIDDLE/BOTTOM
11	37	MIDDLE/BOTTOM
12	38	MIDDLE/BOTTOM
13	39	MIDDLE/BOTTOM
14	40	BOTTOM
15	41	BOTTOM
16	42	BOTTOM
17	43	BOTTOM
18	44	BOTTOM
19	45	BOTTOM
20	46	BOTTOM
21	47	BOTTOM
22	48	BOTTOM
23	49	BOTTOM
24	50	BOTTOM
25	51	BOTTOM
26	52	BOTTOM
27	1	TOP
28	2	TOP
29	3	TOP
30	4	TOP
31	5	TOP
32	6	TOP
33	7	TOP
34	8	TOP
35	9	TOP
36	10	TOP
37	11	TOP
38	12	TOP
39	13	TOP
40	14	MIDDLE/TOP
41	15	MIDDLE/TOP
42	16	MIDDLE/TOP
43	17	MIDDLE/TOP
44	18	MIDDLE/TOP
45	19	MIDDLE/TOP
46	20	MIDDLE/TOP
47	21	MIDDLE/TOP
48	22	MIDDLE/TOP
49	23	MIDDLE/TOP
50	24	MIDDLE/TOP
51	25	MIDDLE/TOP
52	26	MIDDLE/TOP

to the top of the pile. So, the result is: *the cards on the bottom move to the top, in clumps. The Bottom and Middle/Bottom cards move to the top, in a fashion entirely like that of stripping, in reverse; the Top and Middle/Top cards wind up in the bottom half of the new pile, in disjointed clumps.*

Take a moment now to familiarize yourself with the stripping charts. Pay particular attention to the columns that say "Original Order." That shows you where the cards wind up after stripping. Note, too, that, no matter what stripping style, the cards tend to stay within their quadrants (groups of 13). Also note that the topmost and very bottom cards will tend to be the least corrupted with other cards (as reflected in the normal stripping chart, where the procedure was not done so perfectly).

What Does Boxing Do?

Boxing is a procedure you won't see very often. It's a cutting of the cards as close to the middle as possible, with the bottom half placed on top (see photo on page 61, and graphic illustration on page 75. *The Middle/Bottom and Bottom cards wind up on top, and the Top and Middle/Top cards end up on the bottom.* This procedure mimics the way most players cut the cards, at the end of shuffling.

...Which Explains Why Dealer Shuffling Is Not Randomizing

So, now that you realize that standardized casino dealer shuffling procedures are simple sequences consisting of a small number of riffles, in combination usually with a stripping shuffle, and, in a minority of cases, perhaps a boxing shuffle...and now that you realize that each of these types of shuffles produces a predictable, regular and unsurprising result...you should now understand *why* dealer shuffling does NOT randomize the cards.

But Wait: Three More Factors To Consider!

But, your understanding of the entire shuffling process isn't complete yet. There is some pre- and post-shuffling card handling that must be included in this picture: 1) the collecting of the spent cards from the discard tray; 2) the placing of the undealt cards on top or within the spent cards; and, 3) the player cutting of the cards after the dealer is finished shuffling.

The reason I list the collecting of the spent cards from the discard tray is that, if you want to follow a group or string of cards, or several groups or strings of cards from the rounds played just before the shuffling begins, you have to understand where they've wound up: in reverse order to when the rounds were played. In other words: the cards from the *final* round are on the *top* of the discard pile, and, conversely, the cards from the very *first* round are on the *bottom* of the pile. This is very important to comprehend.

Now, where the dealer places the undealt cards is very important, too, for two reasons: 1) it affects the subsequent order of the cards after the shuffling procedure; and 2) perhaps there are cards within the undealt cards that you are hoping will appear after the next shuffle, in which case you would want to know where they wind up, after the shuffling's done. So, watch where these cards are placed. Knowing what you now know about the effect each shuffling act has on the cards, you'll be able to follow them if you pay attention to where they were placed.

Finally, the player cutting of the cards after the dealer shuffling determines what cards will come back -- especially in multi-deck games. Don't forget -- with a 1-deck game, depending on the number of players, you might see a true penetration in the 90 percentile range. In that most favorable of situations, it would be almost inevitable that you'd see most of the same cards you saw in the rounds prior to the dealer shuffling sequence, no matter where the cut card is placed. That truth goes down with each additional deck, however, to the point where, with 6- and 8-deck games, you won't see much more than 60% of the cards before the shuffling procedure begins. So, the undealt cards will amount to 40% of the cards with those multi-deck games. Therefore, with 6- and 8-deck games, it should be clear to you why, if a player cuts the cards in a section that contains all of the undealt cards from the past rounds, why the predictability factor arising from the shuffling process would be almost entirely lost. That also explains why the placement of the cut card in those games will produce the most variation in results.

But, let me make this clear: from the most favorable 1-deck game situation to the most daunting multi-deck game, there are right places and wrong places to put the cut card. This fact pertains to you even if you're not cutting the cards, because you should be aware of whether the player who's done so has created Heaven or Hell for you. We'll get into this in Chapter 12.

For now, understand that most players don't know any better, and tend to cut the cards in the middle, no matter what. This produces a result akin to that produced by dealer boxing, which I demonstrated to you on the prior pages.

Now Do Your Homework

Here's what you should do now, before we get into more advanced applications of what you've learned in this chapter. Go to your favorite casinos, at your leisure, and, like a reporter, observe what types of shuffling they do, and in what sequence. Is it a riffle-strip-riffle-riffle procedure? Or just a riffle-strip-riffle? Or a riffle-strip-riffle-box?

Also, pay close attention to where they put the undealt cards -- on top of the spent cards? Somewhere in the middle? On the bottom?

Once you know the answers to these questions, write this information down as soon as you can, away from the view, of course, of casino personnel. Do it in a restroom, or a restaurant, or a parking lot.

Then, at home, take out as many decks of cards as you need to simulate that shuffling process. I recommend you use new decks, because they come in a readily identifiable order, and that you use a different color or patterned deck for each deck you use, so you can follow where the cards finally wind up after carefully recreating what you've seen at the casino. Each deck will have its cards arranged in the order you see in the top photo on page 10: they'll be together in sequence and in suits, with the Hearts on top, starting with the Ace, and then the Clubs, starting with the Ace, and then the Diamonds, in reverse order, starting with the King, and then the Spades, in reverse order, starting with its King.

You might want to practice doing the various shuffles with an old deck of cards whose order you don't mind rearranging, before attempting to do this exercise. When riffling, start slowly as the bottom cards begin to riffle together -- see how carefully you can accomplish this. With stripping, try to create equal sized clumps of cards. With boxing, try to cut the cards exactly in half. (Don't do any washing for this exercise! The order of the cards, as they come with the new decks, is what will tell you where the cards ulti-mately wind up.) Or -- better yet -- since you're probably not going to produce as careful a result as dealers typically do -- here's what I suggest you do until you learn to shuffle in a professional manner: 1) with riffling, count off 26 cards, so you know each half is equal in size, and then place the bottom card of one half down on the table, and then the bottom card of the other half on top of that, and so on, until you arrive at a perfect example of riffling; 2) with stripping, choose one of the styles I demonstrated, and strip by counting off a proper number of cards for each section and then move each section onto the table, from top to bottom; and 3) with boxing and player cutting, count off 26 cards from the top, and move those topmost cards to the bottom.

Now -- if you're going to use more than 1-deck -- make note of where each deck you're using is located in the original stack before you shuffle the cards, so you know the original position of each card within those decks and, therefore, where they wind up after shuffling is complete. If, for instance, you're playing with 4 decks, and the deck you got in Paris is the third deck from the top, then, later on, after the shuffling is done, you'll be able to notice, for instance, that the A♥ from that deck (the top card) had originally been in the 105th position -- because you originally made a list of what decks you were using, with the order of the cards of each deck listed, from top to bottom.

This exercise will be easiest if you use a computer, using a spreadsheet program. In one column, which you'll label "Original Order," number all of the cards you're using, in their original order, starting with the top card; in another column, which you'll label "Card," list the suit and value of each card; in a third column, which you'll label "Relative Original Position," list each card by its relative position -- for each card in the top quarter, type

"Top," and then for each subsequent quadrant, label them: "Middle/Top," "Middle/Bottom," and "Bottom." Then, shuffle the cards. Once done, set up a new spreadsheet section where you will list where each card wound up -- placing each card in order, from top to bottom, in its new position. From top to bottom, flip over each card in order, filling out each column for every card you turn over, until you go through the entire stack of cards. Now, number the new order of the cards in a new column, starting your numbering with the top cards. (Of course, you do not need a computer to do this. You can use a pencil and piece of paper, perhaps a piece of graph paper, to make your spreadsheet grids.)

This will tell you where the cards wind up during the shuffling process. In analyzing the results, what you'll want to do is look at every conceivable portion of each deck you used (the top, middle top, middle bottom and bottom portions) and then figure out where those cards wound up in the final mix. That way, whether you want to locate a group of good cards you had wanted to follow, a bad group of cards you were hoping to avoid after the shuffling, you'll have a real good idea of where they are.

If you want to see where the cards you would have played from prior rounds would have ended up, take a look at where the cards from the bottom half of your original stack end up. That's where the cards from the first round of action are. (Remember -- the dealer discards the rounds in reverse order: the *first* round going on the *bottom* of the discard tray, the *final* round going on *top*. Because of the way most dealers collect the cards after each round is through, *the dealer's cards are typically on top of the pile of the cards from each round.*)

You should do this exercise for every casino that you go to regularly, until the principles involved become so obvious to you that you are pretty sure where the cards are going. Eventually, you should get so good at shuffling analysis that you can enter a new casino and figure out what their shuffling method does to the card order (and the cards you want to follow), on the fly.

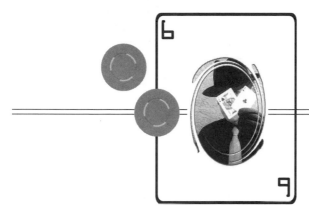

Amazing Repeating Phenomena

Now that you are aware that shuffling does not alter the arrangement of the cards very much, it should come as no surprise to you that many of the same cards revolve together from shuffle to shuffle, resulting in many useful *repeating phenomena*, from which you can profit. To my knowledge, much of what I am about to document has never been discovered before. For years, I've noticed that the cards have a long-term *personality*; now, with my most recent computer studies, I've amassed ample concrete *proof* that this concept is beyond refute, *and* I've uncovered the *reasons* behind it.

The Reasons The Phenomena Exist

The minor way in which standardized casino shuffling changes things (vis a vis the order and the proximity of one card to another) is just one factor that causes the creation and existence of repeating phenomena. The second major reason for it is the way in which *dealing tends to undo some of the effects of shuffling, to bring many of the shuffle-separated cards back together.*

This often means, for instance, that many of the same characteristic group of cards that appeared in one round will reappear together in the same rounds, from shuffle to shuffle, for quite some time. Sometimes it results

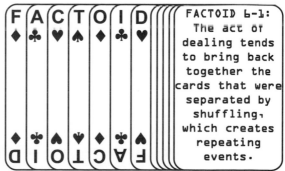

FACTOID 6-1: The act of dealing tends to bring back together the cards that were separated by shuffling, which creates repeating events.

in some of the same cards being dealt to either the same player, a fellow player, or the dealer. Sometimes you'll see the same or similar order of cards being dealt. It's not uncommon, either, for the same *hand,* or at least two cards from one hand, to rotate between different players over the course of many shuffles, or the same general limited set of cards. I'll give examples of each type of repeating phenomenon I've identified, in a moment.

How Will This Benefit You?

How might this new knowledge of card repetition be of help to you? *If you realize that there are factors that repeat from shuffle to shuffle, that the cards have something akin to a short-term "memory," then you'll gain important information regarding a predictability that will help you in betting, in making strategic decisions, in deciding whether to play more than one hand or not, and in deciding whether to leave or not, just to name a few benefits.*

Now, I've proven all of this to myself over the course of many, many months, and much of the data I've accumulated would just bore you to tears, so I'm not going to overwhelm you with the details. The charting of the progression of many thousands of cards from shuffle to shuffle, while interesting to me, would be very hard to present here without getting overly detailed. What I'm going to do instead is simply open your eyes to what's going on, and then let you know what you can do to take this information and run with it.

The Role Dealing Plays

Let's look at Example 6-1 on the next page, which will give you an idea of what I'm talking about. It's not necessarily the best example; in fact, it's not among the more amazing. It's just one, chosen at random, and analyzed, to show that any set of cards from shuffle to shuffle displays many similarities.

In this example, you'll see the order of the cards as they appeared after two consecutive shuffles. Rounds were played in between these events, of course. (Remember, by the way, that the one variable that can't be anticipated in the final reordering of the cards is the placement of the cut card by the player. Wherever this is put determines which cards will reappear first, following the shuffle. *It does not, however, destroy the general relationships, which persist between the cards.*) As I mentioned before, the cut card was placed approximately in the middle of the cards during my research, to mimic the habit by most players of doing just that.

First, take notice of the fact that the A♦ and J♦ appear *in the exact same position after the second shuffle as they had after the first.* And, because this set of cards came from my trials with three virtual players, the dealer got the same Blackjack in the first round following both shuffles! This is an ex-

EXAMPLE 6-1:

Numerical Order	Original Card Order	Order After 2nd Shuffle
BURN CARD	2D	2S
1	QC	JS
2	2H	6D
3	3S	JH
4	AD	AD
5	2C	3C
6	JC	AS
7	6C	8S
8	JD	JD
9	6H	QS
10	8H	9H
11	10S	4S
12	KC	3S
13	3D	2D
14	QH	8H
15	3C	KS
16	4H	5H
17	3H	6C
18	5S	7H
19	QS	QH
20	10C	AH
21	7S	4C
22	JH	7C
23	7D	2H
24	9S	6H
25	9D	KD
26	AH	10D
27	2S	JC
28	QD	8D
29	JS	9C
30	10H	QC
31	KD	3D
32	5H	7S
33	KH	10C
34	8C	10H
35	9C	9D
36	7C	KC
37	6D	8C
38	KS	9S
39	8S	4H
40	AC	3H
41	5C	2C
42	5D	QD
43	6S	AC
44	4D	7D
45	AS	10S
46	9H	5C
47	4S	5D
48	7H	5S
49	4C	KH
50	10D	6S
51	8D	4D

ample of *up card and hole card repetition* -- two very real phenomena, which we'll look at in greater detail soon; and, because both cards returned to the same hand, in the same order, we can also say that this is a case of *exact hand repetition*. It's also an instance of another repetitive phenomenon -- *repetitive positioning*, where individual cards are in precisely the same position in the order of the cards that they were after the previous shuffle. This type of thing happens with a small number of cards practically *every shuffle.*

How does that happen? They don't stand *still* during the shuffling process. A quick analysis of the A♦ and J♦ example reveals the mechanism of how *hands are recreated following a shuffle*, and how this is governed by the number of players at the table. First, the A♦ and J♦, formerly next to each other in the dealer's hand and discarded together, wind up with three cards between them during the shuffling process. With the riffle-strip-riffle-riffle technique used in my research, it's clear that the stripping process did not separate the two cards; what most likely happened was that each riffling effectively placed one card between the pair. With three players at the table, that ensured that the cards would be brought back together during the dealing process.

Why? It has to do with the orderly way the cards are dealt. When three betting spots are being taken, for instance, the cards that are dealt as the first and second cards to both the players and the dealer, were *four* apart from each other following the shuffle. The simple *rule of thumb* is that *cards separated by a distance equal to the number of players plus one might very well wind up in the same hand, by the way the cards are dealt in blackjack.* This is how *dealing* brings cards squeezed apart by *shuffling* back together as partners in the same hand again (not necessarily of the same player).

OK. Let's return to Example 6-1. Here are some other interesting facts. Immediately following the second shuffle, an analysis of the card order shows that *more than 20% of the cards are still next to the same lower neighbor they had been next to after the prior shuffle (for example -- look at the cards in positions 41 and 42 after the first shuffle, the 5♣ and the 5♦; now look at positions 46 and 47 after the second shuffle -- these same two cards are still together, in the same order, just a bit below where they were following the first shuffle!).* In addition: more than 20% are still *equidistant* from their previous *fourth* lower neighbor; more than 40% are only seven or less cards away from their past lower neighbors, and nearly 50% are just eight or less cards away from their previous lower neighbors (and therefore, the likelihood they will be brought back together in the same round by dealing after the second shuffle is quite high); *33%* are *six* or less cards away from their prior lower neighbors; 15% are seven cards or less from the position they were in after the first shuffle, and nearly 30% are within 13 cards of their previous position; and there are many, many other significant recurring relationships going on here.

For instance, look at the 14 cards in positions 38 through 51 after the second shuffle. *Three of these are right next to their lower neighbors from before*, one is just one card away, three are only 2 cards distant, one is three cards away, another four cards away, and two others are 6 and 7 cards away from their prior lower neighbor. *Only two of these 14 cards are separated by more than seven cards from the cards they sat upon after the previous shuffle* (this was caused by the stripping part of the shuffling process).

This is definitely an example of what I call an *orbiting association -- a collection of cards that returns pretty much intact, from shuffle to shuffle.* Not only that -- this particular group of cards is representative of a particular *kind* of orbiting association: these are *proximate cards.* Proximate cards are those that orbit very closely together, from shuffle to shuffle. All orbiting cards don't necessarily maintain close relationships with their neighbors. These do.

And there are other things I could point out -- how, for instance, the 2♥ and J♣ are Player #2's first and second cards in the first round after the first shuffle, and how that hand ends up in the dealer's possession, as the up card and hole card, in the third round after the second shuffle. This is a type of repeating pattern we'll call *partial hand repetition.* This is where at least two cards from one hand return together in a hand following the shuffle.

There Are Repeating Events After Every Shuffle

The above example is not a rare case. This kind of thing can be pointed to after virtually *every shuffle (and repeating patterns can go on for quite some time, by the way).* Take a look at Example 6-2 on the next page, which shows you what happened in the second rounds following two consecutive shuffles.

This is a good example of an orbiting association (look at how few 10s there are, for starters!). There are fewer proximate cards here, but there are many interesting repetitive patterns going on. Indeed, if you look at the round on the bottom of the illustration, you'll see that *nearly 60% of the cards repeat from the same round in the previous shuffle period.* You have a case of hand repetition, with the 8♦ and 8♣ arriving in the same hand together from shuffle to shuffle (although not, in this case, with the same player). And two of the players and the dealer experienced *card repetition* (one person getting the same exact card from shuffle to shuffle). The third player got the 6♥ both times, the fifth player got the Q♠ in both rounds, and the dealer was dealt the 9♣ twice in a row. In addition, the 5♣ and the 7♦ were dealt one after the other in both rounds (they were right next to each other, proximate cards, following both shuffles), as were the 8♥ and the 8♦ (with the 2♣ riding along, close beside them both times).

Furthermore, this kind of orbiting association is the type we especially

EXAMPLE 6-2:

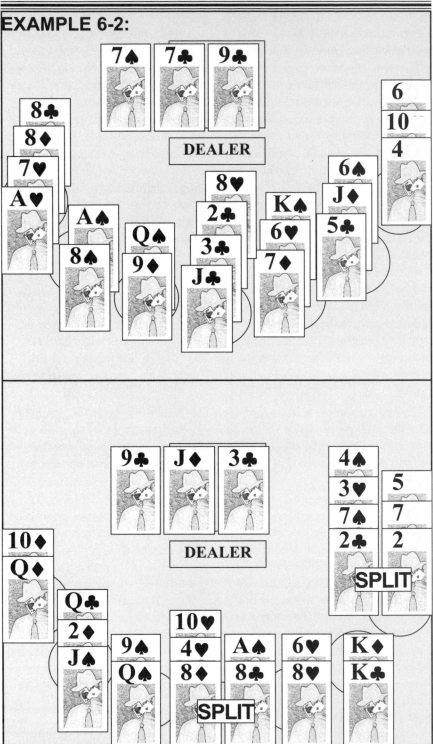

like, because it causes the dealer to bust more than is normal. For example, in the round pictured on the top of the page, the Aces were nearly played out before the dealer's cards were dealt, and in the round shown on the bottom of the page, they were *completely* played out before the dealer's cards were dealt. We'll get into this in more detail later, but *this alone increases dealer busting to significant levels.* Also, the dealer in both cases had a stiff, and, due to the nature of the mix of cards in the orbiting association, the cards that could have *made* the dealer's hands *were all but played out.* In the first situation, the dealer had a 16, and the cards that would have helped the dealer the most were nearly used up -- three 4s and three 5s had already been dealt (three of the 2s had also been dealt before). The second situation was very similar -- the dealer had a 13 and *all of the 2s, 4s, 5s, 7s and 8s had been used up, and most of the 3s...So, here you had an orbiting association that tended to give the dealer stiffs and then rob the dealer of the cards that would have turned those stiffs into an acceptable score. There was a definite personality emerging in the repetitive phenomena going on here, one that would signal me to raise my bet level (beyond my normal outlay), for as long as I noticed it persisting.*

If you're wondering about how long this kind of repetitive phenomenon could go on, the answer is: it depends largely upon where the cut card is placed following future shuffles. If they don't divide the cards that create repeating events, those events can sometimes last the length of time a set of cards is in play!

As a matter of fact, let me show you two great examples of just how long repeating events can last. We'll call the first one "The Incredible Orbiting 4s & 7s," and the second, "The Case of the Amazing Repeating Blackjacks."

The Incredible Orbiting 4s & 7s

The Incredible Orbiting 4s & 7s example (from my 7-player card runs) goes on for 58 shuffles and 116 rounds, and only ended because the cards were replaced, as they were after every two hours of action or so. Shuffle after shuffle, at least one party (often more than one) would get a 4 and 7 as part of their hand -- and the vast majority of these would repeat over and over in later shuffle periods! This kind of long-term pattern was caused by the fact that the 4s and 7s were in close proximity to each other; shuffling wasn't separating them much, and dealing was bringing them back together, and so they were repeating as part of an orbiting association. It was rare that at least two 4s and two 7s were not represented within the round, and there were often more (sometimes with all the 4s or 7s in the same round).

Rather than give you the details, here are some of the facts that stand out:

❶ There were *34 hands* that contained at least one 4 and one 7.

❷ The 4♦ participated in *14 of the 34 hands (41%)* where there was a 7 present.

❸ The 7♠ was a member of *12 of these 34 repeating hands (35%)!*

❹ The 4 ♠ was in *10 of the 34 hands (29%)* in which a 7 was also dealt. The same can be said of the 7♦.

❺ The 4♦-7♥-7♠, which came in the 1st Round, 1st Shuffle of this example, spawned six other repetitions (three of 4♦-7♥, and three of 4♦-7♠), one of which came in the 2nd Round of the next shuffle! This accounts for 21% of the repeating groups.

❻ The 4♥-7♦ appeared in six different hands together (18%).

Because of the recurring proximity of the cards involved, *eight of the 34 repeating hands (nearly 25%) contained three of the repeating cards* (either two 4s and one 7, or one 4 and two 7s)!

Many of the repeating events occurred within a few shuffles of each other (and, not infrequently, consecutive shuffles), adding to the accumulated evidence proving the existence of a nonrandom phenomenon here. For instance, in the shuffle immediately following the 1st Shuffle, in which the 4♦-7♥-7♠ were dealt to one player in the First Round, the 4♦-7♥ were again dealt in the same hand (although to a different player). The 4♠-4♣-7♣ were dealt in the 1st round in one shuffle period, and a pair from that group, the 4♣-7♣, were dealt in the same hand, in the same order, again in the 1st round, following the very next shuffle. That can be said about many other such couples -- including the 4♠-7♠ which were dealt together in 5 of the repeating hands, often repeating as a team in the next or following shuffle.

In addition, many of the cards returned the to same player's hands in short order -- for instance, the first player received the 4♠ in the 1st round of one shuffle period, then in the 1st round two shuffles later, and in the 1st round two shuffles after that.

The evidence is beyond reproach. But I want to show you more.

The Case of the Amazing Repeating Blackjacks

The Case of the Amazing Repeating Blackjacks is an example whose repeating-Ace events continued through 59 shuffles and 117 rounds! The round that set things in motion was one in which the 3rd baseman was dealt this hand: 3♠-A♠-A♥-A♦-8♠-4♥. The dealer's hand at the same time was A♣-6♣. Would you have recognized what this would do to the following rounds?

With four Aces now in very close proximity to each other (because the 3rd baseman's hand was collected right after the dealer's cards during the discard process), *this created an orbiting association that caused the Aces to appear in pairs, trios and quarters together in the same round in virtually every shuffle period afterward (until the cards were replaced)!*

Unfortunately, this also led to the dealer getting nearly *twice* his normal share of Blackjacks, which often happens when Aces travel together -- 11, which amounted to 9% of the rounds (normally, the dealer's Blackjack rate is 5%). But, get this -- in *four* of those Blackjacks (36%), the Ace was the A♣; in *two* of those times, the A♣'s partner was the Q♦ (attesting to the relative consistency of the relationships between the cards)! In fact, *the A♣ was the Ace in four of six consecutive dealer Blackjacks*, which is further proof of the repetitive nature of the cards.

Here are some more facts that will really blow you away! You know that hand of 3♠-A♠-A♥-A♦-8♠-4♥ in the round I said set things in motion? Guess what? Two of those cards returned together in the same hand three shuffles later (the 3♠ and the A♦), and then, the very next round, both of those cards and *another* one of the original four were back in the same hand (the dealer's this time) -- the 3♠, A♠ and the A♦ (*and in the same order*)! If this doesn't speak to the repeating tendencies of the cards, I don't know what will!

But there's more! Here's a case of hand repetition involving one specific Blackjack pair! The A♣-Q♦, which gave the 2nd player in the 1st round of one shuffle period a Blackjack, was dealt as a Blackjack (as Q♦-A♣) to the 5th player of the 2nd round following the next shuffle, and then returned in the 2nd round following the very next shuffle, unfortunately to the dealer, as a Q♦-A♣ Blackjack pair. Convinced yet?

There were a number of cases where the same player got the same Ace two or three shuffles in a row, or in short order...participants who got more than their share of Aces (such as the 1st Baseman)...I mean, this example alone could make the subject of a great thesis! But, I've proved my point. Before we get bogged down in details, let's move on to something *even more important.*

I want to add, however, that all of this shows that, when there is a repeating phenomenon involving Aces, the dealer is frequently the one who benefits the most. If I'd been at this table, I'd probably have left by the third dealer Blackjack.

Dealer Up Card Repetition

One type of repetitive phenomenon that bears more examination is dealer up card repetition. Needless to say, this can either be a boon to the player, or a bust, depending on which cards are coming up again and again. If they're Aces, pay them respect and leave the table!

That's right -- dealer up cards are not random. They tend to repeat. Each set of cards will have a different set of repeating up cards. Furthermore, the specific kinds of cards that repeat as up cards help create a recurring personality -- which is either good or bad. I don't think this phenomenon has ever been identified before, and yet it's powerful information.

How can you use this information? Once you identify which types of up cards are repeating, you'll be able to predict whether player-friendly or player-unfriendly up cards are most likely to come following the next shuffle. That will help you determine how to bet, and whether or not to leave the table.

An Amazing 88-Round Example

Let's look, for instance, at an example I chose at random. This was from a 4-player, 1-deck game study, in which 88 rounds were played, representing 30 shuffles, with the same cards. That's equivalent to about an hour or more of action at a table. (How many rounds are played per hour depends upon the pace of the dealer and the number of players at the table. Don't forget -- if there are seven players at the table, it'll take longer to finish the round than if you were going it alone. Plus, there are variables that affect this at the casino -- time wasted due to: shuffling; waiting for players to make up their minds; dealer changes; dealer attention to chip tray organizing; occasional interruptions by security personnel to do an accounting of the chips; and dealer/player banter.)

OK. First of all, if cards really play randomly, as you have been led to believe, then all 52 cards should be represented in this 88-round example.

Yet this is not the case. *Just 42 of the 52 different cards appeared as up cards! That means that 10 -- nearly 20% of the cards -- did not show up as up cards at all, in more than one hour of action! Plus, of the 42 cards that appeared as up cards, more than half -- 28 of them -- repeated at least once; many, in fact, repeated twice, some three times, and one even made five appearances!*

The evidence of up card repetition is unmistakable: **74 of the 88 rounds -- 84% -- included up cards that repeated!** *Let me say this in a different way: of the 52 cards that make up a deck,* **28 of them (54%) accounted for 84% of the up card appearances!** *This is even more impressive: of the 30 shuffle periods in this example, 100% included up cards that repeated. Let me repeat that: EVERY shuffle produced up cards that either repeated from before, or would repeat in the future.*

This is clearly not evidence of *randomness*. Quite the *opposite*.

Proof Beyond A Reasonable Doubt

Closer examination reveals even more incredible relationships that carried over from shuffle to shuffle. Here are just 10 examples:

♦ There was a case where two cards repeated as up cards *following the same shuffles!* Both the A♦ and the K♥ appeared as the up cards following the first and fifth shuffles. Two of the three up cards in those periods were the same! But that's not all. The A♦ repeated *in the same round in which it appeared the first time!*

- The 10♥ made *five* appearances as an up card within 38 shuffles -- *four of the five were in the last seven shuffle periods.*

- The A♣ made three appearances in 11 shuffles -- the last two times were just three shuffles apart and *both were in the second round.*

- The dealer showed an A♠ in three of 16 consecutive shuffles, *the last two times in the third round.*

- The 10♠ was an up card in the second of three rounds, and then *showed up again as an up card in the same round following the very next shuffle!* It also reappeared 3 shuffles later -- making *three* appearances within *five* shuffles. *In just 12 rounds, the 10♠ accounted for 25% of the up cards!*

- The K♠ took a bow three times in 15 shuffles. The last two occurrences were just three shuffles apart -- and both were in the second round!

- The 10♣ was an up card *three times in four shuffles.*

- The 8♣ was a *four-time* up card within 19 shuffles. It first showed up after the third shuffle, in the second round. Seven shuffles later, it came back as an up card, *again in the second round.* Just three shuffles later, it was an up card again, this time in the first round. Eight shuffles later, it repeated as an up card *in the first round as it had the last time.*

- The dealer showed an 9♠ in four shuffle periods (within a range of 24 shuffles), the last two of which were two shuffles apart.

- The 5♥ was an up card three times, *all of which were in the second round.*

To put this in its proper perspective, you need to understand that, with an average of three rounds per shuffle in this 4-player, 1-deck example, each card should appear just once every 17 shuffles -- if randomness is the rule in blackjack. So, when I say that the 10♥ appeared five times in just *15* shuffles, that's really amazing, because *it's nearly **six times** the amount of times the law of probability says it would have appeared in a random environment.*

Both the 10♣ and the 10♠ appeared *three times in four shuffles;* that's **13 times** what is supposed to happen in a random world.

But get this -- *nearly 50% of the up card repeats occurred within four or less shuffles.* (The

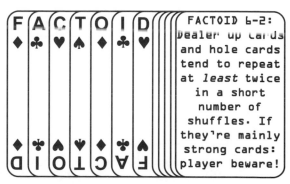

FACTOID 6-2:
Dealer up cards and hole cards tend to repeat at *least* twice in a short number of shuffles. If they're mainly strong cards: player beware!

mode average between repeating up card appearances, in fact, was *three shuffles.*) *Almost 20% of the repeats occurred within just one or two shuffles!* And about 50% of the recurring up cards came back *two or more times.*

Pretty remarkable. All of this is even more incredible when you come to the realization that *this is how the game plays out, deck after deck after deck. With dealer up cards casting such a long shadow over the results of each round, it's not hard to see how this sort of phenomenon creates at least a short-term predictable sameness -- which might be good or bad from the standpoint of player results -- from one shuffle to another.*

Moreover, I have found after extensive study, that *the dealer's hole cards also tend to repeat.* AND, *up cards often repeat as hole cards and vice versa,* over quite a number of shuffles! (For example, the 10♥, a five-time up card, was a hole card three times. The 9♠, an up card four times, made *three* visits as a hole card. The 10♣, a three-time up card, was a hole card *four* times -- a number which is more than two times what would be expected if this were a random game, especially considering that these appearances were within constricted ranges in the 88 round/30 shuffle example.)

So, what we're looking at here is something that needs to be understood and respected. Especially when you realize that the subset of cards that are participating in such a repeating phenomenon at any given time can greatly affect your game. In this example, the 9s, 10s and Aces were overrepresented as up cards and hole cards, especially during the last 24 shuffle periods. These are not the up cards you want the dealer to have. As you might surmise, dealer Blackjacks were significantly more frequent than is normal (5% is the average; these Blackjacks occurred over the course of 52 rounds, encompassing 18 shuffles, representing a Blackjack rate of nearly 12%!! -- well more than twice what would be expected, if the game consisted of random events).

What did this mean to the four virtual players? *All* wound up losers (as you can see in the chart below), and *this was largely due to the mix of cards*

Player	Wins	Losses	Pushes	Net	Loss Rate
1	34	49	6	-15	17%
2	39	48	2	-9	10%
3	33	53	3	-20	22%
4	39	41	10	-2	2%

involved in the repeating syndrome of the up card and hole card during these rounds.

How To Respond To Repeating Up Cards

This proves my point, first made in *Blackjack The SMART Way*, that the quality of the cards -- good, bad or neutral -- tends to *persist* for some time. Therefore, *it's something you should anticipate, look for, and react to in your card analysis.*

While it would be difficult to do a detailed analysis of which up cards, for instance, are repeating the most, it shouldn't be too hard to pick up on occasions when the dealer is getting Aces and 10s in numbers that are well above their Circle of 13 proportions. *And dealer Blackjacks should be like red lights flashing in your face.* You now know that, if there were an unusual number of dealer Blackjacks during the last shuffle period, this repeating phenomenon ensures the likelihood that there will continue to be a high number of them after the shuffle. I always pay attention to the exact identity of the Ace involved in dealer Blackjacks at pitch game tables, by the way. If one of the them returns after a shuffle, in a dealer Blackjack, I'll lower my bet or leave the table if these are contributing to a player-unfriendly situation.

Your response to this repeating syndrome is simple: *pay attention to the general mix of dealer up cards. If they are heavy in 9s, 10s and Aces, and you've noticed you've been suffering losses as a result, leave the table. You now know that the kinds of up cards you're seeing won't change much in the immediate future.* Indeed, it often takes the introduction of a new set of cards to alter your fate (and, believe me, the casinos are aware of this phenomenon, even if no one's written about it before -- why do you think they replace the cards when players are on a hot streak?). The reverse is true, too, of course: *if the dealer's been getting more than his or her share of weak up cards (and the repeating hole cards have been causing the dealer to lose more than is normal, which, roughly speaking, is slightly less than 50%, with pushes taken into account), then you should bump up your bet outlays to a higher level, commensurate with the increase in your winning rate.*

The Repetitive Splitting Phenomenon

The last and least of all the repeating phenomenon I'll mention here is the repetitive splitting phenomenon. This indeed can benefit or hurt you, but it is a short-lived thing, and one that is just icing on the cake of your assessment of the quality of the cards. If the repeating phenomena that are most responsible for your future are producing good results, then, a player's splitting of Aces is a happy happenstance, because many split cards are followed within a short period with at least one repetition of that event, if not two, and an opportunity to split Aces often is a good one. The splitting of 9s also offers the prospect of probable good results. The splitting of 8s, on the other hand, often leads to losses. But, whether you should raise or lower your bet upon noticing a splitting event is doubtful.

Nonetheless, let's look at this, so you realize that this, too, is a syndrome that is going on, as well. I found three examples quickly.

First, there was the case where the 1st player received two 7s (the 7♦ and the 7♣, in that order), which he then split. The 7♣ received the 9♦, and then chose to stand. Four shuffles later, the same player received the same two 7s (in reverse order)! AND, the 9♦ was again dealt to one of those 7s, in a situation where he again chose to stand on that stiff!

Second was the situation where a player received the 3♦ and 3♥, and split them. Four shuffles later, another player was dealt the very same 3s as his first two cards (in reverse order), and split them.

Finally -- to demonstrate how long the underlying card proximities don't change much from shuffle to shuffle -- there's the example of the two 9s (the 9♥ and the 9♠), dealt as one player's first two cards in one shuffle period, and split, which then returned to another player's hand thirteen shuffles later, in the same order, as their first two cards, and again in a splitting situation.

How To Respond To All Repeating Phenomena

This general advice goes for all repeating phenomena: *once noticed, you should respond in one of three ways: raise your bet accordingly, lower your bet appropriately, or leave the table.* The standard in reacting to them should be that they change things *significantly*, one way or another. Some repeating events are just interesting to note, but not easy to capitalize on, such as the repetitive splitting phenomenon. Others, like orbiting associations, often come with telltale signs of good things to come, or bad. Repeating 4-7 combinations are good -- starting off with an 11 offers good chances of success. *Associations that cause the dealer to bust are best, and call for a healthy increase in your betting pattern. Repeating dealer Blackjacks, on the other hand, or patterns that give the dealer more than his or her share of 10s -- as up cards and hole cards -- are causes for concern, and call for immediate cautionary action.*

How NOT To Respond To Repeating Phenomena

The average player, by the way, seems to be aware that the quality of the cards tends to be consistent for quite some time, even though they might not be aware of it on a conscious level. I say this because many will drop out of the action for a round or two, or reduce the number of betting spots they've taken when the table is bad, in the hope of changing the order of the cards enough to make things better (they'll sometimes even verbalize this intention). However, you should realize by now that this is *not* likely to do anything at all. It's not only a waste of your time to try this tactic, it's a waste of your money. If the table's so bad that you would think about trying this, it's time to move to a different table. *The power and persistence of orbiting associations is such that you cannot disrupt them with such an attempt. (And, incidentally -- orbiting associations even exist at tables where there's just one player; it just takes longer to pick up on what they are, because so few cards are seen at a time.)*

To Be Continued...

There will be more on how to identify repeating phenomena later on, in Chapter 12, on "Strategic Card Analysis & Your Real-time Card Strategy."

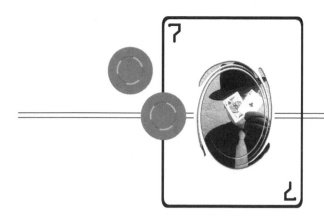

Gains Stages,
Betting Spot Discoveries
& More Precise Betting

So you have learned that card relationships are not altered very much with standardized casino dealer shuffling, which leads to a repeating nature to the dealer's and players' cards. In fact, you have seen that there are repeating phenomenon that tend to be *specific to one betting spot*.

Now that you understand this, it should be no surprise that you can tap into a *predictability* factor regarding the identity and *quality* of the cards you are likely to get in the future, and use that information to great advantage in making the most intelligent bets. This is what we will look at here.

What I'm going to show you will absolutely blow you away! I will introduce you to a number of new discoveries I've made that will undoubtedly transform and fine-tune your game forever.

You will learn about a new way of measuring how well your betting spot is doing, through *Player Progress Patterns*, *Win/Loss Margins*, *Gains Stages* and *Get Out Points*. This information is extremely important. In *Blackjack The SMART Way,* in the chapter on "The X Factor," I spoke of analyzing how good your betting spot was: was it horrible, bad, neutral, good, or great, in terms of your *table win rate -- the percentage of hands you've won or lost* -- and other factors. We then used that information to determine what level you should be at, in my 3-Level Notch-Up, Notch-Down Bet Management System. In this chapter, you will not only see justification for this approach, but I will also give you a solid method to *quantify* how well your betting spot is doing -- and then I will tell you how to use these numbers to determine: how to bet; when to leave; and, how well your betting spot might do in the foreseeable future.

The Prophets Of Randomness

Now, if *instead* the pundits who say the cards play out *randomly* are correct, then for every 52 cards dealt to each betting spot, over the course of many rounds and shuffles, we should find that *each* of the 52 cards is represented. And there should be no repetition of any of the cards in the form of an identifiable *pattern*. But -- as you will see in detail -- those pundits' theories crumble when you see further proof in this chapter that the cards, per each betting spot, are anything BUT random!

The Personality Of Each Betting Spot

I first introduced this concept in *Blackjack The SMART Way* -- that is, that each set of cards displays its own personality in terms of dealer and player busting, win rates, etc. Here, you're going to find *proof* that *each betting spot also experiences long-term repetitive card trends*. Because, as you have seen, players are getting roughly the same set of cards from shuffle to shuffle, you can identify something akin to a *personality* for each betting spot!

...All of which explains, for instance, why one player may be consistently doing well from shuffle to shuffle, while the others are doing poorly. You must have noticed before that players who have taken the betting spots to your left and right often experience differing fortunes than yours -- which are often consistent from shuffle to shuffle, *regardless of what the count is, and regardless of how the table is doing as a whole.*

Introducing Win/Loss Margins

By charting the many, many card runs I've done and continue to do for my ongoing computer studies, many truths became apparent -- including proof of my theory that good cards tend to stay good for quite some time, bad cards tend to stay bad for quite some time, and neutral cards tend to stay neutral for quite some time. Plus, these charts verify my assertion that past history gives us a jump on future probabilities, such as our likely win rates.

What I did was to look at how well each betting spot did over time, in terms of wins and losses, factoring in player gains from splitting, and the halved losses that came from surrendering. (The only thing I did not add into this picture was gains and losses from doubling, and the extra profits from blackjacks -- these would have clouded the real picture.) From now on, we'll call this measure of how well each betting spot fared its *Win/Loss Margin, or WLM, for short.*

For instance -- let's take the example of a situation where you'd won 5 hands, lost 4, and surrendered once. Here's the equation you would use to determine your Win/Loss Margin:

+5   **(for the wins)**

-4   **(for the losses)**

-.5   **(for the surrender loss)**

= .5   **Your Win/Loss Margin**

How will we use these numbers? For starters, charting a player's progress using *WLM* numbers is very revealing. This will become apparent to you, as you study some of the WLM charts I produced in my computer studies, as presented on the following pages.

For one thing, these charts will show you that there are but a limited number of what I'd like to call *Player Progress Patterns, or PPPs,* that a player will encounter. A PPP is the shape of the chart line you get when mapping your WLM numbers from round to round and shuffle to shuffle. By your PPP's *shape,* you can discern your progress trend -- is it up, down, neutral, etc.? It is visually obvious. In addition, PPP charts make it graphically clear how prolonged each player progress trend is. *In the charts you're about to see, therefore, is proof that there ARE palpable long-term trends that develop because of the nonrandom nature of the cards.*

The great thing about this new discovery is that, if you have a familiarity with these patterns, you can learn to detect what PPP you're in, while playing at the casino. This information is dynamite: it will tell you, among other things, how you've been doing and how you're likely to do in the near future, enabling you make more informed decisions. This is yet another new tool I am giving you, to use in your arsenal.

Stock-Style Charts That Tell The Story

When you chart Player Progress Patterns by looking at Win/Loss Margin (WLM) numbers, you come up with graphs that look very similar to the stock charts that Wall Street uses to follow a stock's relative health. You can see this instantly in the charts on the following two pages. None of the PPPs (the lines that result from charting WLMs over time) are unbroken straight lines, no matter what the general direction.

One reason for this is that, very much like stock progress patterns that become clear in the chart of a stock's price as it varies from day to day, your fortunes will go up and down, and will trade, so to speak, in a narrow range, when looked at in the microcosm of a short run of rounds.

Plus, a blackjack player's world is similar in other ways to that of the Wall Street stock trader:

❶ You, like the investor, have to constantly monitor how you're doing, to know when to get out, or when to increase your investment.

❷ Like typical stock traders, most blackjack players tend to stay with

CHART 7-1:

Player Progress Patterns

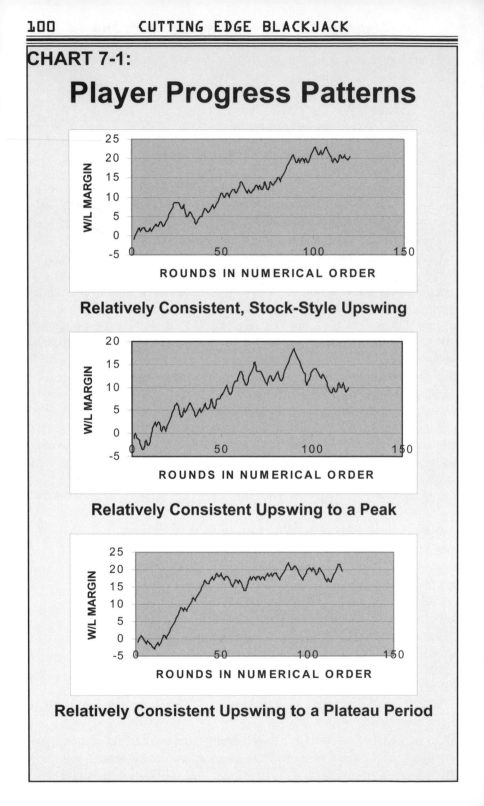

Relatively Consistent, Stock-Style Upswing

Relatively Consistent Upswing to a Peak

Relatively Consistent Upswing to a Plateau Period

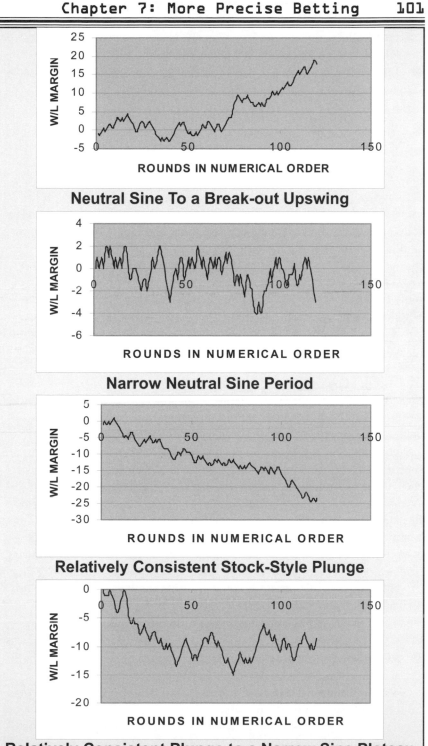

Neutral Sine To a Break-out Upswing

Narrow Neutral Sine Period

Relatively Consistent Stock-Style Plunge

Relatively Consistent Plunge to a Narrow Sine Plateau

losing tables too long, and, conversely, throw back gains by staying too long during an up cycle that's already peaked.

 Like an investor, you can make smarter decisions if you understand how well your "chart" is doing.

Looking At The Sines, Plateaus, Peaks And Break-outs

PPP charts, like the ones on page 100-101. These reflect how well each player fared over the course of time in which just one set of cards was in play. First, notice how few types of player progress patterns there are, defining the relative health of a player's betting spot over time. You'll immediately see, too, that these patterns reveal that each betting spot has a clear personality, because they tend to last quite a long time -- through many shuffles and rounds, and because they are unique to each betting spot. Seen in another way, you could say that many of these patterns have a certain *predictability* about them. You can see that, given their length, you can be fairly certain of where you're going once you've detected which pattern you're on.

A word of explanation: the horizontal axes on the charts denote the rounds played, in numerical order, so we can follow the progress of one betting spot or player, through many, many shuffles -- with each chart representing the playing out of one set of cards. The vertical axes show how players are doing vis a vis their Win/Loss Margins; the positive numbers denote periods where players' wins outnumber their losses, and the negative numbers denote periods where players' losses outnumber their wins.

(Note that I do not refer to the positive periods as times where players are showing profits, or winnings. That's something different. Whether or not each player is winning depends upon that player's betting method. For example, even if a player is in the midst of a super upswing as represented by these player progress pattern charts, that player can lose his or her entire bankroll if he or she places all of it on one hand that results in a loss. So, even if their wins outnumber their losses -- which is what we're measuring here -- a player might wind up a big loser by poor betting. What we're going to want to do is to take what we can learn from these charts and come up with an intelligent betting system to reflect the reality they present.)

First, let us identify the different types of Player Progress Patterns, or PPPs, you might encounter:

❶ **Relatively consistent stock-style upswings.** Although there might be short and shallow setbacks of several Win/Loss Margin points, this pattern features a steady rise in your Win/Loss Margin. These are your profit phases. While it's possible that these might begin in negative territory, most significant upswings -- the ones you profit from most -- begin in positive territory.

❷ **Narrow neutral sine wave-style periods.** These are up and down periods where your Win/Loss Margin goes up and down in a narrow range, much like a sine wave (see below), usually straddling the neutral Win/Loss Margin zero point, where your wins equal your losses.

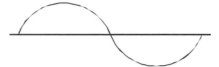

❸ **Relatively consistent stock-style plunge periods.** These are periods where your losses clearly outnumber your gains, and, therefore, your Win/Loss Margin points are steadily decreasing -- whether in positive or negative territory.

❹ **Plateau periods.** In these periods, your Win/Loss Margin hardly varies at all. Very similar to neutral sine wave periods, except these can happen at any point level, and your fluctuation might be so narrow that your pattern is nearly flat, rather than being more like a sine wave. These are not typically profit periods, no matter what your WLM Range is. At best, you're holding your own here. Pay strict attention to any changes that might signal an end to these periods, vis a vis whether the pattern that follows is likely to be profitable or harmful.

❺ **Break-out periods.** Whether going up or down, these are periods that suddenly and consistently veer off from the general trend that came before.

❺ **Peak periods.** Periods of shorter duration than the others listed above, where you reach your maximum Win/Loss Margin points level (in positive territory), and then back off from that level. Interestingly enough, these periods often feature two or more identical peak points, and two or more near-peak points (of within 1 point of the peak). They typically last about a half dozen to 10 or so rounds in duration, often through several shuffles.

These periods can be found together in any combination, in any one player progress pattern chart, over the course of the many rounds and shuffles in which one set of cards is in play (many casinos replace the cards every two hours -- or every 120 rounds, give or take; others keep them in play longer). Note that NONE of these patterns can be described as a straight line in any direction. Stock-style is my way of describing the two-steps-forward-and-one-back type of pattern that typifies the game of blackjack -- which you can see clearly in the jagged progression lines in the charts on pages 100 and 101.

A word of caution -- some casinos overmanage the tables, and quickly replace "hot" cards with new decks, when they notice players accumulating chips. This only validates what I'm teaching you in this chapter regarding the personality of each set of cards. These casinos are obviously aware that player progress patterns tend to last for many, many rounds and through many, many shuffles, as you can see in the charts in this chapter.

By the way, if you notice new cards being brought in at an odd time, outside of the ordinary for that casino, when your progress pattern was in a consistent upswing mode, my suggestion is that you leave immediately. You cannot win if the casino always replaces the cards when they are decidedly in your favor. (For more information on casino countermeasures, read Chapter 11 in *Blackjack The SMART Way*.)

The Numbers Proving This Are Astounding

Now, one reason these periods are not terribly hard to identify, when experiencing one, is the prolonged average length of all but the peak periods. In fact, the numbers that bear this out are absolutely amazing!

My research is ongoing into this matter, but, here's what I've found so far: the number of times players find themselves in downside patterns (where players' WLM numbers are negative) is roughly equal to the number of times players find themselves in upside patterns (where players' WLM numbers are positive).

Looking at my 1-deck runs only, the *AVERAGE length of an upside pattern was nearly 54 rounds! This carried through many, many shuffles -- roughly a dozen or two, give or take* (it depends on the number of players at the table, and, therefore, the number of rounds between shuffles). *The average length of a downside pattern was 57 rounds, also carrying through one to two dozen shuffles, give or take!*

What's more: **49% of the patterns studied lasted anywhere from 41 to 183 rounds!!!** For those who are still questioning whether trends actually exist in the game of blackjack, or that a set of cards can manifest a consistent

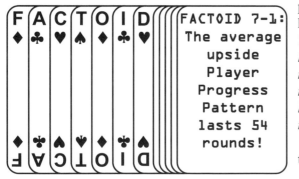

FACTOID 7-1: The average upside Player Progress Pattern lasts 54 rounds!

personality, let me add here that: *more than 72% of the patterns lasted 20 rounds or more -- a convincing majority. In fact, 83% lasted 15 rounds or more!!!*

The numbers speak for themselves.

(Incidentally -- there were patterns that lasted through more than 120 rounds that were still going strong when the cards were replaced by a new deck! This was true, also, of the devastating downside pattern that afflicted a player for 182 rounds, from a situation where the player was playing head-on with the dealer.)

What Does All Of This Mean?

Now, don't get me wrong. Just because you're in an *upside pattern* -- your WLM numbers are in the positive range -- doesn't mean you're on a rocket to the stars. In fact, you can be in an upside pattern and actually be *losing* ground, down in the winnings you had made, as you back off the peaks you had reached. Or, you can be in positive territory where you're in a neutral pattern that doesn't get you very far, and, if your betting system is not conservative, you can actually start heading south in chips. On the other hand, you can be in a *downside pattern* -- your WLM numbers are in the negative range -- and you might find yourself on a minor winning streak that's bringing you back to even money, or better, that offers you a golden opportunity to recoup losses.

We'll be drawing a number of important conclusions from all of this, but, for now, understand that Player Progress Patterns tend to persist for quite some time.

Seeing Is Believing

OK -- let's go from the general to the specific.

Let's look at player progress patterns of "players" at different virtual "tables" plucked from my computer runs -- that is, we'll see how different betting spots fared at one table, during the course of many rounds and shuffles, each virtual table playing out a different set of cards than the others.

On pages 106-111 you'll find charts for three different trials. In these trials, all seven betting spots were played. The course of action for each trial equalled about 2 hours' worth of rounds (figuring here that 60 rounds were played each hour); then, the cards were replaced with a new set.

In these representations, you'll notice that, while some players appear to be on a similar progress pattern, others are experiencing different fortunes. Typical of the average table at the casino, some players are doing well, others not so well.

However -- not every table is alike, either, as I pointed out in *Blackjack The SMART Way.* In the chapter on "The X Factor," I taught you how to evaluate a table as being either horrible, bad, neutral, good, or great -- either globally, in terms of whether you should join a particular table, or, more importantly, how good the table was doing for you, at your particular betting spot. There were one or two skeptics among the reviewers who questioned whether a table could actually display such a long-term personality. With charts such as the ones on pages 106-111, any skepticism should melt away. With these charts, you now have the convincing visual representation of this phenomenon.

(Continued on page 112.)

CHART 7-2:

Player Progress Patterns At Table A

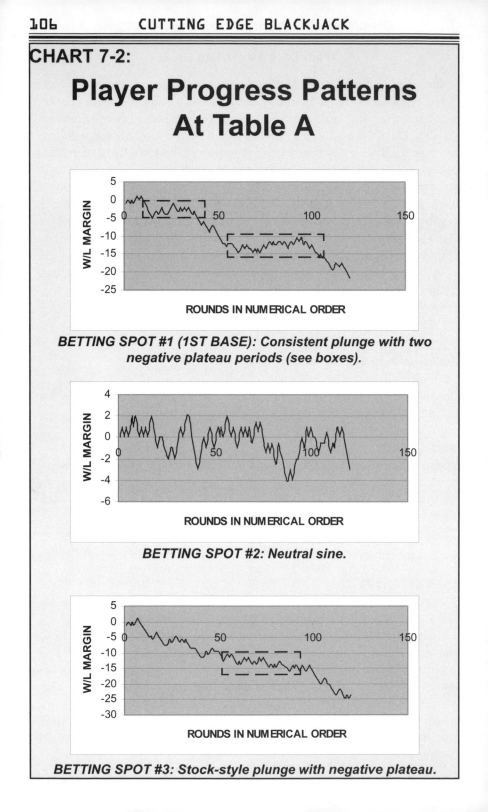

BETTING SPOT #1 (1ST BASE): Consistent plunge with two negative plateau periods (see boxes).

BETTING SPOT #2: Neutral sine.

BETTING SPOT #3: Stock-style plunge with negative plateau.

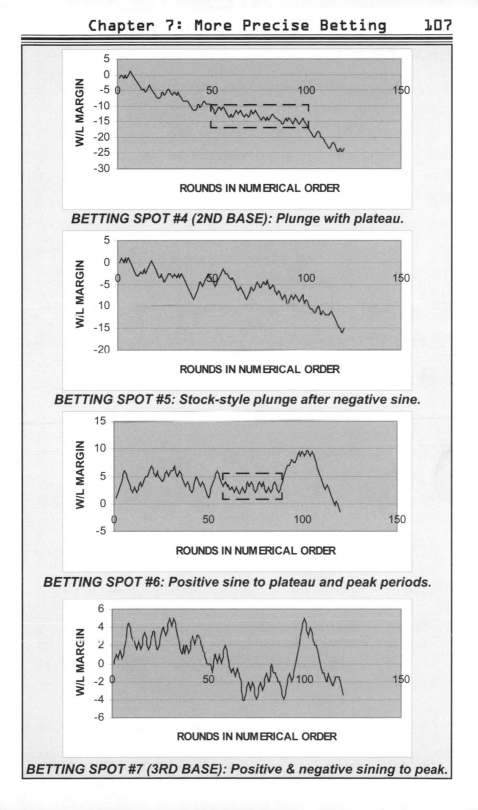

BETTING SPOT #4 (2ND BASE): Plunge with plateau.

BETTING SPOT #5: Stock-style plunge after negative sine.

BETTING SPOT #6: Positive sine to plateau and peak periods.

BETTING SPOT #7 (3RD BASE): Positive & negative sining to peak.

CHART 7-3:

Player Progress Patterns At Table B

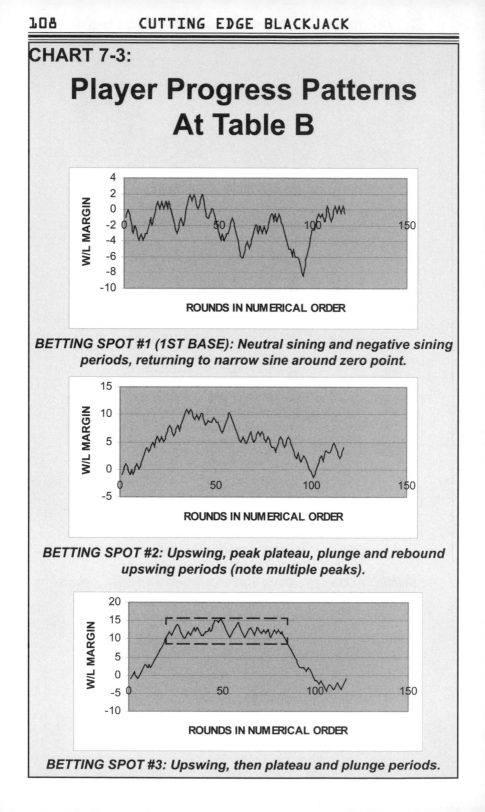

BETTING SPOT #1 (1ST BASE): Neutral sining and negative sining periods, returning to narrow sine around zero point.

BETTING SPOT #2: Upswing, peak plateau, plunge and rebound upswing periods (note multiple peaks).

BETTING SPOT #3: Upswing, then plateau and plunge periods.

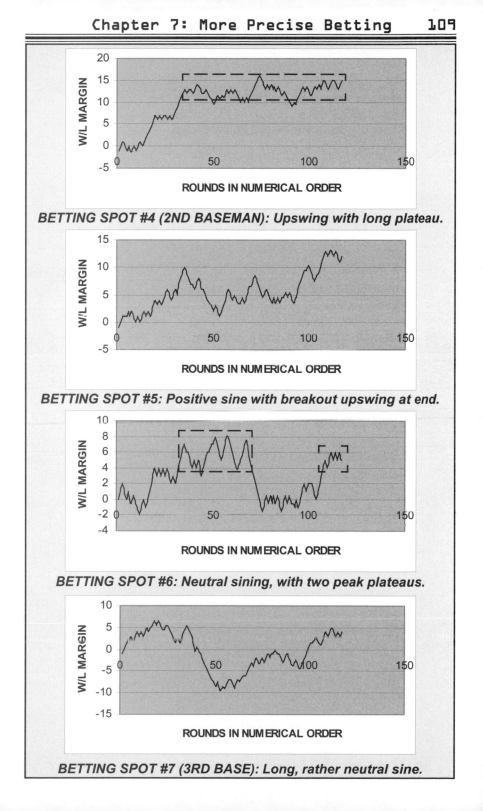

BETTING SPOT #4 (2ND BASEMAN): Upswing with long plateau.

BETTING SPOT #5: Positive sine with breakout upswing at end.

BETTING SPOT #6: Neutral sining, with two peak plateaus.

BETTING SPOT #7 (3RD BASE): Long, rather neutral sine.

CHART 7-4:

Player Progress Patterns At Table C

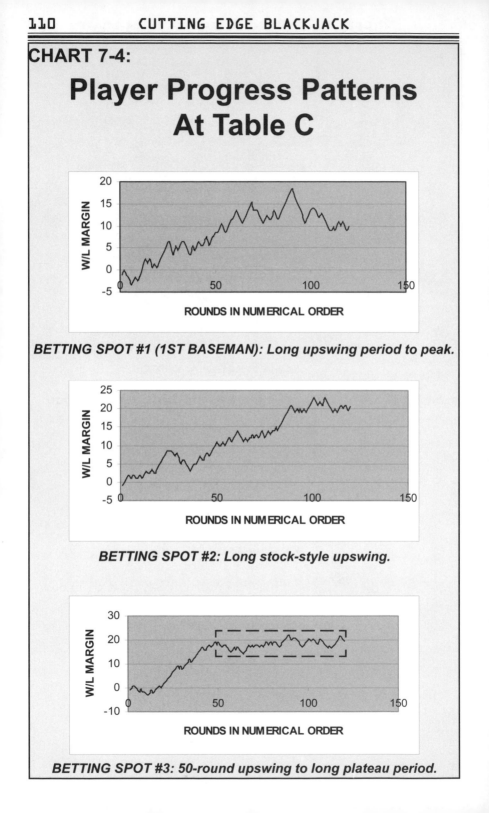

BETTING SPOT #1 (1ST BASEMAN): Long upswing period to peak.

BETTING SPOT #2: Long stock-style upswing.

BETTING SPOT #3: 50-round upswing to long plateau period.

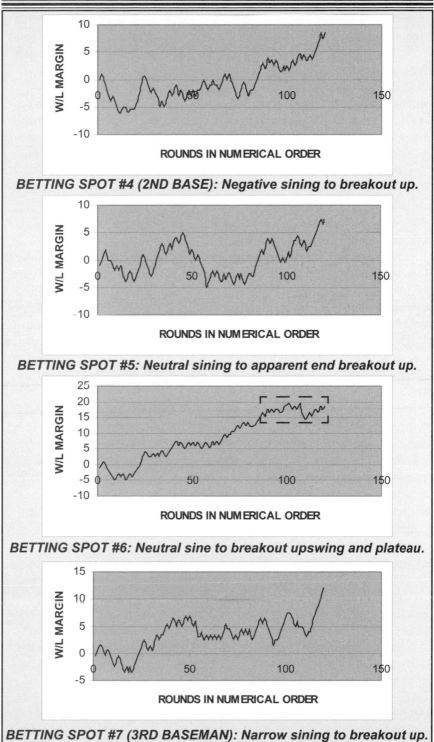

BETTING SPOT #4 (2ND BASE): Negative sining to breakout up.

BETTING SPOT #5: Neutral sining to apparent end breakout up.

BETTING SPOT #6: Neutral sine to breakout upswing and plateau.

BETTING SPOT #7 (3RD BASEMAN): Narrow sining to breakout up.

(There long has been a debate in the blackjack world over whether or not winning and losing *streaks* exist as palpable phenomenon. The word streaks, to me, implies that luck is somehow turning one way or another, inexplicably. Luck has nothing to do with what I'm identifying here, when I talk about the personality of the cards, and the individual betting spots. Now, you may look at the charts on the preceding pages and conclude that streaks do exist. However, there are real reasons for the long-term trends and player progress patterns in these charts, as you will see. So, on one hand, I caution you against thinking that the game is streaky. However, you are correct in thinking that players can take advantage of winning and losing player patterns -- so long as you can identify the trend you're in correctly. More on this later.)

On pages 106 and 107 you see the graphic manifestations of a blackjack table that, for four of the seven players, is horrible. In fact, the player progress patterns for these betting spots -- 1, 3, 4 and 5 -- are fairly similar. However, as you can see clearly from the unique pattern of betting spot #6, one player had a very different experience at this table. This player could have come away a big winner, had that player wisely chosen to leave before his or her spot dropped too far below its peak at a WLM number of about 10. The 3rd baseman, too, might have come out a winner with a wise betting approach. But, the player at betting spot #2, suffered with a frustrating up and down neutral sine pattern that, for most players, would have led to an eventual loss.

Some important things to note here are that: 1) each betting spot experienced cards of a specific personality or trend; and 2) these personalities were expressed in long-term trends, specific to each betting spot (and sometimes contained more than one long-term pattern -- such as the peak periods seen at the end of the charts for betting spots 6 and 7). While four of the patterns are similar, they are not exactly the same. More to the point, it is the three divergent player patterns that demonstrate the unique forces that determine the course each betting spot will take.

As we review the charts on pages 106-111, notice, too, how apparent it is that each table's cards do express an overall personality, even if some of the players successfully buck it. The table as expressed in the charts on pages 106-107 is a rather tough one for most. The personality of the tables as depicted on pages 108-111, however, are far different. Most of the players at the table represented on pages 108-109 would justifiably conclude that this table had been good for them (especially if they knew enough to get out at the right point). Most of the players at the table represented on pages 110-111 would instead say that table had been GREAT for them.

In these charts lies proof of the concepts I first presented in *Blackjack The SMART Way* regarding identifiable trends you will encounter at each blackjack table -- trends that can be identified through analysis, which I'll get to very soon. Tables (actually, a *particular set of cards*) indeed can be labelled as being horrible, bad, neutral, good or great; so can the individual betting spots. The fact that the trends that produce such strongly identifiable phenomenon are such *long-term* trends, lasting through many tens of rounds, and dozens of shuffles, proves my point that each set of cards displays a personality, as does each betting spot.

What Causes These Long-Term Patterns?

It is the personality of the dealer cards that causes the striking similarities in the charts. It is the personality of each betting spot's cards that leads to the patterns that are unique to each spot. This becomes readily apparent when you put the chart patterns of two or more players together on one graph, as I did below, for players 4 and 5, at table C:

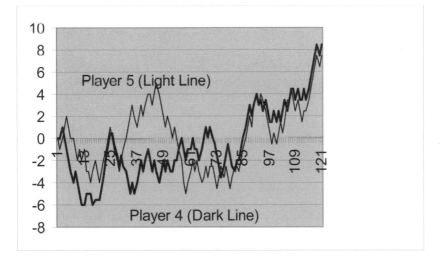

"Now -- wait a minute!" I can hear some of you reacting. "What are you saying??? For there to be a long-term, consistent personality, as you put it, for each betting spot, each betting spot would have to be getting roughly the same restricted selection of cards for a protracted number of rounds and shuffles! Is that what you're suggesting?"

No. This is exactly what's happening -- especially at 1- and 2-deck tables. (At multi-deck tables, this phenomenon will occur to a lesser degree, depending on where the cut card is placed.) This is yet another amazing phenomenon I have discovered -- that each betting spot tends to draw to it a select, repetitive group of cards, due to the nonrandom nature of dealer shuffling, which creates a sort of persistent personality and, therefore, predictability.

CHART 7-5:

Player Progress Patterns At Table D

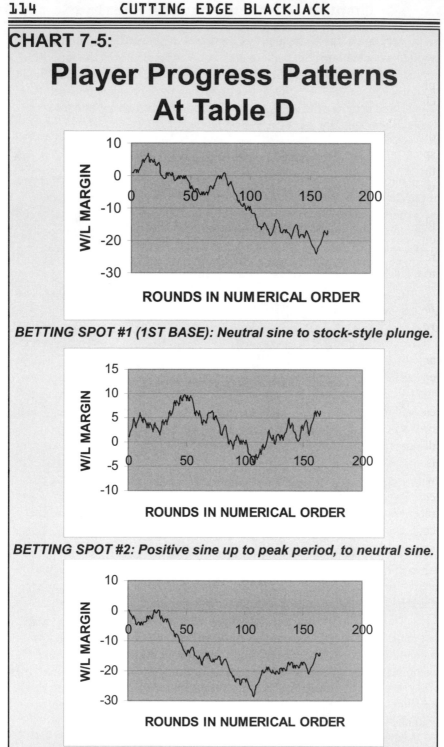

BETTING SPOT #1 (1ST BASE): Neutral sine to stock-style plunge.

BETTING SPOT #2: Positive sine up to peak period, to neutral sine.

BETTING SPOT #3: Negative sine to plunge with plateau.

How Betting Spot Cards Repeat

To demonstrate this, I've chosen to show you an example from my 3-player, 1-deck card runs, for simplicity. (See the player progress pattern charts for Table D, on the prior page.

We'll look at just one of the betting spots, #2, because this is the one that displayed a personality that differed markedly from the other two betting spots. (If player fortunes were dictated solely by the strength or weakness of the dealer's cards, by the way, this would not have occurred -- ALL players would have gone the same way.)

If this had been an actual situation with an actual player at a casino, the player at betting spot #2 would hopefully have known enough to have gotten out with his or her gains as close to the peak as possible (maybe *not*). For research purposes, however, all virtual players played out their betting spots to the end.

The point I'm making is: ***don't get the mistaken impression that it's smart for you to play out your betting spot to the bitter end, disregarding how your cards are faring.***

OK. Now, we're going to look at player #2's cards from several different angles, to convince ourselves that betting spot personality is a real phenomenon, and that it's caused by the repetitive, nonrandom nature of the cards.

If blackjack were a game with random results, we'd expect to find that each of the 52 cards was represented in the roughly same proportion -- that no card or set of cards was disproportionately represented. Therefore, if we discover, by looking at player #2's cards over a protracted period, that there is a repeating phenomenon featuring a specific collection of cards, AND, if we discover, with further investigation, that this type of phenomenon is a *continuous* reality -- that is, that there are ALWAYS small groups of cards repeating no matter what microcosm of rounds we look at -- then we can conclude with assurance that each betting spot indeed has its own repetitive personality.

Because player #2's progress pattern reaches a convincing and prolonged peak period at around 10 WLM units, unlike the other two players' patterns, I thought we should analyze this period first and see if we could identify not only a repeating phenomenon behind this, but also a more specific reason for this upswing.

For this, we have to examine rounds 27 through 54 -- 28 rounds, encompassing 8 shuffles -- which includes the peak period we're examining -- and the accompanying upswing that led to the peak. During this period, player #2 drew 70 cards. This amounts to 1.35 decks of cards.

Now, *if the cards played out randomly, as some would like you to believe, we should find that player #2 had at least one of each of the 52 different cards represented in this bunch* (in fact, statistically speaking, you'd expect each card to appear roughly 1.35 times).

INSTEAD, what we find is that *9 of the 52 possible cards were no-shows: they were not dealt to player #2 at all, during this prolonged period. That's nearly 20% of the cards!!!* Player #2 did not get the 2♣, 3♣, 4♦, 5♠, 6♠, 7♦, 7♠, Q♦ or A♦! (This is illustrated graphically on pages 118-119.)

In addition, we notice that *most of the cards the player DID receive were under-represented in the mix.*

Then, what we find is that *certain cards showed up repeatedly, well beyond their expected representation: Aces as a group, for instance, were overrepresented to the tune of 149%; 10s,102%; 9s,130%; and 8s,149%. In contrast, 7s, 6s, and 4s were greatly under-represented -- their proportions were 37%, 56% and 56% of what you might have expected, if equally represented with the other cards, as in a random system.*

And so we have our answer for why this player did so well during these 28 rounds: not only was there a select group of repeating cards, but they were strong cards: Aces, 10s, 9s and 8s. And seven of nine of the no-shows were weak cards whose absence strengthened the mix in favor of the strong cards.

From now on, we'll refer to the small set of cards that repeats beyond its expected proportion and frequency, thereby creating a consistent personality to the cards dealt to each betting spot, as the *lead cards*. Player #2's lead cards in this example included: the A♠, which was dealt to player #2 FOUR TIMES in SEVEN SUCCESSIVE SHUFFLES -- appearing in 57% of those shuffles; the A♥, which was dealt THREE TIMES in FIVE SUCCESSIVE SHUFFLES -- 60% of those shuffles; the J♥, which was dealt THREE TIMES in FOUR SUCCESSIVE SHUFFLES -- 75% of those shuffles; the J♣, which was dealt FOUR TIMES in FIVE SUCCESSIVE SHUFFLES -- 80% of those shuffles!; and, the 8♥, which was dealt FOUR TIMES in FOUR SUCCESSIVE SHUFFLES -- 100% of those shuffles!

If you're not convinced yet, consider this: of the 70 cards dealt to player #2 in this peak period:

❶ *Just 3 cards -- the A♠, J♣ and 8♥ -- accounted for nearly 20% of them!*

❷ *Just 9 cards accounted for 30 of those 70 cards -- nearly 43% of them (if we look at the cards that repeated three or more times)!*

❸ *Just 15 of the 52 cards accounted for 38 of the 70 cards dealt to player #2 -- making up more than 54% of that player's cards! Of these 15, nine were 8s, 9s, 10s and Aces.*

No wonder this player was on a winning upswing! Betting spot #2 was not only experiencing a repeating parade of a select few cards, those repeating cards featured primarily the *strongest* cards. This was no inexplicable lucky streak.

Now, this period is by no means an anomaly. It is typical of ANY

period we want to look at. The repeating card phenomenon which leads to a specific and prolonged personality for each betting spot is unmistakably real.

For example, let's look at the cards dealt to player #2 in the first 10 shuffles at Table D. In this period, which covers 32 rounds, that player received 87 cards total (equivalent to 1.67 decks of cards). During this time: *there were 12 cards this player was NEVER dealt -- nearly one quarter of the 52 possible cards!!* This is very significant. Statistically speaking, each of these 12 cards should have appeared at least once, if not more, if we were looking at a random situation!

This is a good time to bring up a point: *the large number of cards that do not get dealt to a specific betting spot during a specific and lengthy period, encompassing many rounds and shuffles, is just as important in creating the personality of each betting spot as the cards that do get dealt. In addition, this amazing and persistent phenomenon is further manifestation and proof of the fact that each betting spot is shaped by a small number of lead cards that creates a specific personality over a prolonged period. The phenomenon of lead cards, if you think about it, would not exist without the parallel phenomenon of no-show cards.*

Now, another important point in analyzing the first 10 shuffles in this example is that the majority of the cards this betting spot did receive were under-represented. This, too, is just as important a factor in creating the personality of this betting spot.

Then, continuing our analysis, we notice that there are a select few cards that repeated far beyond their expected proportions or frequencies -- these are our lead cards.

For example: *the Ace♠ appeared FIVE TIMES in SIX SUCCESSIVE SHUFFLES (and this card continued to repeat into the peak rounds we examined before); the Ace♥ appeared FOUR TIMES in EIGHT SUCCESSIVE SHUFFLES -- 50% of these shuffles (this card also continued to repeat far beyond expectations into the peak period we just examined)! Aces, in fact were overrepresented in this group of cards to the tune of 165%...and so on.*

Once again, if you're not convinced yet, consider this: of the 87 cards dealt to player #2 in the first 10 shuffles, encompassing 32 rounds:

❶ *Just 4 cards -- the Ace♠, Ace♥, 7♣ and 5♥ -- accounted for nearly 20% of them!*

❷ *Just 15 of the 52 possible cards accounted for 57% of those 87 cards.*

❸ *Just 27 of the 52 cards accounted for more than 85% of those 87 cards!*

This sort of phenomenon -- as consistent as it is, over time -- would never occur if the cards played out in a random situation. These amazing statistics are evidence of the fact that each betting spot is receiving a repeating set of

CHART 7-5:
The Strong Lead Cards Behind
Player #2's 8-Shuffle Peak Period...

EACH APPEARED
FOUR TIMES

EACH APPEARED
THREE TIMES

EACH APPEARED
TWICE

...And The Seven Weak No-Shows That Helped, By Their *Absence*

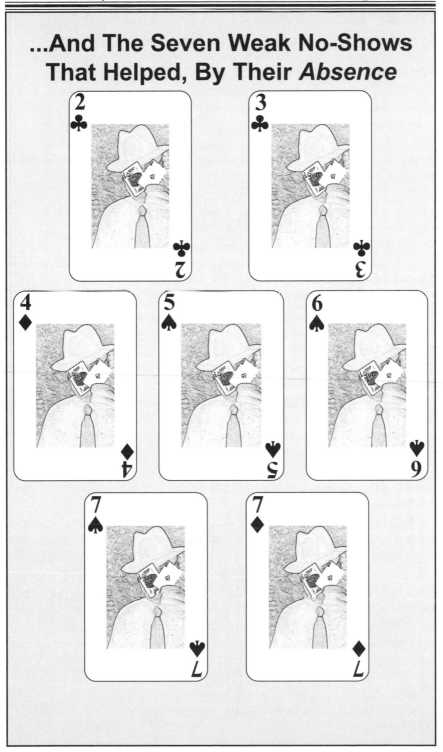

select cards that defines its fortunes over a protracted period, in a consistent, identifiable way.

Not only that -- it gets much more astounding, when you notice that: not only do many of the same cards from one round repeat *together* in later rounds, but *many of the repeating cards repeat in the exact same card order and/or round in which they had appeared before!*

For instance, three of the A♥'s four appearances took place in the 3rd round of action; plus -- it was the first card dealt to player #2 in two of those rounds!!! Three of the Ace♠'s five appearances were in the third round of action, two of which were as the third card dealt! And it goes on from there.

To see a more detailed illustration of this, look at the chart on the next page. There, I chose to analyze player #2's cards over a series of shuffle periods to demonstrate how player cards tend to repeat, and, often, in the *same rounds and order.* I chose specifically to look at repetition involving the cards dealt to player #2 in shuffle #8. The evidence is unmistakable.

Notice, by the way, that when cards repeat in a different position than they did previously, they often continue to repeat in that new position in later shuffles. Also pay attention to how many cards repeated together, in the *same* shuffle periods. There's even one card pair, the 4♣ and A♠, that are dealt together *twice*, just three shuffles apart -- the first time in the second round, the second time in the third round, as the first and second cards!

(NOTE: By way of explanation, the cards -- the A♥, 6♦, and J♣, etc. -- are set off by shading in the top column, to denote the different rounds in which they appeared; numbers in the cards' columns, stand for the round in which they appeared, and the order in which they were dealt -- so "1:1" would stand for the first round, first card; and the # column lists the number of times each card which appeared in shuffle 8's rounds were dealt in other shuffles.)

In fact, the periods detailed above weren't even the most impressive! For instance, there's the 10-shuffle, 33-round period where the K♣ was dealt to player #2 in EIGHT OUT OF TEN SUCCESSIVE SHUFFLES; and that same player was also dealt the J♠ AND 8♣ in FOUR of SIX SUCCESSIVE SHUFFLES; the K♦ in THREE of FOUR SUCCESSIVE SHUFFLES; the 9♦ in THREE of FIVE SUCCESSIVE SHUFFLES; and the 10♥ and A♦ were dealt in THREE of SEVEN SUCCESSIVE SHUFFLES.

During this time, player #2 was dealt 88 cards (1.69 decks worth of cards), but TEN OF THE 52 POSSIBLE CARDS -- NEARLY 20% OF THE CARDS -- WERE NOT DEALT AT ALL TO PLAYER #2! Statistically speaking, each of the 52 cards would have been received by player #2 nearly twice (1.69 times), if the cards in fact played out randomly, as is obviously NOT the case.

SHUFFLE	#	A♥	6♦	J♣	K♠	6♠	4♣	A♠	4♥
1	1	3:1							
2	2		3:1						2:1
3	1					3:1			
4	1	3:2							
5	3			3:2			2:1	2:2	
6	4	3:1		1:1	1:2	2:3			
7	1							3:3	
8	(8)	1:1	1:2	1:3	2:1	2:2	3:1	3:2	3:3
9	1							3:3	
10	1							4:1	
11	0								
12	2	3:2		1:2					
13	3		1:1				3:1	1:2	
14	1			1:1					
15	4	2:1		3:2				2:2	1:1
16	3	2:3		3:2	3:1				
17	0								
18	2				4:3	1:3			
19	2		2:2					1:2	
20	2		1:1		2:1				
21	1			3:2					
22	2			2:4			3:1		
23	0								
24	2		1:2		3:2				
25	0								
26	2			1:5		3:2			
27	0								
28	2	2:1				3:4			
29	0								
30	2		1:2					4:1	
31	0								
32	1		3:3						
33	0								
34	1			1:2					

Incidentally, *just five cards accounted for 25 of the 88 cards dealt to player #2 (nearly 30%)!! Just 12 of the 52 different cards (23% of the deck) accounted for 46 of the 88 cards dealt to player #2 (more than 52%)!!* And, looking at the grand scheme of things, you'd discover another astonishing fact -- *just 24 of the 52 possible cards accounted for 70 of the 88 cards dealt to player #2! Less than half the deck accounted for 80% of player #2's cards!!*

Once again, all of this is proof of a repeating card pattern that creates a prolonged sameness or personality of the cards at any one betting spot. It also provides the answer as to why player #2's player progress pattern looked pretty good in the 33-round period we just examined.

I could go on ad infinitum, but I don't believe that any reasonable person would remain unconvinced at this point.

How Long Will The Bet Spot Card Personality Stay The Same?

How long each group of cards holds sway at any one betting spot before gently giving way to another group of repeating cards varies. As the cards evolve slowly over many shuffles, the *lead cards -- the small set of repeating cards that dominate the personality or behavior of each betting spot --* gradually change, often leading to a change in the player progress pattern. Break-out patterns, peaks, drop-offs -- they're no mystery, nor are they typically short-lived phenomena. They are the result of a change in the lead cards that are in rotation.

So -- how long might one set of lead cards hold sway?

Sometimes looking at a microcosm of cards gives you an insight into a larger pattern. For instance -- if you look solely at the history of the cards from one shuffle, such as those in shuffle 8 from player #2 of Table D, you arrive at some very interesting results -- as you can see, on the prior page. In this example, the eight cards in shuffle 8 repeat at their maximum for about a dozen shuffles -- from shuffle 5 to 16 -- greatly coloring the personality of this player's hands during those shuffles. However, they are a clear presence for an even longer period of time -- they show up in groups of 2 or more rather consistently for nearly 30 shuffles, from shuffle 2 to shuffle 30. Now, these cards are not, by any means, *all* the lead cards that are producing the player progress pattern during this period -- we are just looking at the cards from one shuffle, for a microcosm of what's going on. Cards from other neighboring shuffles are also orbiting in the mix, in this card runs example. But it gives you an idea of how long lead cards circulate before giving way to others.

Now, although, as I say, the duration of player progress patterns due to repeating cards varies from one set of cards and players to the next, I think all of the evidence you've seen in this chapter points to typical patterns lasting -- at *minimum* -- a dozen or so shuffles and 30 or so rounds, encom-

CHART 7-6:

Player Progress Pattern At Table E

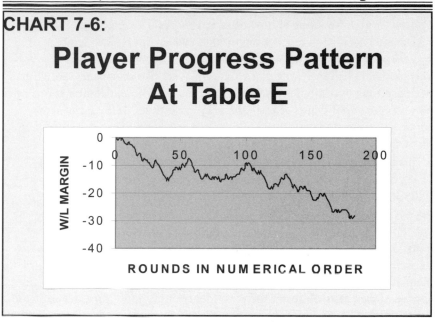

passing at least a half hour of action at the table (depending on the number of players present). Don't forget -- I pointed out earlier that the mean average length of an upside pattern was *54 rounds*.

Understanding that the typical multi-player table sees 60 or so rounds per hour, you should realize that this means you can fairly expect each PPP you're on to continue for at least 30 to 60 or so minutes of action.

In fact, *some repeating card patterns go on for the entire length of time a set of cards is in play.* You've already seen player patterns in this chapter that lasted 120 rounds. Yet, they can go on much longer than that. In Chapter 5 (on shuffling), you saw that some cards retained a similar order 30 to 60 shuffles after the cards were first introduced. Let's look, for instance, at one player progress pattern that lasted *183 rounds*.

Take a look at the 1-player progress pattern on the top of this page. This player was on a consistent negative ride for *the entire time this particular set of cards was in play, which amounted to 183 rounds of action.* The player's chart contained three prolonged progress patterns: an initial plunge period of more than 40 rounds, which led to a negative sining plateau period of more than 50 rounds in the middle, which then led to a final plunge period of well more than 50 rounds. (This should give you an idea of how persistent the personality of the cards can be.)

The Number of Players Makes A Difference

Interestingly enough, this player, at Table E, was dealt *the very same cards, in the exact same order, from shuffle to shuffle, as the seven players at Table B were dealt (see pages 108-109, for Table B's Player Progress*

Pattern charts). Yet, look at how different the results were!

You see, I decided to test my theory that tables with *higher* numbers of players perform *better* for players than tables with lower numbers of players. So, I dealt the cards that solitary players like the one at Table E had been dealt in my computer research card runs, to different combinations of players -- the very same cards, in the very same order. If the *exact* same cards that *pummeled* the solitary player did *well* for players at packed tables, that would certainly be one form of proof that my theory was valid.

This theory was certainly validated, in tests like this one. *Compare for yourself the results at Table E versus Table B. You'll see why I concluded that solitary players can expect lower win rates over time than players at packed tables.*

Another legitimate conclusion you might draw from this is that *a set of cards plays out differently, depending on the number of betting spots being played.* Just because a set of cards is good for a 7-player situation doesn't mean it will be good for other player combinations. The personality of the cards and the personalities of the individual betting spots *vary,* according to the number of betting spots being played, and the patterns that develop as a result of the division of cards among a particular number of betting spots. No one set of cards is likely to be good for all combinations.

OK -- so it should be obvious now that you need to learn to know how to quickly detect what PPP you're on. Then, you need to know how to respond to the various types of PPPs. For this, you need a bit of background in the fascinating world WLM *Ranges* and *Gains Stages* -- further manifestations of typical betting spot behavior. But, first -- how can you keep track of the numbers that propel your PPP charts?

Keeping Track of Your Win/Loss Margin

The key to taking advantage of all the knowledge you'll gain in this chapter is deciding upon a simple way to remind yourself of what your current WLM is at any point in time at the casino. I cannot overemphasize the power you'll tap into by doing this.

Now, there are many ways to do this, and I encourage you to come up with your own method -- preferably one that you believe casino bosses won't pick up on. You don't want to tip them off that you have a system.

You can use your feet -- tilting or twisting your left foot at various angles to indicate that your Win/Loss Margin is a certain number of *negative* WLM units, using your right foot in a similar way for *positive* WLM units.

You can use a watch. Some watches have a twistable dial on the face; you can twist this notch by notch to indicate where you're at in WLM units, so long as you can remember whether you're in positive or negative territory. To throw off casino employees from the real purpose, you could continu-ously play with the dial as if this were a nervous tick of yours -- only setting the dial upon the right number when the dealer starts to deal the cards.

You can use your chips. I like the idea of using one particular stack as the *signal stack* -- the pile that indicates your WLM either by the number of chips or the total value.

I've suggested one method in Illustration 7-7, on pages 126 and 127. In this method, you'd place your bet slightly north of the center of your betting spot to indicate when your WLM is in a positive range, and slightly south of the center when your WLM is in a negative range (try not to make the position extreme; move it just two or three millimeters above or below center line, so as not to tip off the dealer that you're using a system). Your stash of chips behind your betting spot would indicate your specific WLM number: in Illustration 7-7, it's the line of chips in front of the rear line of stacked chips that would indicate, by the number of chips in the stack, what your WLM number is.

A variation of this method would be to forgo using your betting spot as the positive/negative indicator, and simply use one stack of chips to tip you off to your WLM number -- perhaps orienting their pattern straight up for when your WLM is positive, and sideways when it's negative. (The half-units you might accrue through surrendering could either be represented by a chip of a differing value on top, or, perhaps you might choose simply to log surrenders as full losses and forget about keeping track of this subtlety -- it wouldn't make a huge difference, if you feel this shortcut would make things easier for you.)

You can be much more subtle about this, too, if you prefer -- arranging all your chips in one line, and pushing a stack with an appropriate number of signal chips ever so slightly north of the other stacks.

Another variation would be to hide your stack of signal chips within other stacks -- it could be the middle of three stacks, or the one furthest to the right, for example.

If you are going to use chips for this purpose, by the way, I recommend that you play with your stacks continuously, to make the dealer feel that you have a nervous tick, rather than being more obvious, with the danger that you'd reveal the real purpose of your chip rearrangements.

Whatever you do, make sure you decide upon your method and practice it until it becomes second nature to you, *before* you go to the casino.

How Would You Know What Your Pattern Is?

Now, numbers out of context don't tell us the whole picture. So, we'll want to know something about what I call *WLM Ranges* -- how these WLM numbers typically behave, over time. Then, we'll discuss seminal profit and loss periods I've discovered, which I've named *Gains Stages*. Both of these forms of analysis will enable you to better detect what *Player Progress Pattern*, or *PPP*, you're on. And, once you know that, we'll talk about how

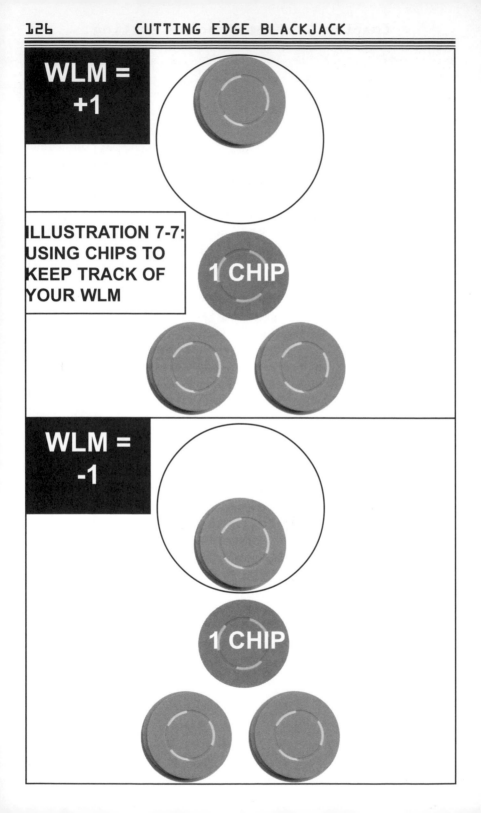

WLM = +1

ILLUSTRATION 7-7: USING CHIPS TO KEEP TRACK OF YOUR WLM

1 CHIP

WLM = -1

1 CHIP

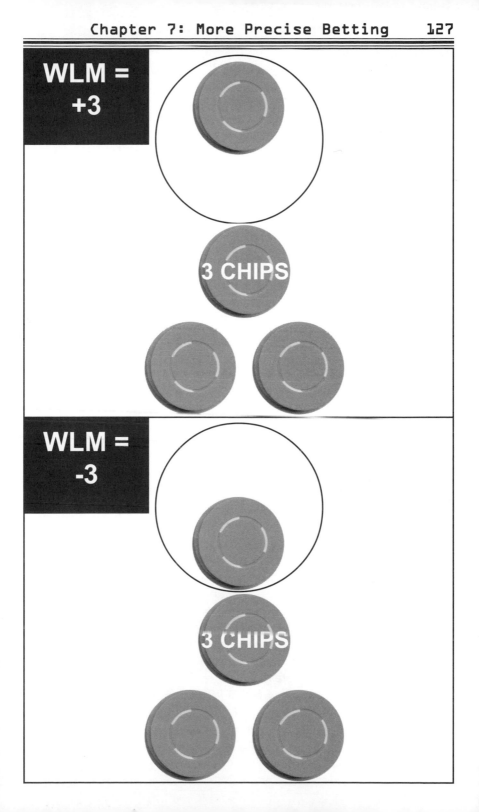

to determine good *Get Out Points* -- when it's time to leave, whether you're up or down.

A *WLM Range* is the distance, in units, between your lowest WLM and highest WLM, in any given period. You might think of this as your fluctuation in fortune over time. For instance, if, at your low point over the course of a particular period you went down to a WLM of -8, and, at your high point during that period you were up to a WLM of -2, your *Range* for that period would have been 6 *WLM units*.

You might find it helpful to determine what your WLM Range is, for each half hour of playing time -- based on the assumption that you will see about 30 rounds of action in a half hour. This is a convenient point at which to take stock of how well you're doing (bring your watch!).

It's interesting to note that the average WLM Range during each half hour of playing time is 7.69 (when analyzing rounds in groups of 30, from the time each new set of cards was introduced). The actual number varies from betting spot to betting spot, during each 30 round period. The lowest recorded Range for 30 rounds was a mere 2.5 units; the highest, 16.5.

Interestingly enough, preliminary data seems to indicate that, the lower the number of players at the table, the higher the average player WLM Range.

A suggestion: if you cannot remember, in general terms, what your range is during each half hour period, you might consider using two stacks of chips to accomplish this. The stack on the left could represent your lowest WLM during the period, and the right stack could represent your highest WLM. The WLM number would be the total number of chips in each pile. Negative WLMs could be represented in any number of ways -- perhaps you might rotate the chip design so it's sideways. (If you're using the method I suggested on pages 126 and 127), the two stacks indicating your WLM Range could be the ones you see pictured in the back row, closest to you.)

If your WLM Range is 6 or less after a half hour, it's likely you're either in a neutral Player Progress Pattern (if your WLM number is within 5 or so of your zero point -- your zero point being where you began), or a plateau period. However -- to be sure, pay attention, too, to your general trendline during the half hour, and where you are at the endpoint versus where you were at the starting point. Regarding the trendline: did you slowly head up or down, or were you vacillating up and down throughout the half hour? This enables you to imagine the shape of your PPP.

At the other extreme, it's more than likely a tip-off that you're either on a Break-out upswing or downswing with a WLM Range of 10 or greater.

If your WLM Range is between 6 and 9, your PPP will become apparent, once again, by paying attention -- during the half hour -- to your general trendline. It's often the case, in this Range, that you're in a sine-wave-style period, but your trendline will tell you for sure.

It's also important to take note of any changes in how your range is doing.

This will help alert you to times when your PPP is changing to a different long-term pattern. What this change indicates will determine whether you stay or leave, and raise or lower your bet.

For instance: if your WLM was travelling in a narrow range of 5 or less in your first half hour, and, all of a sudden, you notice it widening rapidly, you'll need to react to that change -- especially if that range is now beyond the 30-round average of 7.69 (or 8). What you do depends upon what your WLM was, on average, during the period you were in the narrow WLM Range period, and what your new trendline indicates. If your WLM had been well up in the positive zone -- let's say +15 -- in that narrow WLM Range period, you'd want to: 1) leave, if the widening range is seeing your WLM go down; or 2) raise your bet levels, if the widening range is seeing your WLM go up. If your WLM was instead -6 in your narrow WLM Range period, however, you might want to: 1) *leave* if the Break-out is to the downside; or, 2) possibly look toward leaving if your Break-out is to the upside, and it stalls just above your zero point.

A narrow range period is often indicative of three types of PPPs: neutral; up-and-down sine-wave; or relatively flat plateaus. Your general trendline tells you the story. A large range (one that's above 8) is usually indicative of a stock-style, relatively straight-line *Break-out period*, either up or down -- *pay especial attention to this!* A good general rule is: *if you know you're in a Break-out downside pattern -- leave the table.* With the understanding that the great majority of PPPs last a long time, you don't want to ride out a Break-out downside pattern, with its severe risks. If you're on a Break-out upside pattern, however, you might want to raise your betting level.

Your trendline, in terms of WLM numbers, will alert you to the shape and direction of your PPP. From that mental picture, you will be able to predict, with good probability, how your fortunes will fare with the start of a new PPP -- understanding that each PPP is a long-term phenomenon, lasting for many, many rounds, and through a dozen or more shuffles.

Gains Stages, Good & Bad Tables, & Get Out Points

One exciting discovery I've made is that you can predict your future fortunes with good probability, using WLM numbers. That is, if you reach a certain positive WLM number, we can then tap into statistical evidence and find out mathematically what

FACTOID 7-2: If you detect that you've entered a breakout downside Player Progress Pattern, it's time to leave the table!

your chances of doing better or worse are. Although I'm continuing my work in this regard and will fine tune this over time, I am confident that you will find the guidelines I am about to give you very helpful.

Let's first talk about what I call *Gains Stages*. Gains Stages are ranges of WLM numbers that are useful in determining how well you are doing, and often helpful in predicting how well you will do in the future.

In *Blackjack The SMART Way,* I spoke of tables being categorized as either horrible, bad, neutral, good, or great for you (see the chapters on "The X Factor" and "Money Management"). Actually, I was talking specifically about how well your particular betting spot at a table was doing. Here, we can use the concept of Gains Stages to quantify each of the categories of betting spots I introduced to you in my first book:

❶ **Horrible: we'll now define this as a WLM of -6 and lower.**

❷ **Bad: -1 to -5.**

❸ **Neutral: 0 to +5.**

❹ **Good: +6 to +10.**

❺ **Great: +11 and higher.**

From now on, we'll refer to these Gains Stages by their numbers, as in Gains Stage #1, #2, etc. (There are reasons why we can characterize how good a table and particular betting spot is and will be in the foreseeable future, based on past performance. Among these reasons are two major forces shaping how well players do -- the repetitive personality of the dealer's cards, and the repetitive personality of each player's cards, both of which we've already discussed at length.)

As you keep track of your WLM numbers during play, a red light should go off in your head every time you enter a new Gains Stage. This changes the probabilities regarding your future rewards.

I need to introduce one more concept to you here, and that is: *a **Pivot Point** is a WLM number that signals that you've entered a new Gains Stage.* For instance, *a WLM of -6 is a Pivot Point indicating that you've entered Gains Stage #1*; the cards can now be categorized as falling into the Horrible category, and, statistically speaking, you're most likely to continue down a slippery slope of further losses. Conversely, the Pivot Point of +6 indicates you've entered Gains Stage #4; you're now in a Good card category, and, statistically speaking, you're more than likely to do well.

How did I arrive at these numbers? *I analyzed all the PPPs that resulted from my computer trials for Probable Future Rewards (PFRs) -- the probability the player would do significantly better -- and the Bounceback Factor -- the probability that a player in a negative zone would return to positive territory, and discovered that WLM numbers are very good indicators of mathematical probabilities. For the first time in blackjack history, you now have a concrete, numerical guidepost to tell you where you are likely to wind up.*

For instance, when you've reached the Pivot Point of +6 in WLM units, my data suggests that you have a greater than 50% likelihood of going on to reach Gains Stage #5. In fact, the preliminary data indicates you'll have approximately a 54% probability of reaching a WLM of 11 or greater, and that your average likely WLM peak -- or PFR (Probable Future Reward) -- will be a WLM of about 12.63.

This is an exciting discovery not only because it allows you to know with a good deal of probability whether your future looks good or not, but also because it tells you *how* good, numerically. This will give you a much better idea of whether or not to raise or lower your bets, and at what point you should either be happy with your gains and leave, or cut your losses and leave. (In Chart 7-8 on the following page, I offer you some of the mid-research numbers I've come up with, in this regard.)

Arriving At A Smarter Betting System

Now, here's how we will use all of this to arrive at new, highly accurate way of betting. You'll still being using the 3-Level, Notch-Up, Notch-Down Bet Management System you first read about in *Blackjack The SMART Way*. But, now, you'll coordinate the Levels with the specificity of the Gains Stages outlined on the prior page . Computer tests have confirmed that this makes the Notch-Up, Notch-Down system even more profitable.

I will suggest two ways of doing so. Both follow the same principles, but the second method is more aggressive. Which one you choose to use will depend on which one suits your personality and budget better.

As you know, there are four Levels in the Notch-Up, Notch-Down system, starting with Level Zero, where all your bets will be the minimum allowed at the table. Levels 1 through 3, though, contain three steps (see page 140).

When you first come to a table, you'll start at Level 1. *Your Level 1, Step 1 bet will be the minimum allowed bet, which we'll define as 1 Unit.* You'll raise your bet by 1 Unit each time you win, thus going up the three steps. After you've made it up to Step 3, you'll return to your Step 1 bet and begin the process again -- until and unless you reach a Pivot Point, as defined on the previous page. If you push, you'll keep your bet constant. If you lose, lower your bet to its Step 1 level. Each Level will operate the same way -- you'll raise your Step 1 bet by one Unit with each win, going back to Step 1 either after achieving Step 3, or after a loss. Each Level's Step 1 bet will be one Unit higher than the lower Level.

Now, here's how we'll connect the Notch-Up, Notch-Down system with the Gains Stages concept introduced on the preceding page. Your Zero Level will correspond to Gains Stage #2. (If you descend to Gains Stage #1, you'll *leave*.) If you achieve the Pivot Point of zero, indicating you're now in

CHART 7-8:

The Probability
of Future Rewards (PFRs)

WLM #	PROBABILITY OF A PEAK OF X+5 OR MORE	PROBABILITY OF A PEAK OF X+4 OR MORE	PROBABILITY OF A PEAK OF X+3 OR MORE	MEAN AVERAGE WLM PEAK REACHED
3	53%	66%	75%	10.52
4	52%	59%	72%	11.26
5	48%	56%	63%	11.80
6	54%	54%	63%	12.63
7	57%	62%	62%	13.50
8	65%	71%	77%	14.97
9	60%	73%	80%	15.87
10	69%	69%	85%	16.85
11	69%	69%	69%	16.85
12	58%	67%	75%	17.33
13	64%	64%	73%	17.82
14	44%	78%	78%	18.89
15	22%	44%	78%	18.89

Gains Stage #3, you'll move up to Notch-Up Level 1. If your WLM climbs up to the Pivot Point of +6, indicating a rise to Gains Stage #4, you'll move up to Notch-Up Level 2. Finally, if your WLM attains the Pivot Point of +11, indicating you've attained Gains Stage #5, you'll move up to Notch-Up Level 3. Conversely, if you *decline* to the next lowest Pivot Point, you'll go back *down* to the next lowest Notch-Up, Notch-Down Level, and follow that Level's Steps again -- unless your losses are so steep that it's actually time to *leave*; I'll tell you how to determine that in one moment.

Now, that's the *conservative* way to apply my betting system. It's akin to investing in municipal bonds and blue chip stocks. For a more *growth* oriented, *aggressive* approach for those who don't mind the added risk in looking to increase their gains, here's what you'll do (see page 141):

❶ **Make the size of your minimum bet one that you feel *comfortable* making (but one that's above the table minimum). *That* will be your *Level Zero* bet.**

❷ **Your *Level 1, Step 1 bet* will be *twice what you've chosen as your minimum bet*. We'll call that your *1 Unit bet*.**

❸ **Each Level's Step 1 bet will be *twice* that of the next lowest Level.**

❹ **(When you go up the Steps in any Level, you'll still raise your bet by 1 Unit.)**

Why This New Method *Works*

There are a number of reasons why the Notch-Up, Notch-Down Bet Management System, coordinated with your Gains Stages, has been proven to be so successful. Number one, it makes sense to bet in graduated Levels because of the steady Player Progress Patterns you have witnessed, which result from the long-term repeating nature of the cards. Number two, it will get your bet up to maximum amounts at the right moment. Number three, because your *confidence level* increases over time (due to your greater handle on what's to come, as you identify and adjust your card strategy according to the predictable patterns you're facing), raising your bet in Levels and Steps makes sense -- because your bets should reflect your confidence level (so long as your PPP looks good). By the same token, lowering your bets to your *minimum amount*, to limit your exposure to *losses* when you've dropped into Gains Stage #2, also makes good sense. That way, your losing days will never wipe out your winning days.

Notice, too, that, as you raise you're bet, you're actually depositing one or more chips gained into your bankroll pile. By continually reaping profits, you ensure greater gains. That's the beauty part of this system.

Knowing Specifically When To Leave

In *Blackjack The SMART Way,* I gave you a good guide as to how you should know when it's time to pack it in and leave the casino. Here, however -- and for the first time in the history of the game, I believe -- I am going to give you specific numerical guideposts in that regard.

First -- understand that it's relatively rare for your PPP to be on a continuous stock-style upswing to the very end of a two-hour playing period. It's much more typical that your peak would occur within that period, and that, if you continued to play to the end of the whole two hours, that you would have fallen from your WLM height, and sometimes, significantly so. You won't become a consistent winner if you give back your gains consistently.

So, given that (and other factors that led me to urge you in Blackjack The SMART Way to play no more than two hours or so during any one casino session), you need to know when enough's enough on the upside of things. You also need to know when to cut your losses, on the downside.

Get Out Points

We'll talk in terms of *Get Out Points (or GOPs)* here, which are *specific WLM numbers that signal you to leave.*

Let's talk about the downside first, because there's just one number you need remember here, and that's the GOP of -6, which is also, coincidentally, the Pivot Point that announces your descent into Gains Stage #1, meaning your betting spot is now in the Horrible category. I recommend you leave when you arrive at this point (if you prefer to play one more hand to see if you can beat the odds and return to even, that's your choice --but DON'T continue to play if you return to even; your likelihood of going on to a modest gain of just +5 WLM units is practically *nil*).

All the evidence points to -6 as being the doorway to the point of no return. It's not the actual point of no return (which is -10), but you're staring it in the face -- and you certainly don't want to play further, when the odds of achieving any kind of worthwhile winning results are ridiculously low.

In Chart 7-9 on the top of the next page, you'll see the numbers I arrived at when I analyzed my research data specifically for what I call a *Bounceback Factor.* That is, *I wanted to know in general what a player's chances were of bouncing back into positive territory after they'd descended into negative WLM territory.* This involved looking at the cumulative data of players whose WLMs drifted south of zero. (You can see how good or bad the bounceback figures are for each negative WLM number considered, by comparing those numbers to those in the bottom row, where the overall player results are reflected.)

Two things to note here. First: the numbers in Chart 7-9 assume that the players get out sometime after bouncing back into positive territory, and that they don't keep playing until they plunge back into the red. If I'd factored in players who don't take gains on the upside, and kept playing indefinitely, these numbers would be considerably less rosy. Second, the "Probability of

CHART 7-9:

Testing The Bounceback Factor

WLM #	Probability of Doing Better	Probability of Doing Worse	Probability of Doing >0	Probability of Doing >+5	Probability of Doing >+10
-1	51.02%	48.98%	87.76%	46.94%	26.53%
-2	40.00%	60.00%	71.11%	35.56%	15.56%
-3	34.15%	65.85%	63.41%	29.27%	14.63%
-4	27.03%	72.97%	59.46%	21.62%	10.81%
-5	19.35%	80.65%	51.61%	16.13%	3.23%
-6	8.00%	92.00%	40.00%	4.00%	0.00%
All WLM #s	55.10%	44.90%	89.80%	51.02%	26.53%

Doing Better" has, as its basis, that the players were able to rise to a WLM of +5. The reason for this was that players would tend to keep playing and NOT take profits if they'd not reached this minimum WLM level. In other words -- if players did not reach a WLM level of +5, it was assumed that they would have kept on playing; if that continued playing resulted in a dip back into negative territory, the players' figures were placed in the "Probability of Doing Worse" column.

You'll see, in Chart 7-9, that *your prospects are particularly bleak once you reach the -6 WLM Pivot Point. For the first time in your descent into the red zone, you now have a less than 50% likelihood of simply returning past your zero point. Your probability of reaching a meager WLM of +5 is a miserable 8%. You have approximately a 60% probability of doing even worse, and practically no chance of achieving any worthwhile gains. This is your Get Out Point on the negative side of things. At a WLM of -6, cut your losses and leave.*

On the upside, determining your Get Out Point is a bit more involved. The first thing you need to know is: what is your Player Progress Pattern? If you've begun a Break-out upswing PPP, then you know that this is likely to continue through many shuffles and rounds -- just keep track of what your WLM number was at the start of this PPP, and then count off a half hour to 45 minutes of action, and be aware of any evidence your PPP at that point has changed for the worse.

During this process, constantly monitor your WLM peak. Your Get Out

Point might be when you detected that your PPP is now in a plunge pattern; or, you might choose to leave if you've achieved a good peak -- of at least 10 -- and you've fallen three WLM units from that peak.

You can also use Chart 7-9 to give you a general idea of what reasonable gains you might expect from each WLM level you achieve, so that you don't get overly greedy and play too long. Here are some related guidelines you should keep in mind:

Reach +6, and figure you are likely to reach +11. Reach +8, and figure you are likely to reach +15. Reach +10, and understand that you should hit a peak of +17 well more than 50% of the time.

However -- just as your achievement of +6 in WLM units, and arrival at Gains Stage #4 indicates once and for all that you've likely got a rosy future, *your arrival at +14 is another Pivot Point, which now bodes diminishing returns. For the first time in your climb into positive territory, you now have a less than 50% chance of accumulating another 5 points. In other words, a peak of 18 is just about all you can expect. So tread lightly once you reach this Pivot Point. Be ready to get out at a moment's notice, once you detect a downdraft in your WLM numbers or PPP.*

You will only reach a WLM of +20 roughly 4% of the time, so don't push it!!! Just for your general reference, the most extreme WLMs that I've recorded on the upside of things, in approximately two hours of action, is a WLM of +23. (On the downside, a solitary player sank to a record low of *-29* WLM units in 183 rounds of action!)

In fact, you're already in rarified air once you reach +14. You'll only do so roughly 18% of the time. It seems like a paradox, but, while you indeed have a greater than 50% probability of achieving a peak that's 5 WLM units higher than your current WLM as you move from a WLM of +6 to +14 (because of the long-term nature of PPPs), nearly 50% of the time, you won't achieve that lofty peak.

Here are some other factors to keep in mind: *while a PPP might dip 5 WLM units on its way to a nice high peak, it almost never bounces back up from a dip of 6 or more WLM units off a positive peak. So, if you experience a dip of 6 units in your WLM number at any time after being in Gains Stage #4 or #5 you should most definitely leave.* Your patience level should never extend to a drop of more than 5 WLM units on the upside of things. And even that might be too lax a stand to take. Whether you want to let any dip go 3 units below your current peak is debatable -- it all depends on what your last peak was, and how happy you'd be with taking home the gains you still have.

In addition, you can ratchet up your Get Out Points, once you're happy with your take-home level. For example, once you go above +10, you might choose to be conservative and make that your GOP -- you might decide to leave if your WLM sinks back to +10. Then, if you continue to do well, and then go above a WLM of +15, you might ratchet your GOP up to that level, and choose to leave if your WLM dips back to +15. And so on.

Also -- knowing how rare it is to climb above +14, you should definitely not allow your peaks of +15 or more dip more than three WLM units, because you've achieved just about all you're going to. Don't get greedy and hope for an impossibly high peak after hitting a hugely successful level. As the Wall Street investor knows: you rarely, if ever, will be able to take your profits at the maximum possible peak. Take your profits once you've reached near-maximum WLM levels and you notice that you're backing off from your high for the day.

One other interesting phenomenon I've discovered is that, *more often than not, once you've reached a maximum PPP peak, you will hit that peak again* -- at least once or twice; and, whether or not you hit that peak more than once, you usually will hit the near-peak number (the WLM number that's 1 Unit below your peak) more than once. If you see this type of plateau-type behavior after a nice long PPP upswing, my advice is: get out if and when you back off from the second or third coming of that peak WLM number. You've probably seen the best you're going to get.

A peak PPP period is shorter than other periods, as I mentioned before, so don't wait more than six to ten rounds before realizing you're in a peak plateau and it's time to leave. Your Get Out Point won't necessarily be the repeated peak point, but, perhaps you'll be smart enough to get out when one WLM unit off that peak.

In other words, *when you reach a high positive plateau (a plateau reaching approximately 14 or more WLM units), you're most likely on the cusp of a downside pattern. High positive plateaus are often a signal that your upswing is over. Get out while the going's good.*

The beautiful thing is that with my WLM method you can now get a good handle on exactly what you can reasonably expect, with regard to win/loss gains. You need guess no more as to whether enough's enough, and continue down the typical cycle of throwing back your gains by playing too long.

Some Final Important Points

Before moving on, let me suggest some additional conclusions that might be drawn from all of the data I've presented to you in this chapter.

❶ For the first time in the history of blackjack, you now have proof that there's a *lot* to be gained from playing at a stable table. You want to play at a table where the number of betting spots stays consistent from round to round. This is a key to establishing the repeating card phenomena I've identified in this chapter, which then enables you to tap into the power of being able to predict, with good probability, what is likely to occur in the near future, at your betting spot(s). You have a number of options if you find yourself at a table where the number of players or betting spots taken constantly changes. You can *leave*. If you are on a good winning PPP and the number of betting spots goes down in number, you might be able to keep your PPP on track by taking additional betting spots to keep things stable (I would recommend that you place the minimum allowed bet on the additional betting spots and not worry too much about micro-managing those spots, so as to concentrate fully on the betting spot that's been producing well for you, and avoid confusion -- you've got a lot to remember vis a vis your betting spot's progress; you probably don't want to overload yourself by keeping track of WLMs, etc., for other betting spots). Now, if the number of betting spots goes *up*, you should lower your bet, because the predictability that comes from betting spot stability is lost. You'll need to start from scratch, if you choose to continue at that point. (This is another reason why a full table is advantageous -- you'll never see a situation where the number of betting spots taken increases. You can adjust for a *reduction* in betting spots, but *not* the reverse.)

❷   If you're the type of player who often thinks: "My luck has got to change!" and then places higher bets as losses mount, you now know how wrong your thinking is. Player Progress Patterns at stable tables last a long time, as I've established in this chapter. They don't turn around in the near-term. In fact, as you've seen, stock-style plunge patterns can last the whole time a particular set of cards is in play.

❸   Blackjack is not the kind of game where you can promise specific hourly gains, no matter what system you use. Some players have been led to believe this is how the game works. By now you should realize that what you win depends upon the quality of the cards you're getting at your betting spot, which varies with each set of cards you play against. You cannot win at all against certain sets of cards, or at certain betting spots.

❹   Knowing the power you can realize from the knowledge you've gained in this chapter, you should again see the importance of playing at 1- and 2-deck tables, if you can. While repeating phenomena do occur at multi-deck tables, the predictability factor goes way down (and is often dependent upon where the player who cuts the cards places the cut card).

❺   Try to start playing when *new cards* are brought in. That way, you'll know that any pattern you're on -- good or bad -- is probably going to *last, for some time*. That kind of predictability is worth money. If you don't do this, you won't know how long your initial PPP is going to continue; you'll have to stay alert to the fact that it can morph into a different pattern at any time.

❻   Start playing when a new *dealer* comes in. You'll have a maximum amount of stability, with regard to the dealer's shuffling style and the predictability of the cards.

❼ Just because a table with x number of players is doing well doesn't mean that, if you join that table, your betting spot will do well. Your arrival changes the number of players and the PPPs you saw before. Plus, you don't have any information regarding the new spot you've taken, because it wasn't being played before. However, if one player leaves when you arrive at the table, or someone reduces their bets by one betting spot, you'd end up with the cards and the PPP of the player who had previously sat in your numerical position (unless you sit in the 3rd Baseman's seat -- you'd then acquire the PPP of the player who had essentially been the 3rd Baseman before). *This insight gives you a good idea of what lies ahead for your betting spot when joining a table!*

❽ If you've been playing for some time, and new cards are brought into the game -- caution is justified, until you discover what their personality is. They will almost certainly produce different results than the previous cards. For this reason, I often *leave* if I've won a good deal of chips and the cards are then replaced. With new cards come uncertainties. You'll risk incurring losses while you're determining how good the new cards will be for you.

❾ *Because Player Progress Patterns and repeating phenomena last so long, you can raise your bet through shuffles*, if the cards are good or great, according to Gains Stages specifications. That is, you need not lower your bet to minimum levels after a shuffle. After the shuffling is done, continue at the place you left off with your 3-Level Notch-Up, Notch-Down Bet Management System, as coordinated with the Gains Stages method.

There's More To Come

In the tradition of other good blackjack books of the past, I felt it acceptable to share with you all of this chapter's very important information, even though my research continues into these, and other phenomena. This type of practice has been done before, and with good reason.

The point is -- whether in the scientific world, or the world of blackjack -- it makes sense to alert everyone concerned to new discoveries once they have been deemed valid.

ILLUSTRATION 7-10:

The Conservative Notch-Up, Notch-Down Bet Management System

LEVEL ZERO/GAINS STAGE 2 (TABLE MINIMUM)

LEVEL 1/GAINS STAGE 3 (3 STEPS)

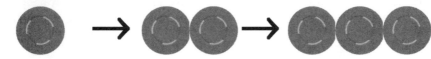

STEP 1   STEP 2   STEP 3

LEVEL 2/GAINS STAGE 4 (3 STEPS)

LEVEL 3/GAINS STAGE 5 (3 STEPS)

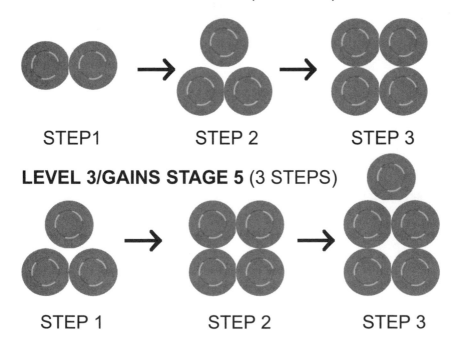

STEP1   STEP 2   STEP 3

STEP 1   STEP 2   STEP 3

ILLUSTRATION 7-11:

The Aggressive Notch-Up, Notch-Down Bet Management System

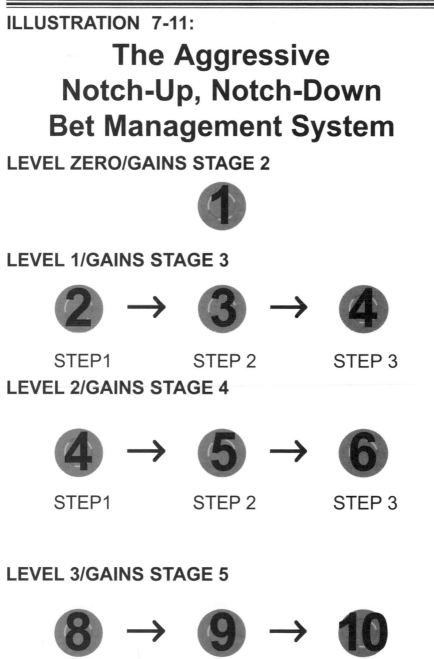

LEVEL ZERO/GAINS STAGE 2

LEVEL 1/GAINS STAGE 3

STEP1   STEP 2   STEP 3

LEVEL 2/GAINS STAGE 4

STEP1   STEP 2   STEP 3

LEVEL 3/GAINS STAGE 5

STEP1   STEP 2   STEP 3

(Numbers = # of Units)

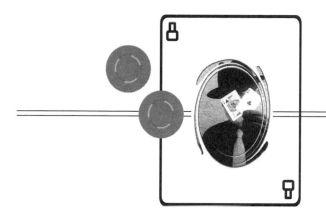

Auxiliary Betting Indicators

Before you're done reading this chapter, one thing you're probably going to tell yourself is: "I didn't realize that the *9s* were such important cards!" (Yes, this is very interesting, indeed! The 9s are much ignored cards!)

While my discovery of the value of the 9s amazed me, in searching for a more precise betting system, as I am always doing, I came to *many* very good realizations about the unique ways in which each of the cards affects the outcome of each round, which I'd like to share with you.

What I'm going to present here are some fantastic discoveries of times where your chances of winning are at least double your normal rate, if not three and four times as much. This certainly justifies your raising your bet to higher levels than you'd normally make, with the Notch-Up, Notch-Down system (which you read about in Chapter 7).

What I did was to investigate how each of the ten different cards in blackjack affects your fortune. What I wanted to determine was how important each of the cards was to both the player, on the one hand, and the dealer, on the other. That is -- if either the player or dealer had a certain card in his or her hand, would that, over time, help or hurt them? My goal was to find indicators that would help guide our betting strategy.

In so doing, I've looked at each card up and down, from many perspectives. For instance, I removed all the rounds in which one card appeared, leaving just the rounds where it did not. This is something blackjack's pioneers did many years ago. But, it reveals just one part of the story. Then, I did a different study, eliminating all the player hands that did *not* contain the card I was examining, except in rounds where the dealer's hand had that card in it -- that gave me an idea of the relative value of that card to the player, because it showed how well players did in relation to the dealer's results with that same card in the mix. In that case, it did not matter whether the card showed up as the player or dealer's first, second, third, or later cards. If it was in the mix, it was considered a factor. And it went on from there. I've analyzed each card's influence on future results in more than a half dozen studies, under varying conditions.

(Please note: because each variation in the number of players produces different player Win/Loss and Gains results, and because my studies have shown we should only consider playing at tables with at least four, if not more players, the focus of this particular effort is how each type of card impacts the results at *multi-player tables*. The answers might be different for solitary-player situations -- which the early blackjack computer studies were primarily aimed at.)

Here are some tips that have come out of these studies. This chapter will primarily be confined for now to the topic of how to predict the future round's results, using the relative oversupply or paucity of a particular card as a betting indicator. These are *pre-round* indicators; once you're within a round of action, card factors are a bit different, as you will see in Chapters 9 and 12.

Let's start with some startling information regarding the Aces.

The Relative Value of Aces

As you might know, the prevailing opinion for years has been: if Aces are *due, raise* your bet! Yet, I've determined beyond a doubt that this is NOT the way to go. In fact, if you were to remove player Blackjacks, the Ace would actually be a BAD card for the player, resulting in *losing* win/loss ratios, and a negative bottom line (your *bottom line* is *what you make or lose*, factoring in not just the numbers of hands won and lost, but also the halved losses due to surrendering, and added winnings from Blackjacks and doubling that a win/loss statement would not address). In other words, *when you get an Ace, unless you have a Blackjack, your score will not compete well against the dealer's, in the long run.*

Shocking, isn't it? But that's because (as I warned you in *Blackjack The SMART Way*), *when Aces are due, the dealer has an above-average probability of getting a Blackjack*, which is the dealer's ultimate trump card, if you will, producing almost 100% player losses.

So, if you were to haphazardly raise your bet whenever Aces were due -- you might make a little money, *if* you had a good share of Blackjacks; but, *if you were not among the players who got Blackjacks, and the dealer DID, you'd come out a certain loser.* Plus, the margin of victory provided by player Blackjacks is quite small, anyway, and not a good reason to raise your bet (even if you *could* predict when you would be one of the players who would get one).

This card is not the money maker you might think it should be. But that reality only emerges if you do your research carefully. That is -- if you only factor in how players fare when they get an Ace, you'd think, wow, this card is dynamite! But the picture changes when you balance that against the victories the *dealer* gets from getting Aces during the same period you're examining. Then, the win/loss equation tilts in the *dealer's* favor -- except, again, for paltry gains players get from Blackjacks. Indeed -- while I found these gains to be in the 4-5% range, *these results actually underperformed the overall gains players got when all the cards were taken into account!*

Yet, you *can* make money off the Aces if you understand what this equation is telling you and you take a different tack. *First: you'll make more money off the Aces if, instead of raising your bet every time they're due, you only increase your bet when they're overdue and the 10s are also likely to appear in greater than normal numbers in the following round (a condition where you're most likely to get a Blackjack).* Don't forget that Blackjacks come along, on average, only about 5% of the time. The rest of the time, the Aces will *hurt* you to some degree, and some caution is warranted. This advice, of course, comes with this proviso: now that you're aware of the repeating phenomenon you learned about in Chapter 6, you should understand that, *if you're caught in a repeating dealer Blackjack pattern, you will want to lower your bet when Aces are due (or leave the table if it's that devastating).*

Get ready for the shock of your life, though. I've uncovered something even better!

If you really want to make money off the Aces, raise your bet significantly when they're thoroughly depleted! The dealer's bust rate is in the 40 percentile range in this condition, and your win/loss rate will be firmly in positive territory (as opposed to when Aces are in the mix)! If you chose to stand on all stiffs given this situation, it would be understandable (but I have an invention, however, which will better guide you as to how to handle your stiffs -- the ducks and bucks, which you'll read about in the next chapter). *My data shows that you will obtain gains of nearly three times your normal rate when all the Aces are gone, and so you should raise your bet to three times the normal level when this condition occurs.*

(For multi-deck players: while the complete using up of a card might take longer and might, in fact, never happen, due to the large number of undealt cards in those games, a close approximation of this condition is reached when Aces have appeared in far greater numbers than you'd expect, in relation to their Circle of 13 proportion in the card mix.)

The Conundrum of the 10s

While most betting systems since the 1960s have also urged you to raise your bet when 10s are due, I, again, can't agree with that philosophy. I have found that dealer busting rates increase when the 10s are *just under* their Circle of 13 proportions. Under those conditions, my data indicate that player gains increase to nearly *twice* their normal level (the normal level, incidentally, depends upon the number of players at the table, as Chapter 3 explained). At 7-player tables, *overall gains of more than 11% were achieved playing according to Blackjack The SMART Way Basic Strategy (see pp. ix-xii) when the 10s were somewhat lacking. This would definitely call for a raise in bet levels, appropriately (a near-doubling of your chances calls for a corresponding bump in your bet).*

(Some of you might think: how does this jibe with your warning in *Blackjack The SMART Way* about the occasional casino that's been caught removing 10s from the decks, in an attempt to hurt players. The answer to that puzzle is this: our strategy is based upon certain expectations. If we make moves mathematically correct for an honest deck, figuring 10s are due when they're NOT because they've been *removed,* that's where the problem lies.)

Unlike other cards, the one study that cannot be done with the 10s is one in which rounds without 10s are deleted. That is because, with four times as many 10s as other cards, you won't *find* any rounds without 10s, at tables at which you and I would consider playing -- that is, those with four or more players. However, I *did* test the 10s' overall value to the player, in which I got rid of all *player hands* that did not contain 10s. The results were similar to those of the Aces. Player gains were just about 5% for the 7-player runs, which was 2% less than they were when all the player hands were included in the study. In addition -- just as I found with the Aces -- the players' win/loss rates were in the negative range (minus 1.25%). It was only the fact that the players' Blackjack rate was nearly 8% that they showed any *bottom line* gains.

The Upper Cards

One surprise that has come from my investigations is how important the 9s are to you. In rounds without 9s, the dealer's busting rate falls to about 21%, and your chances are rather bleak: player losses are nearly 9%, with the corresponding win/loss rate (which does not consider gains from doubling and Blackjacks) *very* negative: ***-15.20%! Therefore, if the 9s are gone, lower your bet significantly (unless there are contrary indicators, such as when all the Aces have been played out -- in that case, the effect of the Ace depletion would cancel out the harm caused by the absolute lack of 9s, and keep you in positive territory; no change in your betting pattern would then be called for, with the two indicators effectively negating each other).*

The 9 has a significant role in causing dealer busting, and that's largely where its value lies (it also acts to hold down the dealer's score profile somewhat, making the dealer less competitive with you). My test of the 9's "Overall Value To The Player" *showed player gains of 11% at the 7-player tables -- nearly double the normal value -- when 9s are in the mix. Therefore, when the 9s are overdue, it calls for a corresponding increase in your betting levels.*

The same can be said to a somewhat lesser extent about the 7s and 8s. It's bad when they're absolutely used up, and good when they're overdue. *Player losses and win/loss rate dips are similar to the 9s when they're gone (in fact, the numbers for the 8 are even worse than the 9). On the other hand, player gains of about 9% can be expected when those cards are present in good supply.* So, *when the 7s and 8s have been played out, that's a call to seriously consider lowering your bets, unless there are contrary indicators.* On the flip side, the increase in gains when they're overdue doesn't quite call for a doubling of your bet, as does the same situation with the 9s. A modest in-between increase of about 50% would be appropriate.

The Lowest Cards

There are paradoxes surrounding the lowest cards -- the 6s are best for the player when they're gone. Conversely, it is *unfavorable* when the 3s and 5s are completely used up.

When 6s are exhausted, player gains are a bit higher than average, calling for a bet increase of about 50%. When 6s are plentiful and, in fact, dealt to the players, player losses as a result are approximately 11%! So, if they're overdue, *lower* your bet 1 Unit below the Step 1 bet size of the Notch-Up, Notch-Down system Level you're on (again, unless there are other cards acting strongly in your favor that would counteract the effect of the 6s). A test of dealer hands that contain 6s reveals player *bottom line* losses of more than 2%, by the way.

The 3s and 5s are very similar in that, *when they're played out, player losses are rather steep -- about 13%.* (Two reasons for that are: the 3s and 5s are often what you need to avoid busting, and achieve a competitive score, when you have a stiff total; and, they result in player bottom line gains that are above average when they're dealt to the dealer. In fact, player gains are nearly three times normal when the dealer gets a 5 among his cards.) So, when the 3s and 5s are spent, a reduction in your bet to your Step 1 bet size minus 1 Unit would be appropriate, in the absence of other cards whose positive influence might outweigh the 3s and/or 5s' impact on your fortunes.

The 2s are best for the player when they're in the mix. Your gains will be about 40% higher than average when they're available. *So, if no 2s have appeared, or few, that would be an indicator to raise your bet by about 40%-50% going into the next round* (once again -- you have to factor this into what all of your indicators are telling you, as a whole). Now, if the 2s are gone, your bottom line will be down about 30% from its average, but you will still experience gains of about 5% (we're not talking about losses here), so no decrease in bet is warranted.

About the 4s...When they've all been dealt, player gains are roughly at their average, positive levels. When they're in the mix, players' gains are below average, but, often, just above even. So, with the certainty of good gains with their depletion, you might raise your bet by 1 Unit when 4s are gone. No reduction in bet is called for when 4s are gone, however.

That being said -- player gains are often three times their normal levels when the dealer gets a 2, 3, 4, or 5 among his cards. So, all things considered, this should be an indicator to raise your bet accordingly when you've had initial rounds following a shuffle where either no such cards have been played, or very few.

Again: measure these indicators against any contrary indicators that might present themselves. The way you do that is to sum up the probable gains and losses I've detailed in this chapter. If I've told you player gains are three times normal levels, that would be about 20%, at 7-player tables. That's the kind of return you'll get, for instance, when Aces are gone, as you now know. But, let's say 5s are spent, too. That would hurt your bottom line by 13%. The net result is a gain of 7%. That's a likely positive gain, so I'd raise my bet to take advantage of that -- move up to Step 3 in your Level, or, if you were already at that Step in the last round, increase your bet by 1 or 2 Units, depending on whether you've decided to go with the conservative or the aggressive versions of the Notch-Up system.

Two more things.

First, if you're at Step 3 of Level 3, and the indicators for the next round are fantastic, you should definitely go above your normal maximum bet, in an amount that reflects your increased chances of winning, as mentioned in this chapter.

Second, if *negative* auxiliary indicators are in great number -- 5s, 7s, 8s and 9s are gone, for instance -- and there are no positive indicators softening the blow, it would be smart to move down to Level Zero in your betting amounts.

Remember, though -- all of this is meant to enhance the results you'll get from the use of my 3-Level, Notch-Up, Notch-Down Bet Management System, in coordination with the Gains Stages method outlined in the prior chapter. That's why I call this chapter *Auxiliary* Betting Indicators.

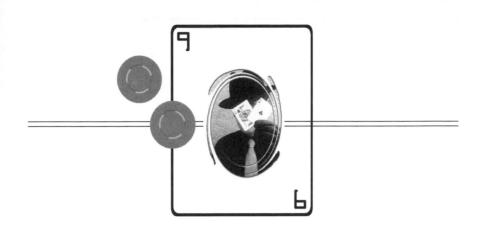

What's Your Up Card IQ?

(Introducing the Concepts of
Weakened Up Cards
And The *Ducks & Bucks*)

A t a book event in Colorado, I was giving a card demonstration, and I asked the audience what they would do with a hand of 12 points versus the dealer's 3. I wanted to see what level they were on.

An indignant young woman, who stayed only for a few minutes, blurted out: "I always *stand* on 12s against the dealer's 3!" She said this as though any fool would know this (even though she was dead *wrong*).

"And why is that?" I asked.

"Because I was taught," she responded, her voice dripping with conde-scension, "that the dealer's 3 *always* busts!" Then she stalked off!

She's not alone in her misconception that some up cards bust ALL of the time. And there are many others I've met who were under the mistaken impression that some up cards bust a MAJORITY of the time. That, too, is wrong!

Then there was the man at a book event in Westchester, New York, who, in passing, blurted out that he routinely stands on hands of 16 points versus the dealer's 10!

"I win 65% of the time doing that!" he said, as if he were a repository of blackjack revelations. He *interrupted* my book event to add that word of "wisdom"! He was *boasting* that he routinely makes a *bad* move!

I tried to explain to him that, playing that way, he would only win when the dealer *busted*, which would be a measly 22% of the time. Therefore, he would, in fact, *lose* roughly 78% of the hands he played that way (the net result being a loss of nearly 56%).

Nonetheless, he shouted back:

"Nope! I win 65% of the time!" And, with that, he disappeared into the mall, apparently uninterested in knowing the truth.

This story illustrates another common defect in players' understanding of the up cards. Yes, surrendering your 16 -- your best move -- is a losing proposition. So is hitting it (if you can't surrender). Versus the dealer's 10, your losses will be 50% by surrendering, and nearly 55% by hitting -- but that's a *savings of about 6% and 1%, respectively, over standing!* (And how he figured to win *anything* is beyond me!)

...And up card misconceptions are not confined to players, either. One reader emailed me, directing me to an author's web site, where I noticed the author claimed that the dealer's up card of 10 is sometimes the player's best card!! This couldn't be farther from the truth.

Having a thorough knowledge of their strengths and weaknesses is fundamental to playing a good game. So, it's obviously time to clear up the confusion that's out there!

How Much Do YOU Know?

Speaking of which, how much do *you* know about each of the dealer's up cards? Do you realize how *much* information is being handed to you by the identity of the dealer's up card? An awful lot! (In fact -- if you play outside the United States, in an area where the hole card is not dealt until after all players have had their turns, your read on the up card will largely determine how you play your hand!)

Do you know how often each up card tends to bust? Do you know what their typical score profiles look like (what average scores each tends to attain) -- for example, how often they reach high winning scores? Do you know how often you can expect to win or lose against them? Do you know how they rank, in terms of player-friendliness? And, most important: do you know their *weaknesses?*

The more you know about how the up cards behave over time, the smarter a player you will be. This aspect of the game always gets short shrift or gets ignored, and yet this is basic stuff. Playing blackjack without this knowledge is like going into the boxing ring without studying your opponent's strengths and weaknesses. You need to locate each up card's vulnerabilities and come up with a smart strategy, to capitalize on those vulnerabilities and *win*.

Up Cards By General Ranking Order

Each of the dealer's ten types of up cards — the Ace, 2, 3, 4, 5, 6, 7, 8, 9 and 10 — has its own idiosyncrasies. Each has a different chemistry in combining with other cards. Therefore, each exhibits unique tendencies toward reaching winning totals and busting. You will use the detailed profiles that follow to identify the up card strengths and weaknesses of which you can take advantage — even if it means taking the path of the smallest losses in a losing situation.

We can only talk about identifying up card characteristics in terms of *tendencies*, because, as I have shown you, these numbers *vary* over time due to all of the variable factors I enumerated in prior chapters: the number of betting spots played; the types of cards that predominate in repeating patterns; changes in the card count or card flow; etc. However, trust me. There's something to be gained here by starting off with a look at the overall picture. Later on, we'll get more specific about how to handle variations in up card behavior. Please understand, therefore, that *the numbers that follow are not to be considered constants; they are just guideposts*.

Also -- the numbers will undoubtedly seem somewhat different from what you might have read elsewhere, but they are highly representative of what you will probably experience in your playing career. This is not just because they were produced by doing a lifetime's worth of *real* blackjack rounds, with *real* cards, instead of doing *random* computer *simulations*. It is also due to the fact that the numbers you're about to see represent a special situation. I am only presenting summations from the 4, 5, 6 and 7-player card runs. As you learned before, dealer bust rates are at their lowest and dealer win rates are at their highest when three or less betting spots are being played. I've warned you not to play under those circumstances, and, so, there's no reason to muck things up here with realities you should avoid.

OK. Let's start by looking at how the up cards stack up against each other. The illustrations on the next four pages will give you a good generalized overview, based upon three important measures: *how often each up card will tend to beat you*; *how often each will lose to you*; and, finally, what each up card's overall *Dealer Advantage (or DA)* is. By way of explanation: *DA numbers* are expressions (in percentages) of whether an up card, in a lifetime of rounds, will cause the dealer to *beat* you or *lose* to you more.

Here's how they are calculated: you subtract each up card's losing rate from its winning rate. A positive DA number indicates that the up card will enable the dealer to *beat* you more than lose to you, by the percentage listed. A *negative* DA number tells you that the up card will *lose* to you more often than beat you, and by what percentage. So, depending on if it is positive or negative, a DA number either expresses a winning rate or losing rate.

One other thing: I have ranked the up cards according to how good the cards are for the *dealer*. Cards in the illustrations' *left* columns, therefore, are the dealer's *strongest* cards, and cards in the *right* columns are the

(Continued on page 156.)

ILLUSTRATION 9-1:

Dealer Up Card Rankings
By Dealer Winning Percentage

5 Strongest: **5 Weakest:**

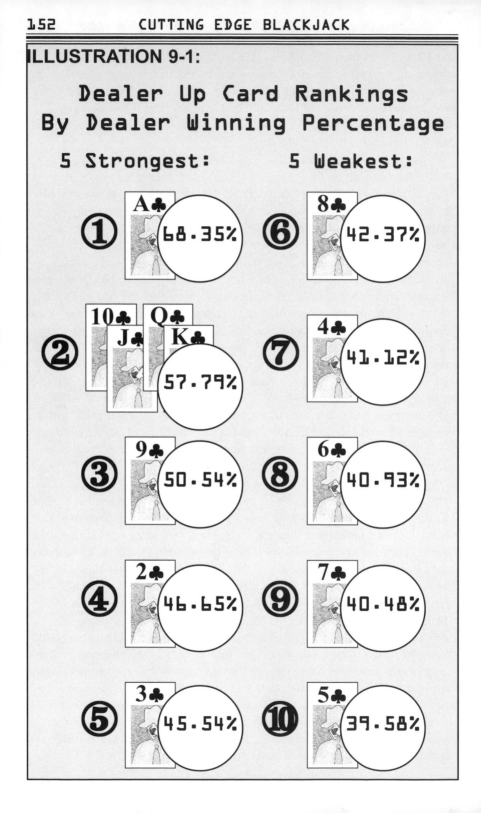

ILLUSTRATION 9-2:

Dealer Up Card Rankings
By Dealer Losing Percentage

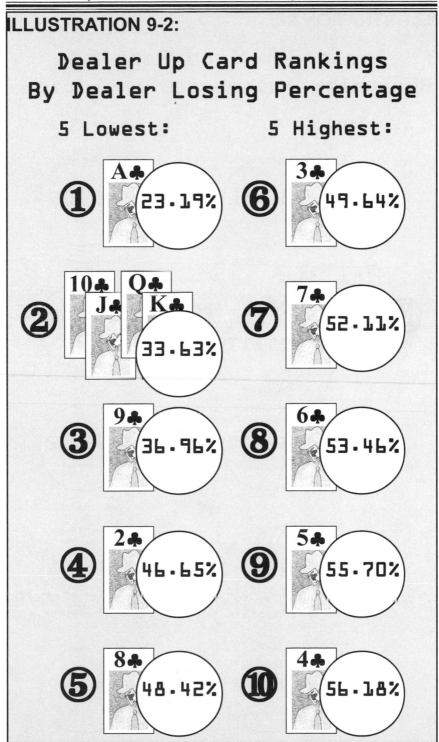

5 Lowest:

① A♣ — 23.19%

② 10♣ J♣ Q♣ K♣ — 33.63%

③ 9♣ — 36.96%

④ 2♣ — 46.65%

⑤ 8♣ — 48.42%

5 Highest:

⑥ 3♣ — 49.64%

⑦ 7♣ — 52.11%

⑧ 6♣ — 53.46%

⑨ 5♣ — 55.70%

⑩ 4♣ — 56.18%

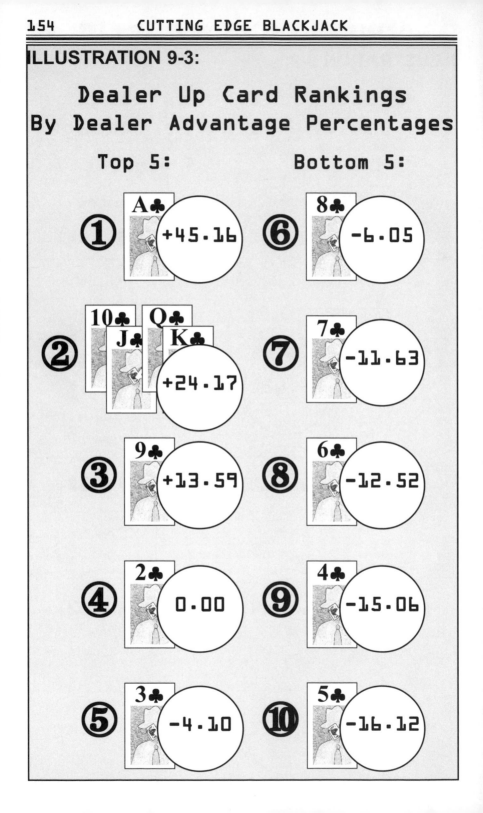

ILLUSTRATION 9-3:

Dealer Up Card Rankings
By Dealer Advantage Percentages

Top 5:   Bottom 5:

① A♣ +45.16   ⑥ 8♣ -6.05

② 10♣ J♣ Q♣ K♣ +24.17   ⑦ 7♣ -11.63

③ 9♣ +13.59   ⑧ 6♣ -12.52

④ 2♣ 0.00   ⑨ 4♣ -15.06

⑤ 3♣ -4.10   ⑩ 5♣ -16.12

ILLUSTRATION 9-4:

Dealer Up Card
Win Rate Summary

	WINS	PUSHES	LOSSES	DA #
2	46.65%	6.70%	46.65%	0%
3	45.54%	4.82%	49.64%	-4.10%
4	41.12%	2.70%	56.18%	-15.06%
5	39.58%	4.72%	55.70%	-16.12%
6	40.93%	5.61%	53.46%	-12.52%
7	40.48%	7.41%	52.11%	-11.63%
8	42.37%	9.21%	48.42%	-6.05%
9	50.54%	12.50%	36.96%	13.59%
10	57.79%	8.58%	33.63%	24.17%
A	68.35%	8.47%	23.19%	45.16%

*Note: Negative DA numbers indicate the player will tend to beat the dealer up card, over time, by the percentage listed.

dealer's *weakest*.

The numbers speak for themselves. But let's focus on some of the results that you might find surprising. Not shocking, perhaps, is that the Ace appears to be the king of the beasts, followed by the 10 and the 9. Everything else, however, will probably be news to most.

I had warned you in *Blackjack The SMART Way* that the dealer's *2* is not one of the best up cards for the player. Here, you can see why. *The 2 is consistently the dealer's 4th best up card!* It gives the dealer the 4th highest number of wins, the 4th *lowest* number of losses, and its 4th highest DA ranking, right behind the Ace, 10 and 9.

Notice, however, that the 2 is a rather *neutral* up card. Its DA of zero shows that you will lose to it roughly as much as you will win against it. Nonetheless, you should not treat this anything like the 4, 5, or 6 -- or even the dealer's 3, 7 or *8* -- against which you will win more, and therefore have more powerful strategy options. A 50-50 winning proposition is not cause for celebration.

Also in *Blackjack The SMART Way* I told you the dealer's **7** is a very good card for you. Here, *for the first time, you can see, in mathematical detail, how weak that 7 really is for the dealer*. You will probably be surprised to learn that *it achieves a very low dealer winning percentage (the percentage of times it beats the players) -- it ranks 9th of the 10 different up cards! And, judging it by its DA number, the dealer's 7 is the 4th best card for the player!*

I had also told you in my first book that the dealer's 8 is not a strong card for the dealer. In fact, as you can see in Illustration 9-3 on page 152, *you will win more hands against the dealer's 8 than you will lose!* Your percentage gain versus the 8 will be approximately 6%, which puts the 8 slightly ahead of the dealer's 3 in terms of its advantages to you. Although this number is just north of neutral territory, the point is that you should NOT *fear* this up card, as is suggested in many books. No, it's actually rather player-friendly!

You might also be surprised to learn that *the dealer's 5 is perhaps the weakest up card*, scoring the very lowest DA number (although it is not that much weaker than the dealer's 4).

```
FACTOID 9-1:
The dealer's 7
is very weak:
   it has the
  second lowest
 dealer winning
  percentage of
 all up cards.
Plus, its DA #
is 4th best for
  the player!
```

Also fascinating is that the dealer's 6 falls behind the 4 and 5 in player benefits. (I'll bet you thought the 6 was your best up card!) I attribute the 6's somewhat lesser value to you partly to the fact that, of the 4, 5 and 6, only the 6 can combine with another card (the Ace) to form a total upon which the dealer would stand (at most casinos). This is also reflected in the average number of cards the 6 receives, over time, per hand, before achieving a score, or busting -- 3.12, which is lower than the average for the 4 and 5, which are 3.47 and 3.36, respectively. In general, the more cards an up card requires before attaining an acceptable dealer score, the higher the likelihood that the dealer will achieve a bustable total. You can see proof of this in the fact that the five cards with the lowest bust rates all have cards-per-hand averages below 3.

(This reality won't change in casinos whose dealers HIT soft 17s, by the way, because, then, the dealer's 6 only becomes stronger against the player. The score of the dealer's up card of 6 in combination with a hole card of an Ace improves more than 46% of the time when the dealer takes hit cards. Even though the dealer busts 25.28% of the time in doing so, the dealer's soft 17 will do better against you when the dealer takes hit cards than if the dealer has to stand on the very weak total of 17.)

Up Card Performance Profiles

Many players harbor the notion that it is an up card's *busting rate* that determines how often they will beat that card. Not so. As you can probably tell from the winning rates just presented, there's another, more important factor at work here. That is: *how often each up card will outscore you.*

This is revealed by each up card's *score profile* -- my term for *how often each up card achieves hands of 17, 18, 19, 20 and 21 points (and, in the case of the 10 and Ace, how frequently they form a Blackjack).*

On the following pages, you will find *Up Card Performance Profiles,* which include not just score profiles, but also busting rates, the average number of cards it takes for the up card to achieve a score, and, another invention of mine -- Tell Numbers (I'll explain what they are in a minute). These Performance Profiles give you another overview of each card's strengths and weaknesses, in great detail. This is a treasure trove of information, and you should really take some time to digest all of it.

What The Tell Numbers Reveal

In order to paint a complete picture of each up card, I found the need to create the idea of *Tell Numbers,* which reveal the strengths and weaknesses of each up card, in terms of the scores each attains, when looked at over the course of many, many rounds. I decided upon the name of *Tell* Numbers because these figures *tell* you what you need to know, and because, like a *tell* in poker, they are akin to inadvertent poker player ticks that give away important information regarding how strong the player's hand is.

(Continued on page 168)

CHART 9-4:

Up Card Performance Profile

Bust/Score/Cards Info

BUST %	AVG SCORE	# CARDS
35.42%	18.97	3.96

Score Profile

%BJs	%21s	%20s	%19s	%18s	%17s
N/A	12.17%	12.89%	13.49%	12.65%	13.37%

Tell Numbers

%BJ21	%20+	%19+	%18+	%17+	%18B	%17B
N/A	25.06%	38.55%	51.20%	64.58%	61.45%	48.80%

CHART 9-5:

Up Card Performance Profile

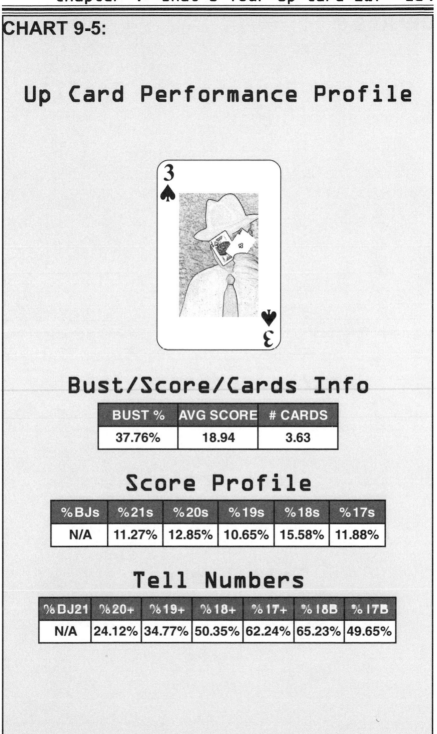

Bust/Score/Cards Info

BUST %	AVG SCORE	# CARDS
37.76%	18.94	3.63

Score Profile

%BJs	%21s	%20s	%19s	%18s	%17s
N/A	11.27%	12.85%	10.65%	15.58%	11.88%

Tell Numbers

%BJ21	%20+	%19+	%18+	%17+	%18B	%17B
N/A	24.12%	34.77%	50.35%	62.24%	65.23%	49.65%

CHART 9-6:

Up Card Performance Profile

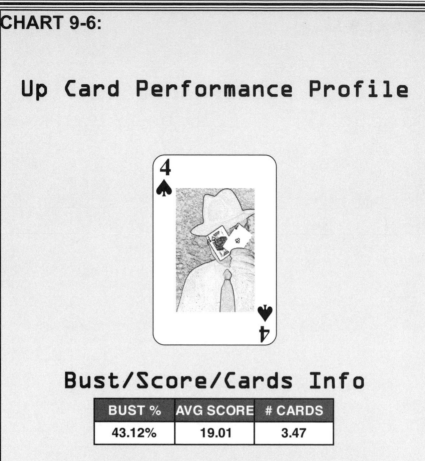

Bust/Score/Cards Info

BUST %	AVG SCORE	# CARDS
43.12%	19.01	3.47

Score Profile

%BJs	%21s	%20s	%19s	%18s	%17s
N/A	12.01%	12.38%	9.96%	10.05%	12.47%

Tell Numbers

%BJ21	%20+	%19+	%18+	%17+	%18B	%17B
N/A	24.39%	34.35%	44.40%	56.88%	65.65%	55.60%

CHART 9-7:

Up Card Performance Profile

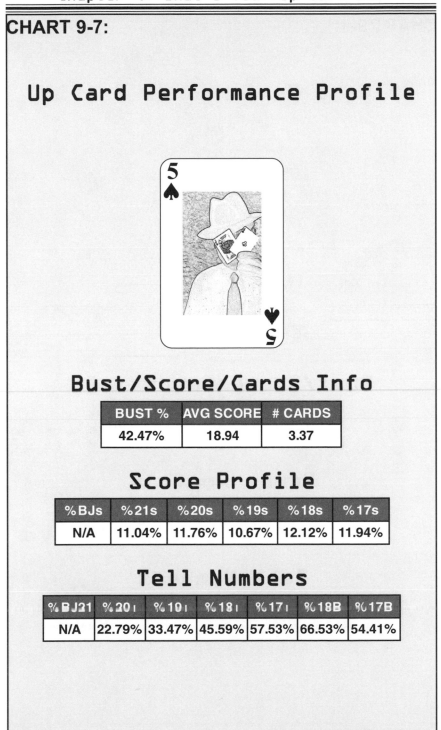

Bust/Score/Cards Info

BUST %	AVG SCORE	# CARDS
42.47%	18.94	3.37

Score Profile

%BJs	%21s	%20s	%19s	%18s	%17s
N/A	11.04%	11.76%	10.67%	12.12%	11.94%

Tell Numbers

%BJ21	%20↑	%10↑	%18↑	%17↑	%18B	%17B
N/A	22.79%	33.47%	45.59%	57.53%	66.53%	54.41%

CHART 9-8:

Up Card Performance Profile

Bust/Score/Cards Info

BUST %	AVG SCORE	# CARDS
41.96%	18.80	3.12

Score Profile

%BJs	%21s	%20s	%19s	%18s	%17s
N/A	10.81%	9.91%	10.00%	11.99%	15.32%

Tell Numbers

%BJ21	%20+	%19+	%18+	%17+	%18B	%17B
N/A	20.73%	30.73%	42.72%	58.01%	69.27%	57.28%

CHART 9-9:

Up Card Performance Profile

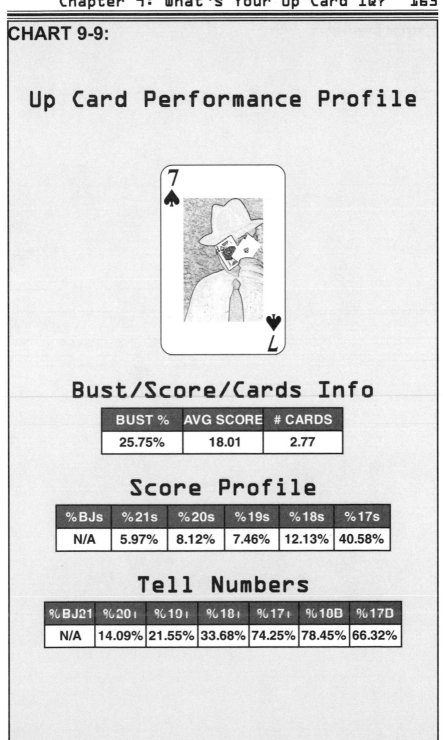

Bust/Score/Cards Info

BUST %	AVG SCORE	# CARDS
25.75%	18.01	2.77

Score Profile

%BJs	%21s	%20s	%19s	%18s	%17s
N/A	5.97%	8.12%	7.46%	12.13%	40.58%

Tell Numbers

%BJ21	%20↓	%19↓	%18↓	%17↓	%18B	%17D
N/A	14.09%	21.55%	33.68%	74.25%	78.45%	66.32%

CHART 9-10:

Up Card Performance Profile

Bust/Score/Cards Info

BUST %	AVG SCORE	# CARDS
23.91%	18.53	2.71

Score Profile

%BJs	%21s	%20s	%19s	%18s	%17s
N/A	7.61%	8.15%	12.91%	36.01%	11.41%

Tell Numbers

%BJ21	%20+	%19+	%18+	%17+	%18B	%17B
N/A	15.76%	28.67%	64.67%	76.09%	71.33%	35.33%

CHART 9-11:

Up Card Performance Profile

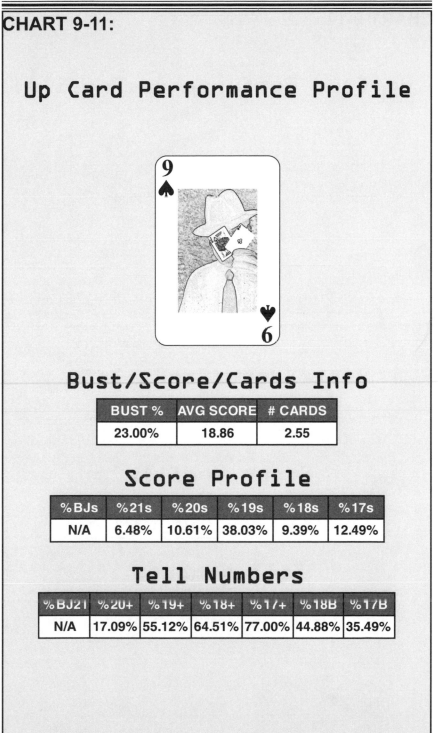

Bust/Score/Cards Info

BUST %	AVG SCORE	# CARDS
23.00%	18.86	2.55

Score Profile

%BJs	%21s	%20s	%19s	%18s	%17s
N/A	6.48%	10.61%	38.03%	9.39%	12.49%

Tell Numbers

%BJ21	%20+	%19+	%18+	%17+	%18B	%17B
N/A	17.09%	55.12%	64.51%	77.00%	44.88%	35.49%

CHART 9-12:

Up Card Performance Profile

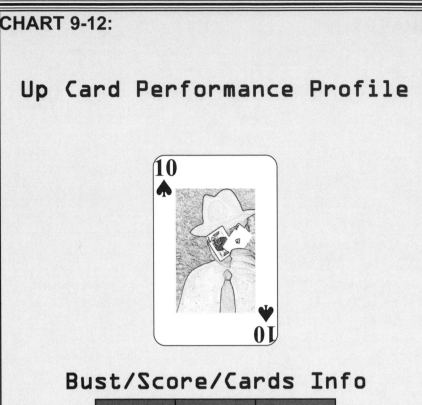

Bust/Score/Cards Info

BUST %	AVG SCORE	# CARDS
20.38%	19.30	2.39

Score Profile

%BJs	%21s	%20s	%19s	%18s	%17s
7.94%	3.65%	35.42%	11.59%	10.35%	10.68%

Tell Numbers

%BJ21	%20+	%19+	%18+	%17+	%18B	%17B
11.59%	47.01%	58.60%	68.95%	79.63%	41.41%	31.06%

CHART 9-13:

Up Card Performance Profile

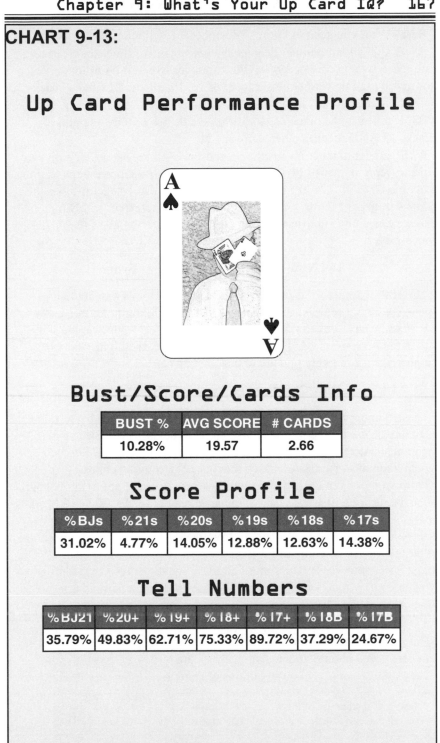

Bust/Score/Cards Info

BUST %	AVG SCORE	# CARDS
10.28%	19.57	2.66

Score Profile

%BJs	%21s	%20s	%19s	%18s	%17s
31.02%	4.77%	14.05%	12.88%	12.63%	14.38%

Tell Numbers

%BJ21	%20+	%19+	%18+	%17+	%18B	%17B
35.79%	49.83%	62.71%	75.33%	89.72%	37.29%	24.67%

Here's what you need to know to decipher the Tell Number symbols:

A "+" sign after a number denotes the percentage of times the dealer's up card reaches that score or *higher*. For example, **18+ Tell Numbers** reveal how often each up card attains a score of 18, 19, 20 and 21 (and a Blackjack, if the up card is a 10 or an Ace).

BJ21 indicates the percentage of times the dealer's 10 or Ace gets a Blackjack AND reaches other scores of 21.

A "**B**" after a number means the percentage of times the dealer's up card tallies a score indicated by the number, or *less*, plus the percentage of times that up card *busts*. For example, **18B** refers to the percentage of times the a particular up card scores an 18, or 17, or busts -- inclusive. Tell Numbers that are especially significant will be referred to later on as *Defining Tell Numbers.* *

Tell Numbers And Your Average Score

The **18B** numbers are especially significant, in light of the fact that the average winning score you will achieve is *19*. That's right. I don't know where some have gotten the mistaken impression that your average score (when not busting) is 18. It's *not. It's 19*. Therefore, the higher the 18B number, the more likely you are to beat that up card.

How Researchers Use These Numbers

These numbers are especially useful to researchers, such as myself. For example, up card score profiles can be used to devise Basic Strategy recommendations. Those profiles are used to determine how often you would likely beat the dealer, based on your point total, in choosing any number of move options. In other words -- researchers want to know how often the dealer will attain each winning score (17, 18, 19, 20 and 21) and beat *you*. The number of pushes are also taken into account. Then, it's determined how often you'll benefit from the dealer's predicted percentage of busts (you're not going to get the benefit of ALL of them, because YOU might bust sometimes). The sum of all these equations results in a prognostication on how much you might win or lose by doing a particular move.

How YOU Might Use Performance Profile Numbers

However -- apart from how researchers use Up Card Performance Profile numbers -- you should understand that they are also very useful to *you!*

For example, let's say you're curious to know how often you'll win by

---

*There was another use of the word "tell" in blackjack, but that is now obsolete. It was used in reference to a dealer's inadvertent giving away of what the hole card was in the course of checking for a Blackjack, but, since the advent of machines that do this function, this type of "tell" has disappeared from a player's palette of tricks.

standing on your stiffs versus a particular up card. You can come up with the answer! Simply look up the bust rate of the card you're facing. That's a good approximation. (Using this method, you can see that the man who said he wins 65% of the time by standing on 16s versus the dealer's 10 is sadly mistaken!)

Or, say you want to know how frequently you'll win by standing on a hand of 17 points versus an up card. The up card's busting figure gives you a general idea. For overall *gains*, subtract the up card's **18+** Tell Number from its busting rate. For example, if you're facing the dealer's 6, your 17 will win 41.96% of the time, when the dealer busts. The dealer will beat you 42.72% of the time with scores of 18 or greater (according to the **18+** Tell Number). Therefore, your overall gains in this situation will be 41.96%-42.72% = -.76%. That is, you'll have overall losses of nearly 1%.

(And, by the way, most of the up card Tell Numbers and Score Profiles give you good approximations of how YOUR hard hand totals would perform. This information is especially helpful, for instance, if you're contemplating splitting a pair of cards -- let's say they're 3s. You could then go to the Performance Profile for the 3 and get ballpark figures for how often you might expect to bust with each split 3, and what your scoring probabilities might be -- which is made simple for you, by the Tell Numbers. Look at page 159, for example. Split your 3s, and your likelihood of busting -- if you intend on pulling to a minimum of 17 points -- is about 38% with each new hand, and your probability of drawing an 18 or better with each hand is above 50%.)

Let's Clear Up A Misconception Regarding Stiffs

OK. Now, probably to the surprise of many, I want you to notice that *no up card busts anywhere near 50% of the time* (when looking at this situation from the standpoint of a *lifetime* of rounds).

So, you ask, if that's true, why should you ever stand on *stiff* totals, when you're destined to *lose* more than 50% of those rounds? I'll bet you thought you'd *win* more than 50% of the time doing that!

When it comes to standing on stiffs, there's a lot of player confusion. Many think they're in *winning* situations when they've been told to stand on stiffs. Not at all.

As you can surmise from the Up Card Performance Profiles, it's sometimes wise to stand on certain stiffs because, in those cases, that will lead to the least *losses*. Don't forget -- in hitting your stiff, you'll bust a lot, and, in so doing, you'll lose some of the benefits of *dealer* busting (you'll bust some of the times when the dealer busts).

Some Surprises In The Performance Profile Numbers

One thing I was astonished to find was that *the dealer's 4 consistently had the highest overall busting rate, not the 5.* This was true, no matter how these numbers varied with each additional round's data. The 6 always had the lowest busting rate of the three.

Here are some other observations:

The dealer's 2's score profile is very strong, which explains why it does so well against you. It ranks *1st* in the percentage of 21s it achieves, and *3rd* in the number of 20s and 19s it tends to attain! Its Defining Tell Number is its **20+** percentage, which shows that *it scores a 20 or 21 more than a quarter of the time, making it 3rd best in that category!*

The 7, once again, shows itself to be among the very weakest up cards. Its average score of 18.01 is the very lowest. Matter of fact, it ranks 10th in most of the Performance Profile categories. Its Defining Tell Numbers are **18+**, which is also the *lowest*, and **18B**, which is the very *weakest! Its 18+ number shows you that it only scores an 18 or better roughly one-third of the time! Its 18B number shows you that your average score of 19 will beat the 7 nearly 80% of the time!* I am sure that you can imagine perhaps some creative doubling and splitting opportunities here, in cases where you're sure your resulting score will likely be 19 or greater. We'll look at this later.

The weakness of the dealer's 8 is also apparent: it has the second lowest average score...the second lowest 20+ and 19+ numbers...and the second highest 18B number! This up card scores paltry totals of 17 and 18 OR busts more than 70% of the time! (Note how much better the 9, the 8's neighbor, so to speak, does in the **19+** category! Almost *twice* as well!) Score a 19, and you've likely beaten the 8. Can't you imagine using this information, in previously unexplored doubling opportunities, similar to what I suggested with the dealer's 7?

What other Achilles heels can you find amongst the Performance Profiles? For one thing, *both the Ace and the 10 score poorly in the %21s category*. That might lead to possibilities. *The 9's 20+ Tell Number is third lowest, indicating it doesn't do well in achieving the highest winning totals*. When you've learned with good regularity how to predict what your hit cards are likely to be, and you're pretty sure you can score a 20 by doubling or splitting, wouldn't you find the 9's limitations profitable?

Take some time to really review all of the information you've just been presented. You might want to take out a highlighter and mark the boxes whose statistics could provide you with an edge at the blackjack table!

Introducing...The *WEAKENED* Up Cards!

Now, I'm going to throw a fly in the ointment. Did you realize that the numbers I gave you for the 10 and the Ace are not really the ones you should consider, when deciding how to move? They're not representative of the dealer's true relative strength at that time. Why?

I've never seen this pointed out anywhere before, but, when you have a choice to make versus these up cards, it means they were checked by the dealer and did not combine with the hole card to form a Blackjack. In other words -- they're *Weakened* Up Cards in that case. The *Weakened Ace* does not have its most powerful partner, the 10, in the hole, and the Weakened 10 does not have its best hole card, the Ace. So, their Performance Profiles are actually not quite as scary as the ones you saw in the preceding section, which represent their *overall* numbers! Including the Blackjacks really cloud the picture. (See the charts on the following four pages. The Weakened 10 and Ace are represented as 10^W and A^W, respectively.)

When you look at the 10 and Ace this way, it becomes apparent that *the 10, in its Weakened condition, is better for the dealer, in most respects, than the Weakened Ace!* So, in this context, you might say that the dealer's 10 is the dealer's strongest performer! The Weakened 10 has a higher average score than the Weakened Ace. In fact, *while the 10^W ranks 1st in that category, the A^W not only ranks 7th, but its average score of 18.83 falls below the average score you will attain over time, that of 19!* The 10^W also does much better in the **20+** Tell Number category. In that regard, *the 10^W attains the highest winning scores nearly one and a half times as often as the A^W!* The 10^W also outdoes the A^W in the **19+** category. Plus, it scores totals of 20 nearly twice as often as the A^W!

Although the A^W's DA number is slightly higher than that of the 10^W, they are so close that they can, for all intents and purposes, be considered *tied* in that important category. That's largely due to the 10^W's higher busting rate. Therefore, the DA numbers do not detract from the useful information presented in the prior paragraph, which reveal the A^W's Achilles heel.

Can't you imagine ways in which your knowing the A^W's weaknesses might lead to better moves and more winnings?

But This Isn't Enough

We want to get more specific, however, if we can, about an up card's potential to beat us. Remember -- the numbers presented in this chapter are largely generalized numbers, based on averages from a large number of rounds featuring a wide variety of differing card situa-

(Continued p. 176.)

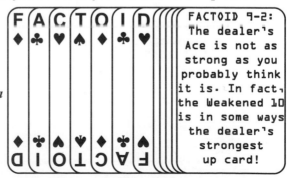

FACTOID 9-2: The dealer's Ace is not as strong as you probably think it is. In fact, the Weakened 10 is in some ways the dealer's strongest up card!

CHART 9-14:

Weakened Up Card
Performance Profiles

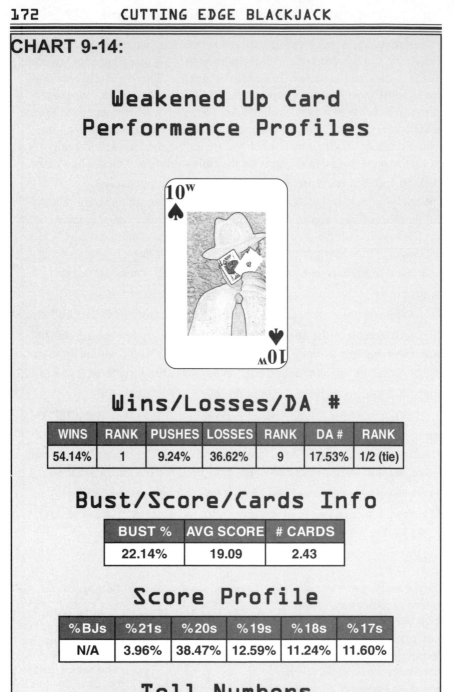

Wins/Losses/DA

WINS	RANK	PUSHES	LOSSES	RANK	DA #	RANK
54.14%	1	9.24%	36.62%	9	17.53%	1/2 (tie)

Bust/Score/Cards Info

BUST %	AVG SCORE	# CARDS
22.14%	19.09	2.43

Score Profile

%BJs	%21s	%20s	%19s	%18s	%17s
N/A	3.96%	38.47%	12.59%	11.24%	11.60%

Tell Numbers

%BJ21	%20+	%19+	%18+	%17+	%18B	%17B
N/A	42.43%	55.02%	66.27%	77.86%	44.98%	33.74%

CHART 9-15:

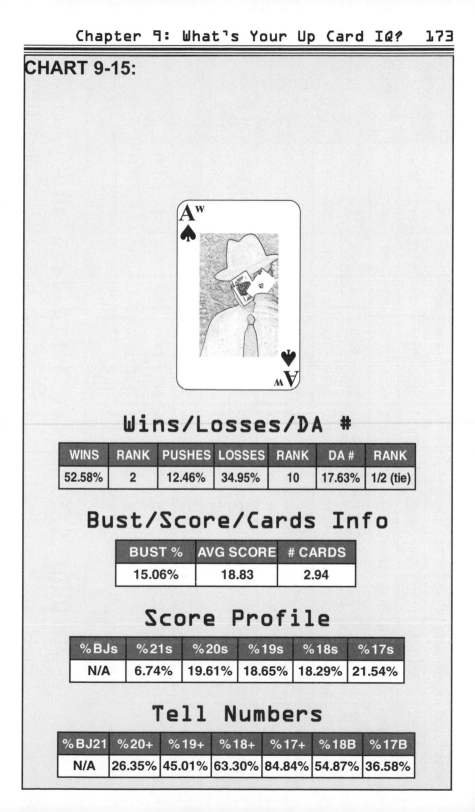

Wins/Losses/DA

WINS	RANK	PUSHES	LOSSES	RANK	DA #	RANK
52.58%	2	12.46%	34.95%	10	17.63%	1/2 (tie)

Bust/Score/Cards Info

BUST %	AVG SCORE	# CARDS
15.06%	18.83	2.94

Score Profile

%BJs	%21s	%20s	%19s	%18s	%17s
N/A	6.74%	19.61%	18.65%	18.29%	21.54%

Tell Numbers

%BJ21	%20+	%19+	%18+	%17+	%18B	%17B
N/A	26.35%	45.01%	63.30%	84.84%	54.87%	36.58%

CHART 9-16: UP CARD VITAL STATISTICS SUMMARY

UP CARD	BUST %	AVG SCORE	# CARDS	%BJs	%21s	%20s	%19s	%18s	%17s	%BJ21	%20+	%19+	%18+	%17+	%18B	%17B
2	35.42	18.97	3.96	N/A	12.17	12.89	13.49	12.65	13.37	N/A	25.06	38.55	51.20	64.58	61.45	48.80
3	37.76	18.94	3.63	N/A	11.27	12.85	12.89	15.58	11.88	N/A	24.12	34.77	50.35	62.24	65.23	49.65
4	43.12	19.01	3.47	N/A	12.01	12.38	10.65	10.05	12.47	N/A	24.39	34.35	44.40	56.88	65.65	55.60
5	42.47	18.94	3.37	N/A	11.04	11.76	10.67	12.12	11.94	N/A	22.79	33.47	45.59	57.53	66.53	54.41
6	41.96	18.80	3.12	N/A	10.81	9.91	10.00	11.99	15.32	N/A	20.73	30.73	42.72	58.04	69.27	57.28
7	25.75	18.01	2.77	N/A	5.97	8.12	7.46	12.13	40.58	N/A	14.09	21.55	33.68	74.25	78.45	66.32
8	23.91	18.53	2.71	N/A	7.61	8.15	12.91	36.01	11.41	N/A	15.76	28.67	64.67	76.09	71.33	35.33
9	23.00	18.86	2.55	N/A	6.48	10.61	38.03	9.39	12.49	N/A	17.09	55.12	64.51	77.00	44.88	35.49
10	20.38	19.30	2.39	7.94	3.65	35.42	11.59	10.35	10.68	11.59	47.01	58.60	68.95	79.63	41.41	31.06
10^w	22.14	19.09	2.43	N/A	3.96	38.47	12.59	11.24	11.60	N/A	42.43	55.02	66.27	77.86	44.98	33.74
Ace	10.28	19.57	2.66	31.02	4.77	14.05	12.88	12.63	14.38	35.79	49.83	62.71	75.33	89.72	37.29	24.67
A^w	15.04	18.83	2.94	N/A	6.74	19.61	18.65	18.29	21.54	N/A	26.35	45.01	63.30	84.84	54.87	36.58

CHART 9-17:   UP CARD VITALS BY RANKING

(Ranked based upon dealer strength. The designation of 1 means the up card is the strongest for the dealer in that category.)

UP CARD	BUST %	AVG SCORE	%21s	%20s	%19s	%20+	%19+	%18B (Rev)*
2	6	3	1	3/4 (tie)	3	3	4	4
3	7	4/5 (tie)	3	3/4 (tie)	6/7 (tie)	5	5	5
4	10	2	2	5	8/9 (tie)	4	6	6
5	9	4/5 (tie)	4	6	6/7 (tie)	6	7	7
6	8	8	5	8	8/9 (tie)	7	8	8
7	5	10	9	9/10 (tie)	10	10	10	10
8	4	9	6	9/10 (tie)	4	9	9	9
9	3	6	8	7	1	8	1/2 (tie)	1/2 (tie)
10	(2)	(2)	(10)	(1)	(5)	(2)	(2)	(2)
10^w	2	1	10	1	5	1	1/2 (tie)	1/2 (tie)
Ace	(1)	(1)	(9)	(2)	(4)	(1)	(1)	(1)
A^w	1	7	7	2	2	2	3	3

*Note: (Rev) indicates that these numbers are ranked in reverse order: the *lowest* 18B number ranks #1.

tions, most of which have little to do with the facts you face in any given round. You should use them primarily as guideposts, for comparative information, and for when you are unable -- for whatever reason -- to get a handle on what to do in a particular round. But, as a general rule, my goal is to get you to become more round-specific.

The reality of how up cards play out is actually much stranger than this.

Up Card Variability

I uncovered the vagaries of up card behavior quite by accident. Early on in my research, acting on a hunch, I divided the results for each up card into consecutive periods in which the up card had made 25 appearances. (This covers roughly 5.5 hours of playing time, or, if you prefer, approximately 325 rounds of action -- a bit more than a day's worth of action for the typical player.) I then did subtotals for each such period.

A funny thing happened. A picture of a *vastly changing landscape* emerged. For each 25 appearances, *up card bust rates, score profiles, ranking and win rates were all over the place!*

Looking at rankings, for instance, I found that, in one span of 325-rounds, the dealer's 4 was the best card for the player, with the highest overall losing rate. In another, the 5 took that honor instead. In comparing similar stretches of time, I found that the dealer's 8 was sometimes the player's 5th best card; at other times, it was only the 7th best up card for the player. There were many such periods where the dealer's 9 busted more than the dealer's 8! Sometimes the dealer's 10 was the strongest card for the dealer (when you factored out dealer Blackjacks).

Busting rates varied greatly, too. For example, you know that the dealer's 2, according to Old School thinking, is supposed to bust reliably and predictably 35% of the time. OK. But, in actuality, there were times – in looking at periods of 325 rounds – that the 2's bust rate was only 16%! That is below that of the 10! At other times, it busted as much as 48% of the time. Chart 9-18, on the following page, gives you a good idea of what you might experience vis a vis the 2's bust rate fluctuation when looked at in terms of periods that cover 25 appearances of the 2 as an up card (also see its companion chart on page 178, which graphically demonstrates the extremes you'll experience). Note that *the 2 busts less than its projected rate in 60% of the periods listed!* Nor is there even *one* instance of the 2 bust rate being 35%, as you've been told to expect. The plain truth is that you will *rarely* find a period encompassing roughly 325 rounds, or 25 up card appearances, where the 2 busts 35% of the time — as it's supposed to do, *all the time;* that is, according to Old School pundits.

Chart 9-20 on page 178 paints a more complete picture of this phenomenon, as it affects all up cards (again, ten consecutive periods of 25 up card appearances were chosen from my data, different periods for each up card,

CHART 9-18:

An Example of How Up Card Bust Rates Vary Per Each 25 Appearances

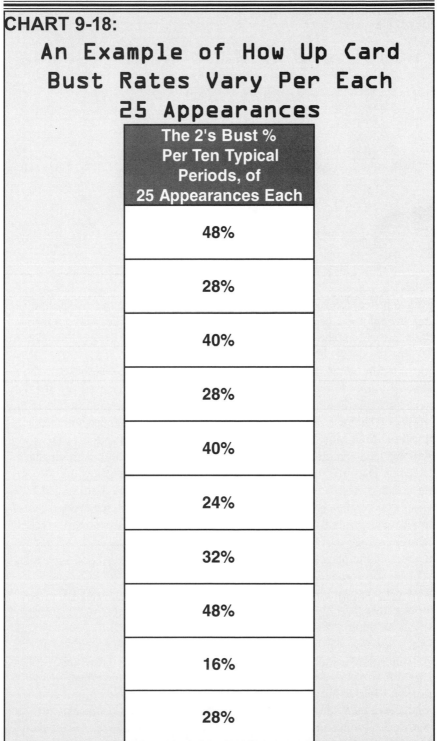

The 2's Bust % Per Ten Typical Periods, of 25 Appearances Each
48%
28%
40%
28%
40%
24%
32%
48%
16%
28%

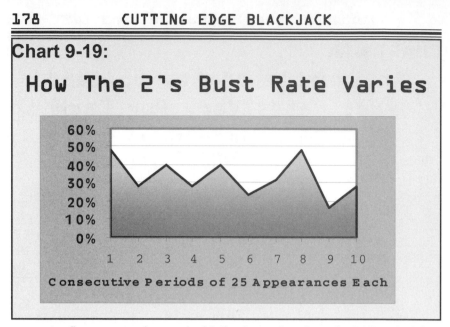

Chart 9-19:

How The 2's Bust Rate Varies

so as to reflect more or less typical behavior -- therefore, the "A" period for the 2 would not necessarily be the same "A" period for the 3, etc.). Once again, not only is the *range* of busting rates striking, but the trend from card to card also speaks of the individual personality of each up card. And take note not only of the range, but also *the relative amount of periods in which each up card goes into high and low busting territory*. For example, the 4 busted 40% or more in 7 of 10 periods (and peaked at the highest rate of any up card). The 5 did so in 8 of 10 periods. But the 6 was significantly less beneficial to players, busting 40% or more of the time *in only 3 of 10 periods!* This kind of analysis is more telling than using old methods that rely upon inaccurate generalized averages. Note, too, that, as you go from the 7 and up, how it becomes increasingly more rare to find prolonged periods where the up card's busting rate is above 30% (in other words, periods which might call for a long-term change in player strategy to reflect the weakness in the up card). This view of things clearly shows the Ace to be, overall, the player killer card, followed by the 10.

(Incidentally, the range of differences in busting rates would be even greater if you examined up card behavior over the course of just 10 appearances, rather than 25. Ten appearances would occur roughly every 130 rounds, or approximately 2+ hours of playing.)

Let's continue our look at the up card of 2, however, because there's something else I'd like to point out, regarding its *Dealer Advantage Percentage*. This varies too! For example, in one 325-round period where the dealer's 2 busted 32% of the time (just 3% less than it was supposed to, if you believe the Old Guard), its DA number reflected a *winning* rate of nearly *25%* (which is 25% higher than it should be, and even *greater* than that of the 10)! At the opposite end of the spectrum, there were similar

CHART 9-20:
UP CARD BUST RATE VARIATION, PER 25 APPEARANCES

25-Appearance Examples, By Order	2	3	4	5	6	7	8	9	10	Ace
A	48%	40%	32%	52%	56%	20%	16%	24%	8%	12%
B	28%	24%	36%	44%	24%	16%	12%	32%	4%	16%
C	40%	48%	40%	44%	32%	28%	20%	8%	8%	8%
D	28%	44%	48%	44%	44%	32%	0%	36%	20%	12%
E	40%	48%	52%	48%	40%	20%	20%	20%	24%	28%
F	24%	36%	40%	52%	32%	16%	40%	16%	36%	16%
G	32%	40%	40%	40%	24%	28%	20%	28%	16%	8%
H	48%	36%	60%	28%	32%	20%	20%	20%	12%	16%
I	16%	36%	32%	48%	36%	36%	32%	40%	32%	16%
J	28%	52%	40%	28%	36%	44%	52%	16%	24%	24%
RANGE:	16-48%	24-52%	32-60%	28-52%	24-56%	16-44%	0-52%	8-40%	4-36%	8-28%

periods where the 2's DA number was -19%, showing steep *losses. That's a large swing in player realities.*

The Conclusion Of This Analysis

I had stumbled upon a happy discovery (which I first introduced to you in Chapter 3): the truth of the blackjack player's universe is that it is constantly *in flux!* It is NOT a world where using cosmic averages said to be *constants* fits the reality, or produces consistent player victories. Quite the contrary. As you just saw, my research showed that those "constants" of old will lead you astray -- *every* day. Up card numbers cannot be counted on to remain the same because *the cards are always out of balance, and in different ways, when comparing your day-to-day experiences.*

So, can you approach each up card with a cookie-cutter type mentality for each round? No! One thing should be clear from our look at up cards per 25 appearances: they have long periods where they're much more vulnerable than at other times, and other intervals where they're significantly more potent adversaries. Now that we've reached this point in *Cutting Edge Blackjack*, you should be able to understand what's behind all of this, too. The underlying causes of these wide swings, and the reason they last so long, is because of *long-term card flow imbalances*, set in motion by the distinctive *repetitive patterns that carry over from shuffle to shuffle,* created by *standardized casino shuffling*. It's no mystery.

So, given all of this, how do you deal with this quandary? Your everyday reality is very different from the one presented in Old School manuals, isn't it? Looking alone at how radically the 2's *busting rate* changed over time in Chart 9-18 (page 177), you can see the need for a *flexible* strategy, and one that has a good deal of *precision -- something that is lacking in the traditional approach to the game*. In the case of the dealer's 2, it would have to inform you to play the 2 more like a *4* at times, and more like a *10* at others!

Introducing The Concept Of *Ducks & Bucks*

Well, here's one way to uncover and react to each up card's probable behavior *of the moment:* through my inventions, the *Ducks* and *Bucks*.

I guarantee that these new concepts will radicalize your game for the better. They will help you identify whether an up card, during any particular round, is weak (it's a *Duck*), or strong (it's a *Buck*), AND how relatively weak or strong it is. What we're talking about is fine tuning your game, to a much greater extent than card counting could ever hope to.

Actually, the purpose of introducing the Ducks & Bucks idea is fourfold:

❶ *To teach you just how variable up card behavior is.*

❷ *To reveal WHY the strength of each type of up card can differ so greatly, from round to round.*

❸ *To show you that you can get real specific, and recognize not only whether the up card is a Duck or Buck, but what variant. This will facilitate your reacting properly to the up card's likely behavior of the moment, to win more hands than ever before.*

❹ *To give you a more definite picture of each up card's overall personality, so to speak, including unique weaknesses you are undoubtedly unaware of, from which you can profit greatly.*

All Ducks have exploitable *vulnerabilities* (even the Ace, although in that card's case, it's a matter of degrees). *All Bucks* need to be treated with due *care* -- and often with greater respect than you ever thought was necessary. Now, once it's clear you're facing one of these animals, *you will usually need to adjust your card strategy, and sometimes in ways you never conceived of before. This is where their power lies -- in their ability to warn you of probable dealer outcomes that stray from what has traditionally been taught as the norm.*

The name Duck (as in sitting Duck) is an acronym that stands for: Diminished Up Card. An up card is a Duck when it is most likely to be paired up with a hole card that would combine with it to form a weak point total -- one that would make it most likely to bust and/or lose to you. (This usually translates into hole cards that, with the up card, give the dealer a stiff total. Sometimes, however, we'll only be interested in hole cards that form a total of 15 or 16 with the up card.) *Every* up card acts like a *Duck* at times, although some Ducks are better than others; some are more prone to busting and/or losing than others. (In referring to Ducks, they will sometimes be abbreviated as symbols. For example, the Ace Duck will be represented as: A^D.)

The word Buck is also an abbreviation -- of Brutal Up Card. A Buck describes the condition in which any of the up cards is coupled with hole cards that combine with them to form two-card totals that are most likely to beat you. These totals might be strong winning scores, or, promising point totals such as 10 or 11 that lead most often to great results. (Bucks will also be expressed from time to time as symbols; to avoid confusing these with Tell Numbers, the postscript K will be used. For example, the Ace Buck will be represented as: A^K.)

(Incidentally, I'm not trying to be cute here. There are two good reasons I choose the acronyms of "Duck" to represent the idea of the Diminished Up Card and "Buck" for the "Brutal Up Card": 1) in simplifying the names, it makes it easier for you to grasp and remember the concepts; and, 2) this shorthand type of name will enable you to alert any playing partners to either the vulnerability or invincibility of the up card by whispering "Duck!" or "Buck!" without drawing unwanted attention to yourself.)

Your job is to acquire the skills to identify when the up card you're

facing is most likely a Duck or Buck of which you can take advantage. In one sense, I am getting ahead of myself a bit here, because this requires, in part, that you know how to determine what the hole card is most likely to be, every round, and also the dealer's hit cards. This is very doable, using methods I've developed, which we'll cover in the Advanced Card Analysis chapter. (In fact, those of you who read *Blackjack The SMART Way* already know how to do this.)

But -- *first* things *first*. For now, it suffices that you get acquainted with each up card's Ducks and Bucks, and the mathematical logic that makes them work. It's a matter of getting in touch with *probabilities.*

It begins with your absorbing and memorizing the information I've presented in the Ducks and Bucks charts. Then, here's what you'll do: each round, you will ask yourself if any cards have been depleted, thereby producing the conditions that would make the up card a Duck or Buck (the cards which, by their absence, create Ducks and Bucks are enumerated in the "Hole Cards Missing" columns in the charts on pages 186-205. With each Duck and Buck's identification, you can be assured of a certain predictable outcome (which is expressed in the columns labelled "Probable Bust Rate"). You'll find your appropriate card strategy response in the columns entitled "Play It Like A" and "Strategy." (If it says "Play It Like A 10," you'd follow the recommendations of my Basic Strategy Charts, on pages ix-xii.)

What Are *Simplified* Ducks & Bucks?

In dividing all the possible hole cards into two categories -- those that make the up cards *Ducks* (more likely to bust and/or lose) and those that make the up cards *Bucks* (more likely to win) -- I realized it might be too cumbersome to take all of them into account, in your attempt to identify them. In addition, the more cards that must be considered lacking, before recognizing up cards as being Ducks or Bucks, the more *rarely* those situations will occur, and the less useful these concepts would be. More to the point, it's not *necessary* for 6 to 8 of the possible hole cards to be depleted for an up card to act like a Duck or Buck. (So, most of the *"complete"* Ducks and Bucks on pages 186-205 are not very usable in a practical sense. They're included only as a reference; so that you might know all of the cards that, by their absence, contribute to those conditions.)

Therefore, I came up with the idea of the *simplified* Duck and Buck. These have a much smaller *subset* of hole cards that defines them, yet they still get the job done. The fewer the cards you need to follow to confirm the condition, the easier it will be for you to capitalize on it -- and *the greater the assurance you will have of having identified an up card as being either a Duck or Buck.* With less possible hole cards in the picture, it makes this method significantly more *accurate.*

The beauty part is that *often the depletion of just one or two cards suffices to make an up card either a Duck or Buck, warranting a strategy change on your part.* If an up card mathematically goes one way or another when just one or two types of hole cards are in short supply, *these are situations that should be easy to spot, with a high confidence level.*

The best part about using *simplified* Ducks and Bucks is that they will simplify your memorization process, and make your life less complicated.

What The Numbers Reveal

Looking at the numbers, it should drive home two points: 1) how senseless it is to use the global bust rates of old, which take all the possible hole cards into consideration; and, 2) how easy it is to divide the up cards into much more meaningful subcategories that alert you to very different probable dealer outcomes, requiring differing responses in terms of your card strategy!

(Note: you should understand by now that bust rates alone are not sufficient in determining card strategy. Each Duck or Buck variant's *score profile* is also key, as you saw earlier in this chapter. However, while I used these score profiles in producing the recommendations on the following pages, I chose not to present the details here because that would have overloaded you with information that's really unnecessary for you to know, and would possibly have led to some confusion as well.)

Now, you'll notice that *up cards often act like several different types of Ducks and Bucks*, depending on how many of the hole cards that make for their condition are lacking in the card balance. That is, we're not only dividing each up card into two different types, but we're also subdividing those further, to get even more precise, so you can play with almost pinpoint accuracy.

The fantastic thing about Ducks and Bucks is that, while your guideposts are the various busting rates that are part of each up card's kaleidoscope, what we're really talking about here are: 1) your chances of winning or losing; 2) the dealer's chances of winning or losing; and, 3) what you have to do to react appropriately to the occasion. The bust rate percentages are really probabilities. They'll guide you to do the move that's most correct, according to the percentages, not the move that wins all the time (such a move doesn't exist).

To keep things as familiar to you as possible, I often tell you to play a Duck or Buck "like" a specific up card. That should be self-explanatory: this means, play them according to my Basic Strategy recommendations for the card the Duck or Buck is being compared to.

Sometimes, however, I've added a modifying adjective with these suggestions; i.e., you might see instructions to play a Duck or Buck like a "*weak* 7," or a "*strong* 10." If these descriptions require strategies you've never used before, I specify exactly what I mean in a separate "Strategy" column.

A few cards are so strong that I've told you to play them like a "Winner" or "Sure Winner." You are undoubtedly unfamiliar with these beasts. A "Sure Winner" *never* busts, and a "Winner" has such a minuscule busting rate that it *nearly always* scores. Your *response* to them will be the same. When facing them, for instance, your 17 will not only be a sure loser, it will be a *huge* loser. Your 17s will lose more than 81% of the hands in which they go up against a Sure Winner, resulting in overall losses of 62% (your overall losses are calculated by subtracting the percentage of hands you win from the percentage of hands you lose: 19%-81%= -62%). So, if allowed, *you will surrender your 17s when facing them* (I'll bet you've never done that!). *If surrender is not allowed, you will HIT your 17!*

Versus the Ace Sure Winner, for example, your overall losses by hitting a hand totalling 17 points would be 56.29%, over time. However, by standing, your losses would be a whopping 73.66% (your 17 would push with the dealer's 17s, but would lose against the higher dealer scores; because the dealer's Sure Winner does not bust, you could not hope for a single win). You cannot stand in that situation -- that is, if you want to play correctly. If you're afraid of players' or dealers' reactions to your hitting a 17, then you must decide whether it's smarter to placate them, rather than to make the right move.

This is just one example of how my Ducks and Bucks system will free you from the shackles of antiquated thinking, and lead you toward ingenious, winning moves you've never made before. You will probably see some players and dealers scratching their heads at your unorthodox decisions, but, that's OK -- it's your money. The good thing is that, as you rake in your dough, casino employees will probably put your wins down to *luck*, which is what you *want*; if they think you're stupid (because they don't recognize the wisdom of card strategies they've never seen before), you shouldn't draw too much unwanted heat.

Get to know these animals. They will dramatically raise your winning rate and your profits. All of a sudden, dealer outcomes will make sense, each round -- not that you'll have 100% success at prognostication, but that you'll be right much more than you'll be wrong. And you'll be winning a much higher percentage of hands than you ever thought possible.

There will be more on this, in the Advanced Card Analysis chapter.

A word of advice: *it's OK if you start small. That is, if memorizing all of the Ducks and Bucks is too much for you right now, then, take out your highlighter and choose one Duck and one Buck per up card -- the ones you feel you can profit from the most -- and begin by looking for those at the casino.*

But don't underestimate the monumental value of the concept of the Ducks and Bucks. The names may sound cute, but the results are *great*. *This is an excellent way to achieve a level of precision never before thought possible in the world of blackjack.*

How To Play Blackjack Outside The United States

One additional thing -- those of you who have played outside the contiguous United States have run into casinos where the game of blackjack is played a bit differently. Namely, there's often no hole card.

The beauty part is that the Ducks and Bucks and other up card information in this chapter will guide you toward the correct strategy. The dealer's first card, face up, still acts like an up card, and any choices you make will be further enhanced by treating the dealer's eventual second card like a hole card; your ability to predict what that will be is based upon the same principles you use to unmask the hole card, and is no more difficult.

Sitting toward 3rd Base is especially wise here, because you'll have better success, with your turn coming right before the dealer's second card. Chapter 12 on "Strategic Card Analysis & Your Real-time Card Strategy" will teach you how to play the non-hole-card games, too. It will show you how to analyze card flows and card composition in card prediction.

One Last Word

One last thing for the very curious only: the hole cards that form a total of 17 points with each up card were hard to put in either the Duck or Buck camp. If you remove these hole cards from the overall picture, yes, the up card's *bust rate* will go *up*, so you might think, aha, that means that these hole cards, by their removal, would make the up card a *Duck*. But, in so doing, the up card's *win rate* simultaneously *goes down!* So, do the hole cards that make for totals of 17 belong in the *Buck* category? The quick answer is: the up card's *busting* rate is more helpful to us in choosing a card strategy than knowing its *winning* rate. That's why I've decided that it will be the *Ducks* that will lack hole cards that give them totals of 17 (or 7, in the case of lower up cards); this raises their busting rates to levels that usually identify situations that justify altering your strategy (as indicated in the Ducks and Bucks charts).

CHART 9-21:

Ducks & Bucks: Characteristics

The Complete Duck

HOLE CARDS MISSING	PROBABLE BUST RATE	PLAY IT LIKE A
Aces & 5s-9s	45.13%	4-6

Simplified Duck A

HOLE CARDS MISSING	PROBABLE BUST RATE	PLAY IT LIKE A
7s-9s	38.38%	3

Simplified Duck B

HOLE CARDS MISSING	PROBABLE BUST RATE	PLAY IT LIKE A
6s-9s	40.67%	4-6

Simplified Duck C

HOLE CARDS MISSING	PROBABLE BUST RATE	PLAY IT LIKE A
5s-9s	43.73%	4-6

CHART 9-22:

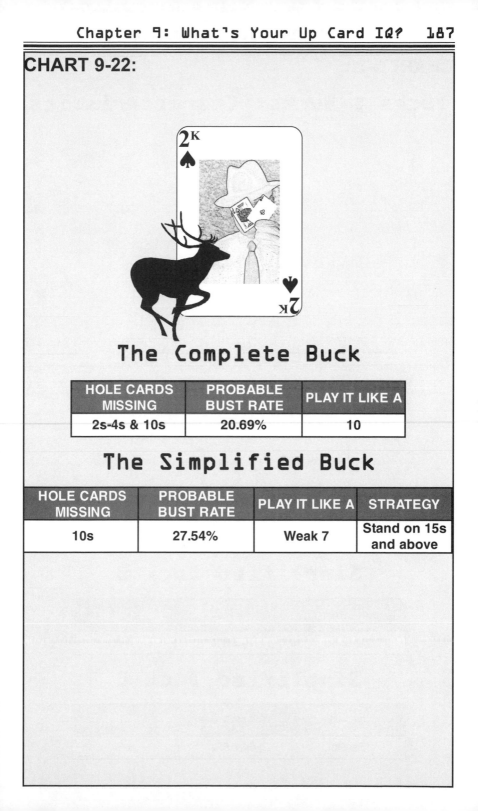

The Complete Buck

HOLE CARDS MISSING	PROBABLE BUST RATE	PLAY IT LIKE A
2s-4s & 10s	20.69%	10

The Simplified Buck

HOLE CARDS MISSING	PROBABLE BUST RATE	PLAY IT LIKE A	STRATEGY
10s	27.54%	Weak 7	Stand on 15s and above

CHART 9-23:

Ducks & Bucks: Characteristics

The Complete Duck

HOLE CARDS MISSING	PROBABLE BUST RATE	PLAY IT LIKE A
Aces & 4s-8s	51.02%	Weak 4-6

Simplified Duck A

HOLE CARDS MISSING	PROBABLE BUST RATE	PLAY IT LIKE A
8s	39.51%	3

Simplified Duck B

HOLE CARDS MISSING	PROBABLE BUST RATE	PLAY IT LIKE A
7s & 8s	40.99%	4-6

Simplified Duck C

HOLE CARDS MISSING	PROBABLE BUST RATE	PLAY IT LIKE A
5s-8s	44.96%	4-6

CHART 9-24:

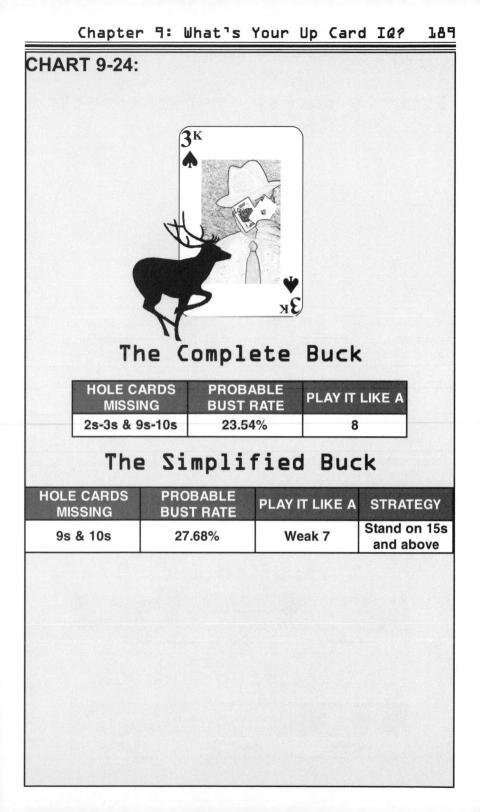

The Complete Buck

HOLE CARDS MISSING	PROBABLE BUST RATE	PLAY IT LIKE A
2s-3s & 9s-10s	23.54%	8

The Simplified Buck

HOLE CARDS MISSING	PROBABLE BUST RATE	PLAY IT LIKE A	STRATEGY
9s & 10s	27.68%	Weak 7	Stand on 15s and above

CHART 9-25:

Ducks & Bucks: Characteristics

The Complete Duck

HOLE CARDS MISSING	PROBABLE BUST RATE	PLAY IT LIKE A
Aces & 3s-7s	56.27%	Weak 4-6

Simplified Duck A

HOLE CARDS MISSING	PROBABLE BUST RATE	PLAY IT LIKE A
5s-7s	47.34%	4-6

Simplified Duck B

HOLE CARDS MISSING	PROBABLE BUST RATE	PLAY IT LIKE A
4s-7s	49.57%	Weak 4-6

Simplified Duck C

HOLE CARDS MISSING	PROBABLE BUST RATE	PLAY IT LIKE A
3s-7s	53.77%	Weak 4-6

CHART 9-26:

The Complete Buck

HOLE CARDS MISSING	PROBABLE BUST RATE	PLAY IT LIKE A
2s & 8s-10s	25.56%	7

Simplified Buck A

HOLE CARDS MISSING	PROBABLE BUST RATE	PLAY IT LIKE A
10s	34.99%	2

Simplified Buck B

HOLE CARDS MISSING	PROBABLE BUST RATE	PLAY IT LIKE A
9s & 10s	31.65%	2

Simplified Buck C

HOLE CARDS MISSING	PROBABLE BUST RATE	PLAY IT LIKE A
8s-10s	28.27%	2

CHART 9-27:

Ducks & Bucks: Characteristics

The Complete Duck

HOLE CARDS MISSING	PROBABLE BUST RATE	PLAY IT LIKE A
Aces & 2s-6s	55.87%	Weak 4-6

Simplified Duck A

HOLE CARDS MISSING	PROBABLE BUST RATE	PLAY IT LIKE A
3s-6s	48.10%	4-6

Simplified Duck B

HOLE CARDS MISSING	PROBABLE BUST RATE	PLAY IT LIKE A
2s-6s	53.41%	Weak 4-6

CHART 9-28:

The Complete Buck

HOLE CARDS MISSING	PROBABLE BUST RATE	PLAY IT LIKE A
7s-10s	20.57%	10

Simplified Buck A

HOLE CARDS MISSING	PROBABLE BUST RATE	PLAY IT LIKE A
10s	29.73%	2

Simplified Buck B

HOLE CARDS MISSING	PROBABLE BUST RATE	PLAY IT LIKE A	STRATEGY
9s & 10s	27.26%	weak 7	Stand on 15s and above

Simplified Buck C

HOLE CARDS MISSING	PROBABLE BUST RATE	PLAY IT LIKE A
8s-10s	24.41%	8

CHART 9-29:

Ducks & Bucks: Characteristics

The Complete Duck

HOLE CARDS MISSING	PROBABLE BUST RATE	PLAY IT LIKE A
Aces & 2s-5s	53.53%	Weak 4-6

Simplified Duck A

HOLE CARDS MISSING	PROBABLE BUST RATE	PLAY IT LIKE A
4s & 5s	48.41%	4-6

Simplified Duck B

HOLE CARDS MISSING	PROBABLE BUST RATE	PLAY IT LIKE A
2s-5s	53.21%	Weak 4-6

CHART 9-30:

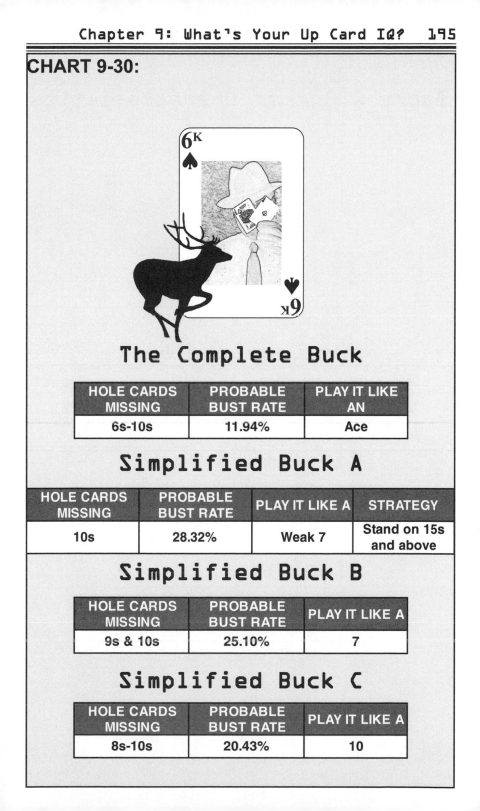

The Complete Buck

HOLE CARDS MISSING	PROBABLE BUST RATE	PLAY IT LIKE AN
6s-10s	11.94%	Ace

Simplified Buck A

HOLE CARDS MISSING	PROBABLE BUST RATE	PLAY IT LIKE A	STRATEGY
10s	28.32%	Weak 7	Stand on 15s and above

Simplified Buck B

HOLE CARDS MISSING	PROBABLE BUST RATE	PLAY IT LIKE A
9s & 10s	25.10%	7

Simplified Buck C

HOLE CARDS MISSING	PROBABLE BUST RATE	PLAY IT LIKE A
8s-10s	20.43%	10

CHART 9-31:

Ducks & Bucks: Characteristics

The Complete Duck

HOLE CARDS MISSING	PROBABLE BUST RATE	PLAY IT LIKE A
Aces & 2s-4s & 10s	58.33%	Weak 4-6

Simplified Duck A

HOLE CARDS MISSING	PROBABLE BUST RATE	PLAY IT LIKE A
10s	37.55%	3

Simplified Duck B

HOLE CARDS MISSING	PROBABLE BUST RATE	PLAY IT LIKE A
10s & Aces	42.18%	4-6

CHART 9-32:

The Complete Buck

HOLE CARDS MISSING	PROBABLE BUST RATE	PLAY IT LIKE A
5s-9s	7.37%	Strong Ace

Simplified Buck A

HOLE CARDS MISSING	PROBABLE BUST RATE	PLAY IT LIKE A
9s	21.93%	10

Simplified Buck B

HOLE CARDS MISSING	PROBABLE BUST RATE	PLAY IT LIKE A
8s & 9s	10.65%	Strong 10

Simplified Buck C

HOLE CARDS MISSING	PROBABLE BUST RATE	PLAY IT LIKE A
5s & 6s	19.35%	Strong 10

CHART 9-33:

Ducks & Bucks: Characteristics

The Complete Duck

HOLE CARDS MISSING	PROBABLE BUST RATE	PLAY IT LIKE A
Aces, 2s, 3s, 9s & 10s	51.67%	Weak 4-6

Simplified Duck A

HOLE CARDS MISSING	PROBABLE BUST RATE	PLAY IT LIKE A
10s	32.08%	2

Simplified Duck B

HOLE CARDS MISSING	PROBABLE BUST RATE	PLAY IT LIKE A
Aces, 2s, 3s & 10s	43.75%	4-6

CHART 9-34:

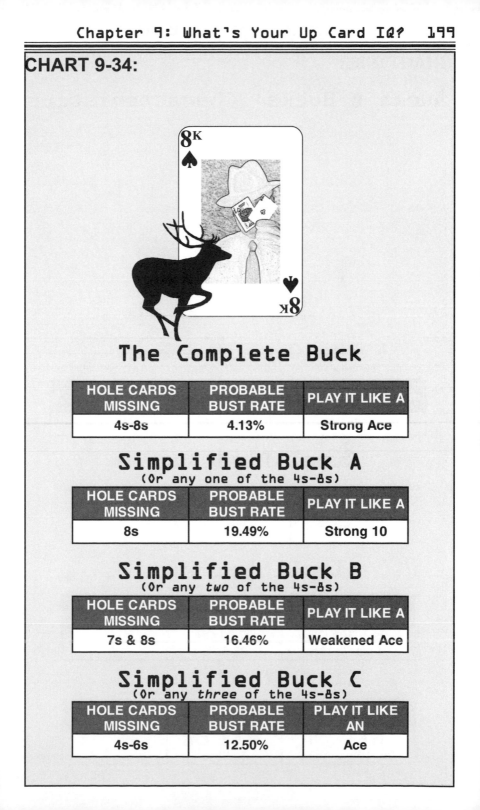

The Complete Buck

HOLE CARDS MISSING	PROBABLE BUST RATE	PLAY IT LIKE A
4s-8s	4.13%	Strong Ace

Simplified Buck A
(Or any one of the 4s-8s)

HOLE CARDS MISSING	PROBABLE BUST RATE	PLAY IT LIKE A
8s	19.49%	Strong 10

Simplified Buck B
(Or any two of the 4s-8s)

HOLE CARDS MISSING	PROBABLE BUST RATE	PLAY IT LIKE A
7s & 8s	16.46%	Weakened Ace

Simplified Buck C
(Or any three of the 4s-8s)

HOLE CARDS MISSING	PROBABLE BUST RATE	PLAY IT LIKE AN
4s-6s	12.50%	Ace

CHART 9-35:

Ducks & Bucks: Characteristics

The Complete Duck

HOLE CARDS MISSING	PROBABLE BUST RATE	PLAY IT LIKE A
Aces, 2s, 8s- 10s	58.69%	Weak 4-6

Simplified Duck A

HOLE CARDS MISSING	PROBABLE BUST RATE	PLAY IT LIKE A
10s	34.41%	2

Simplified Duck B

HOLE CARDS MISSING	PROBABLE BUST RATE	PLAY IT LIKE A
9s & 10s OR Aces & 10s	37.78 OR 38.64%	3

Simplified Duck C

HOLE CARDS MISSING	PROBABLE BUST RATE	PLAY IT LIKE A
8s & 10s OR 9s, 10s & Aces	39.66% OR 42.93%	4-6

CHART 9-36:

The Complete Buck

HOLE CARDS MISSING	PROBABLE BUST RATE	PLAY IT LIKE A	STRATEGY
3s-7s	2.96%	Winner	Surrender 4s-7s, 12s-17s. No splitting.

Simplified Buck A
(Or any one of the 3s-7s)

HOLE CARDS MISSING	PROBABLE BUST RATE	PLAY IT LIKE A
7s	18.22%	Strong 10

Simplified Buck B
(Or any two of the 3s-7s)

HOLE CARDS MISSING	PROBABLE BUST RATE	PLAY IT LIKE A
6s & 7s	15.10%	Weakened Ace

Simplified Buck C
(Or any three of the 3s-7s)

HOLE CARDS MISSING	PROBABLE BUST RATE	PLAY IT LIKE AN
5s-7s	12.46%	Ace

CHART 9-37:

Ducks & Bucks: Characteristics

The Complete Duck*

HOLE CARDS MISSING	PROBABLE BUST RATE	PLAY IT LIKE A
7s- 10s	55.02%	Weak 4-6

Simplified Duck A

HOLE CARDS MISSING	PROBABLE BUST RATE	PLAY IT LIKE A	STRATEGY
10s	30.58%	Weak 7	Stand on 16s and higher

Simplified Duck B
(Or any *one* of the 7s-9s plus the 10s)

HOLE CARDS MISSING	PROBABLE BUST RATE	PLAY IT LIKE A
9s & 10s	35.93%	2

Simplified Duck C
(Or any *two* of the 7s-9s plus the 10s)

HOLE CARDS MISSING	PROBABLE BUST RATE	PLAY IT LIKE A
8s-10s	43.43%	4-6

*The 10's ducks and bucks are based on *weakened* 10s; so, while not listed, *there are of course no Aces in the hole.*

CHART 9-38:

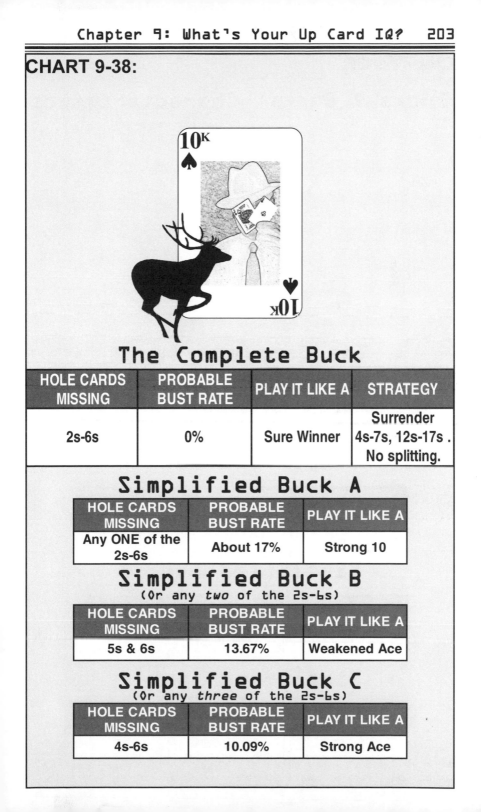

The Complete Buck

HOLE CARDS MISSING	PROBABLE BUST RATE	PLAY IT LIKE A	STRATEGY
2s-6s	0%	Sure Winner	Surrender 4s-7s, 12s-17s . No splitting.

Simplified Buck A

HOLE CARDS MISSING	PROBABLE BUST RATE	PLAY IT LIKE A
Any ONE of the 2s-6s	About 17%	Strong 10

Simplified Buck B
(Or any *two* of the 2s-6s)

HOLE CARDS MISSING	PROBABLE BUST RATE	PLAY IT LIKE A
5s & 6s	13.67%	Weakened Ace

Simplified Buck C
(Or any *three* of the 2s-6s)

HOLE CARDS MISSING	PROBABLE BUST RATE	PLAY IT LIKE A
4s-6s	10.09%	Strong Ace

CHART 9-39:

Ducks & Bucks: Characteristics

The Complete Duck*

HOLE CARDS MISSING	PROBABLE BUST RATE	PLAY IT LIKE A
6s- 9s	32.63%	2

Simplified Duck A

HOLE CARDS MISSING	PROBABLE BUST RATE	PLAY IT LIKE A
Any ONE of the 6s-9s	17-17.68%	Strong 10

Simplified Duck B

HOLE CARDS MISSING	PROBABLE BUST RATE	PLAY IT LIKE A
Any TWO of the 6s-9s	About 20-21%	10

Simplified Duck C

HOLE CARDS MISSING	PROBABLE BUST RATE	PLAY IT LIKE A
Any THREE of the 6s-9s	About 25%	7

*The Ace's ducks and bucks are based on *Weakened* Aces; so, while not listed, *there are of course no 10s in the hole.*

CHART 9-40:

The Complete Buck

HOLE CARDS MISSING	PROBABLE BUST RATE	PLAY IT LIKE A	STRATEGY
Ace-5s	0%	Sure Winner	Surrender 4s-7s, 12s-17s. No splitting.

Simplified Buck A

HOLE CARDS MISSING	PROBABLE BUST RATE	PLAY IT LIKE AN
Any ONE of the 2s-5s	About 12-13%	Ace

Simplified Buck B

HOLE CARDS MISSING	PROBABLE BUST RATE	PLAY IT LIKE A
Any TWO of the 2s-5s	About 10%	Strong Ace

Simplified Buck C

HOLE CARDS MISSING	PROBABLE BUST RATE	PLAY IT LIKE A	STRATEGY
Any THREE of the 2s-5s	About 6%	Winner	Surrender 4s-7s, 12s-17s. No Splitting.

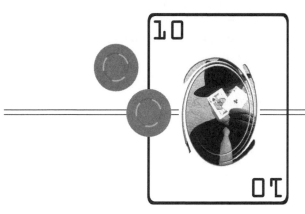

How To Count Cards At 1- And 2-Deck Tables

So...you're a card counter. And you're smart -- you only play the 1- and 2-deck pitch games. But what about all those face-down cards?

I am always surprised at how few players are aware of how handicapped they are because of those face-down cards -- the hands at the 1- and 2-deck pitch game tables that players are required to place face-down, out of sight, during the course of a round.

I've met literally *thousands* of blackjack players in my nationwide travels -- while playing blackjack, doing book signing events, and giving blackjack seminars. When someone identifies themselves as a card counter, I'll often ask them how they manage to count cards at pitch game tables, where the odds are the best, but where so many of the cards of the other players are placed face-down, out of view. I mean, if you are a card counter, you need to, by definition, *count all the cards* that were dealt before your turn arrives. Isn't that the idea?

You'd be surprised how many otherwise intelligent players nonchalantly respond that it is not terribly *important* that they know what those face-down cards are! In fact, most will tell you that it is *impossible* to figure out what those cards are. They don't seem terribly concerned about a problem that greatly threatens their game, and which has prevented them from doing real-time card counting!

What's more, it seems to me that they have convinced themselves that it's sufficient simply to count the cards as the cards are exposed *after* the round is finished! That's strange, because many of these same players seem to believe that there is little that they don't know about the game.

(That's one reason why this chapter -- when advertised -- provoked such a positive reaction. It is, to the best of my knowledge, a historic first.)

The Handicap Born of the 1960s

Perhaps this mass misconception results from the many decades that have passed since the near-devastating rule changes that brought about those face-down cards.

For centuries, players had it made. The game, invented in France as "vingt et un," or, 21, during the late Renaissance period, was designed to be a 1-deck game, with all the cards dealt face up, for all to see. Then, in the 1960s, in response to the relatively new practice of card counting, the casino industry instituted harmful new rules and restrictions (also, for the first time, multi-deck games appeared, also in an attempt to confuse card counters).

As a result, the 1-deck games that still exist -- and their younger multi-deck cousin, the 2-deck games -- require players, when standing on their first two cards, to conceal their first two cards under their chips to indicate that they are standing. This practice is also required when players want to stand after taking hit cards. Plus, the extra card players receive when doubling down is dealt face-down.

The Card Counter's Paradise Lost

In effectively hiding many of the in-play cards, card counters no longer have as much of an advantage as they had enjoyed previously. The good players who were around before the early-60s rules changes keenly understood their loss. A good amount of accuracy is gone.

But what is really interesting is that, in the many decades that have passed, and, indeed, as of this writing, *no one, to my knowledge, has proposed a sound, effective way of attempting to restore the advantages blackjack players lost.*

Apparently today's card counters are using card counting solely in relation to their betting strategies, and not for their playing strategies. But that's not using card counting to its full potential.

Being above all else a player, I have been determined to solve the riddle of how to figure out what those face-down cards are. Knowing what the count is at your turn can be very helpful in deciding what move to make.

Look at Examples A and B from my computer card runs on the next page, for instance. Wouldn't it be extremely helpful if you were able to figure out what the count was in deciding how to play your cards in these situations? We'll review those examples and others later in this chapter. (Please note: *this chapter is based upon my All-Inclusive Counting System, where the 2s through 7s are each assigned a count of +1, and 8s through 10s each count -*

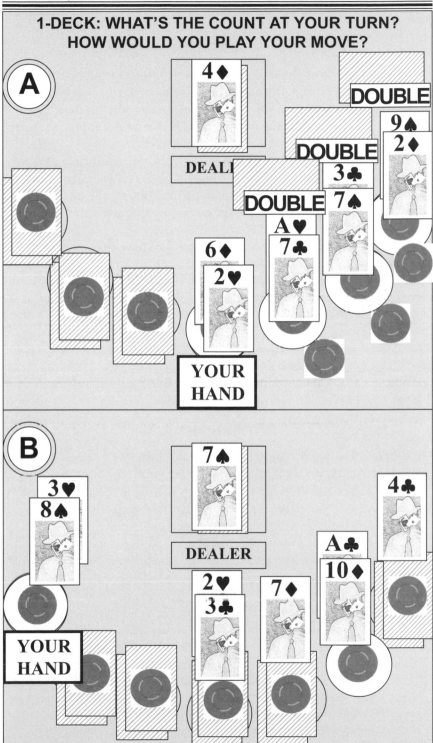

**1-DECK: WHAT'S THE COUNT AT YOUR TURN?
HOW WOULD YOU PLAY YOUR MOVE?**

1. Aces have no point value.)

Going Head-To-Head Is Not The Answer

Now, before some of you raise the possibility of getting around all of this by going one-on-one with a dealer, let me note here that playing head-on against the dealer *is* one way of negating the problem. But head-on play presents its own very daunting problems and is inadvisable for the average player.

Plus, in many of the ever-rising number of casino locales, blackjack tables are in such short supply that you often don't have the option of going one-on-one with the dealer even if you wanted to. The pitch game tables -- which are greatly outnumbered at most casinos by the multi-deck shoe games -- are rarely unoccupied.

If you are a high roller or a whale, of course, you have the option of going into some private back room area to play all alone, just you and some casino personnel. I don't believe this is a good solution. I've heard of far too many players who have lost big-time doing this. This practice presents its own unique risks. Suffice it to say, at the very least, you are guaranteed to suffer from the effects of intense casino scrutiny.

But, more to the point -- the major reason this chapter is necessary is that most players *prefer* the tables where there are other players, even with the dilemma that they cannot see those face-down cards, nor account for them.

All of that, I hope, will change with this chapter.

The Opportunity To Win More

There are a few questions you might have that I need to address here:

Q: **Will the methods in this chapter increase your win rate?**

A: If you're a card counter, and you've been playing in the dark, so to speak, with regard to the face-down cards, most certainly. With more information at your disposal, you become a better player, capable of making smarter decisions regarding how to play your hand.

Q: **Are these methods going to enable you to win every hand?**

A: No. No method can promise that. Ask any good poker player about bad cards. You cannot will your hand to reach 21 points. What you can do is increase your odds of winning by making the smartest possible move.

Q: **Are these methods going to be 100% accurate?**

A: No. But, then again, neither is card counting to begin with. Even if the count were to be +19 in a 1-deck game, you wouldn't have a 100% confidence level that the next card would be a high card. Plus, at count levels you see most often -- counts in the single digits -- card counting methods will give you *far* less than 100% accuracy. So, if you're comfortable with the level of accuracy you can achieve with card counting, then, you should be even happier with the level of accuracy you will achieve with the method I am unveiling in this chapter.

How Good Is This New System?

Although, as I always do, I am continuing my research and might refine this with new discoveries down the road, preliminary tests indicate that what I've come up with is impressively accurate. This should turn the tables, so to speak, to the players' advantage!

Here's how it stacked up in initial tests, which were based upon there being 7-players at the table, to make the per-round analysis that much more relevant (and tough!):

♦ On a complete round basis, *my method was either absolutely correct or accurate to within 1 or 2 points nearly 90% of the time!*

♦ Of the rounds where the estimate was off, more than *80% were within 1 or 2 points of the actual count -- well within an acceptable standard of error.* And that's after *all* 7 players' hands were taken into consideration! (In a real game situation, you'd know your own hand, and would have one less hand to worry about than was considered in this computer study, and so your per-round accuracy rate would be even higher!)

♦ On a hand-to-hand basis, *it proved to be nearly 80% dead-on accurate.*

I think you will agree that this method certainly passes the test. I offer it to you now, with the hope that it will be as helpful to you as I have found it to be. In the absence of anything else, it should certainly fill a void for you.

A Stab In The Dark

Interestingly enough, someone emailed me not long ago, upon reading mention of this chapter on my web site, and he suggested that the problem posed by the face-down cards had already been solved by another author!

That author's solution, according to the emailer? That players should assume all pairs of face-down cards to total -2 when the dealer's up card is a 7 through Ace; otherwise, they should assume those cards to total zero.

I think you will recognize shortly that this not only is a gross oversimplification with very little malice of forethought, but that it also totally overlooks the fact that there are different categories of cards that might be found face-down on the table, each of which requires its own special approach. (As you will see shortly, this method failed miserably when tested for accuracy.)

The Various Categories of Face-Down Cards

Let's start there. Let's list the various situations in which 2-card hand combinations might be hidden from our view when it's time for our turn. We can't tackle the problem until we understand that there are a number of reasons cards might wind up face-down, and that each reason filters out what types of cards they might be. Here are the different face-down card categories with which you must become familiar:

♦ **FIRST CATEGORY: Cards players slip under their bets immediately, when standing on their first two cards.** These are the cards that account for the majority of the face-down cards you'll have to reckon with. Within this category are subcategories we must identify, necessitated by the differing rules players follow, depending on what the dealer's up card might be. A player would not take a hit card, for example, if they had a hard total of 13 and the dealer's up card was a 4 through 6. One subcategory, therefore, would be cards we'd find slipped under players' chips when the dealer showed a 4 through 6, where most players would tend to stand with all stiffs (hard 12s through 16s). We would certainly not have to anticipate finding stiffs amongst the cards players immediately slip under their chips when the dealer showed a 7 through an Ace. In other words, each subcategory has its own mix of cards that we have to take into account.

♦ **SECOND CATEGORY: Cards players slip under their bets to stand AFTER receiving one or more hit cards.** This category of face-down cards is of a completely different complexion than the preceding category. There are even more subcategories we must divide these cards into, based upon not only what up card the dealer is showing, but, also, how many points the players eventually draw with hit cards, before standing.

♦ **THIRD CATEGORY: Cards held in the hands of players to your left.** It is not always possible to sit in the 3rd Baseman's seat, as I recommend in *Blackjack The SMART Way*, so if there are players to your left and they are indecisive, or if they need more cards, they will be holding their first two cards when your turn arrives. There are some players who will, inexplicably, hide their cards from you when you try to peek. They act as though you're trying to cheat on a test by looking at their answers! They don't understand that it is to everyone's mutual benefit to share this information. No matter. I will offer you a means of dealing with that unusual situation. For now, understand that this is one category of cards that might be hidden from your view.

♦ **FOURTH CATEGORY: The dealer's hole card.** While vexing, the dealer's hole card is never part of any card counting system, so, for the time being, we won't worry about it. My Strategic Card Analysis method (detailed in Chapter 12) enables you to guess what this is with good success.

♦ **FIFTH CATEGORY: The extra cards the dealer deals players, facedown, when they double down.** These cards will be almost impossible to determine. Fortunately, these cards account for only a fraction of a percent of the face-down cards, so it's not a huge loss if fellow players don't take the opportunity to peek at these cards as they're allowed, and show you or tell you what they have. You can't see the hole card, either.

Two Preliminary Assumptions Are Necessary

Of course, you might have noticed that I have made a big assumption in categorizing the various types of face-down cards. That is: to uncover the identity of those cards in the various situations players face, I have had to assume that all players at the table are following some form of commonly accepted Basic Strategy, and are doing so with consistency. Otherwise, any attempt at doing so would fail.

If you cannot make any presumptions about what card combinations players tend to stand on, or if you have to take into account the various styles of mistakes the worst of the beginners might commit versus each up card, this whole effort would become too difficult. (Don't forget -- if you have to start with the idea that amongst the players are those who have little or no clue as to what they are doing, then, to take them into account, you'd have to have the ability to analyze the games of the players at your table and determine which players were playing haphazardly, and then figure out what particular mistakes they'd be expected to make. Impossible.)

So, if you understand this necessary assumption, you should also agree, then, that any horrible players at your table will throw off your ability to use the method you're about to learn at its peak efficiency. *If you realize that there are players at your table making absolutely goofy and unpredictable moves, then, obviously, you cannot account for what cards they might place face-down at all. This illustrates another reason why I say that horrible players tend to mess up your ability to win. You should leave a table where you notice players are making moves without rhyme or reason.*

The Hands We Need Not Worry About

Fortunately -- and this should be obvious -- certain hands will be exposed to us by the time it's our turn. Players will turn up their cards if they: bust; have a blackjack; double; split; or, surrender. I mention this only to remind you why you might not see certain types of hands accounted for in the course of this chapter -- for example, hands that total 10, when facing the dealer's 2 through 7, where players would be doubling, and placing their first two cards face up for us to see.

The Variety of Hand Combinations

OK! Here's how it works. We will start by listing all of the possible two-card hand types that players might stand on, and in what situations.

On the chart on the following page, you will see that I have divided them into three major types:

❶   Card combinations that would instantly be slipped under player chips and stood upon, without the player requesting any hit cards.

❷   Card combinations that might sometimes fall into the first type, above, but not always. I refer to these as "hybrid hands" -- sometimes players stand on them; sometimes players request a hit card on top of them. It all depends upon what up card the dealer is showing.

❸   Card combinations players would stand on only if they had decided to take hit cards.

I have also listed in that chart the counts associated with each hand type, and the percentage of times players might expect to be dealt those types of two-card combinations. (The percentages were determined by analyzing my computer research results.)

I might have added one more type, that of cards that are rarely, if ever, stood upon, such as pairs of Aces and 8s, but only advanced players might do that, and only on rare occasions at that. In addition, pairs of Aces and 8s only crop up about .4% of the time, each, so those aren't worth even worrying about.

Notice that some combinations are subcategorized into neutral and positive manifestations. For example, hard 12s might be made up of a high card and a low card, such as a 10 and 2, resulting in a count of zero (neutral); or, they might be made up of two low cards, such as two 6s (which are not always split), resulting in a count of +2. Those two subtypes have different effects on our count, and aren't always going to be stood upon in the same situations.

In the pie chart, titled "Two Card Hand Types Overview" (on the top of page 216), you will see that players will get hands in the first type -- ones they always stand upon -- slightly more than a quarter of the time.

In the "NEVER" section, which is shown on the pie chart but not listed on the next page, are Blackjacks, which each player should get nearly 5% of the time, as well as pairs of Aces and 8s -- these are the ones we need not concern ourselves about, because they will never be among the face-down cards.

In a moment, you will see how all of this information comes together.

Most Up Cards Require Different Approaches

Here's how we will tackle the problem: we know that two factors determine whether your average player will stand on his or her cards -- namely, what up card the dealer shows, which is the most important factor; and the player's point total, which is really a secondary consideration, as you will

Two-Card Hand Types

ALWAYS UNDER CHIPS:	COUNT	%
HARD 17s: 10s & 7s	0	5%
HARD 17s: ALL OTHERS	-2	1%
HARD 18s (EXCEPT PAIRS OF 8s)	-2	5%
HARD 19s	-2	5%
HARD 20s	-2	9%
SOFT 19s (ACE-8)	-1	1%
SOFT 20s (ACE-9)	-1	1%
SOMETIMES UNDER CHIPS:		
SOFT 18s (ACE-7)	1	1%
PAIRS OF 9s	-2	0.4%
HARD 12s NEUTRAL COUNT	0	8%
HARD 12s POSITIVE (EXCEPT PAIRS OF 6s — SEE BELOW)	2	1%
HARD 13s NEUTRAL COUNT	0	7%
HARD 13s POSITIVE	2	1%
HARD 14s (EXCEPT PAIRS OF 7s — SEE BELOW)	0	7%
HARD 15s	0	7%
HARD 16s	0	6%
ONLY AFTER PLAYER HITS:		
SOFT 13s/3s (ACE-2)		1%
SOFT 14s/4s (ACE-3)		1%
SOFT 15s/5s (ACE-4)		1%
SOFT 16s/6s (ACE-5)		1%
SOFT 17s/7s (ACE-6)		1%
HARD 5s		1%
HARD 6s		1%
HARD 7s		3%
HARD 8s		3%
HARD 9s		4%
HARD 10s NEUTRAL		1%
HARD 10s POSITIVE		3%
HARD 11s NEUTRAL		3%
HARD 11s POSITIVE		3%
PAIRS OF 2s		0.4%
PAIRS OF 3s		0.4%
PAIRS OF 6s		0.4%
PAIRS OF 7s		0.4%

Two-Card Hand Types Overview

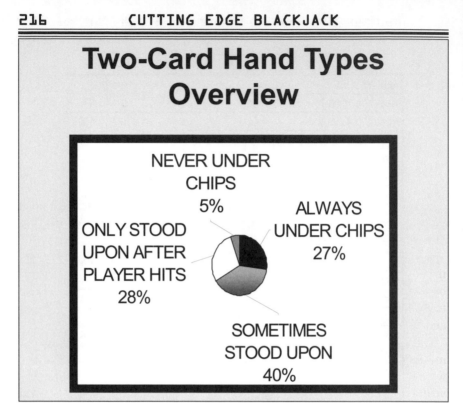

see.

We will use the *Cutting Edge Blackjack* Basic Strategy on pages ix-xii as the strategy we'll assume the other players are using. That way, we'll avoid the confusion of trying to keep track of too many different systems. *Cutting Edge* Basic Strategy has some important differences with other Basic Strategies, but it's not radically different.

Since the dealer's up card is the most important factor influencing player decisions, let's start there. Although Basic Strategy is very similar for the dealer's up cards of 2 and 3, they're different enough that we need to attack them separately. Fortunately, the dealer's 4 through 6 are handled the same, so we can lump them together when trying to figure out what's what. The up cards of 7 through the Ace are played similarly but there are enough differences to warrant individual treatment.

So, here we go. Let's divide the puzzle into its component parts and conquer it. We'll analyze how players tend to play versus each dealer up card, and see what conclusions we can draw.

Lists That Tell The Story

Now, we need to determine which two-card hand *types* players tend to stand on, within all the different types of face-card *categories* (which were listed on page 212). Each face-down card type plays out differently, and so we have to analyze each of them separately.

We'll tackle the card types in order, starting with the First Category face-down cards -- *cards players slip under their bets immediately when standing on their first two cards* -- understanding that this varies per dealer up card.

I'll walk you through my research process, using situations involving the dealer's up card of 2, to give you an understanding of the logic behind all of this.

Using the master list of two-card hand types on page 215, let's pick out the ones that players would most likely immediately stand upon versus the dealer's 2, because of Basic Strategy considerations. There are 13 such hand types that would fit this particular situation, as you can see in Chart 10-1 on the following page. With the assumption that most players stand on hard totals of 13 and up, and soft totals of 18 and up, when the dealer shows a 2, the list reflects all the various two-card permutations of those totals, listed by their respective card count totals. Notice that, with the hard 17s, we need to distinguish between the ones whose count totals zero (composed of 7s and 10s) and those that total -2 (composed of 8s and 9s).

To make this list work, I will plug in the percentages that I have determined, through my computer research, to reflect the correct proportions in which these various two-card combinations will appear, over time -- not versus the 2 in particular, but against all the dealer up cards (the percentages were rounded off for easy comprehension). This is necessary in order to give proper weight to the list's component parts, and get a handle on which card count totals predominate. Once we determine what the mathematical mix of face-down hands is, a profile then emerges which contains -- with some analysis -- a solution to part of our puzzle!

Understanding The Research-Generated Numbers

By summing up everything we've come up with (see the chart on the top of page 219), the secret identity of one subcategory of face-down cards has now been revealed! Let's examine what this means.

First, this summation indicates that, when the dealer has an up card of 2, and you spot players immediately standing on their first two cards, a majority of those hands will have a count total of 0. (Those neutral hands, of course, total zero because they are composed of one high card and one low card. Bear this in mind -- this added information will become more significant to you in the following chapter.)

Second, we cannot choose to ignore the fact that 43% of the time, those face-down hands will total something other than 0. While 8% of that is scattered thinly among three different count totals, that doesn't hide the fact that 35% of the time -- more than one third of the time -- these hands will total a count of -2. So...how will we account for that 35%? While that's a minority percentage, it nonetheless represents a sizable chunk of the hands

CHART 10-1:

First Category Face-Down Hands Versus The Dealer's 2

2 Card Hand Types	Count	%
Hard 13s neutral count	0	7%
Hard 13s positive	2	1%
Hard 14s (Except Pairs of 7s)	0	7%
Hard 15s	0	7%
Hard 16s (Except Pairs of 8s)	0	5%
Hard 17s: 7s & 10s	0	5%
Hard 17s: 8s & 9s	-2	1%
Hard 18s	-2	5%
Hard 19s	-2	5%
Hard 20s	-2	9%
Soft 18s (Ace-7)	1	1%
Soft 19s (Ace-8)	-1	1%
Soft 20s (Ace-9)	-1	1%

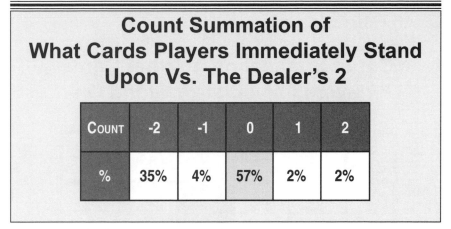

Count Summation of What Cards Players Immediately Stand Upon Vs. The Dealer's 2

COUNT	-2	-1	0	1	2
%	35%	4%	57%	2%	2%

we'll encounter in this situation.

Before I answer that question, let's follow through with the process we've begun, and list all the card count summations for *all* of the dealer up cards (see the chart on the following page). Then, we can unravel this part of the riddle in relation to *all* of the up cards, not just the 2.

The Answer To The Cards Players Immediately Stand On

Looking at the complete listing of card count results for all the various types of dealer up cards on the next page, can you see the pattern that has emerged? *The card count totals for cards players immediately stand on tend to reach one primary total,* depending on the dealer up card, *while having a significant secondary total that must be taken into account* when we design our method of demystifying those face-down cards.

It's fortunate, too, that only two of the five possible count totals seem to matter here -- namely, the count totals of -2 and 0. That will make the process of memorization simpler, when we put all of this information together in a cohesive system.

What else can we learn?

That, when players stand on their first two cards versus the dealer's 2 through 6, most of those hands consist of a high and low card (and total zero); however, a strong minority of those hands are composed of two high cards (and total 2). It is nearly the reverse situation for the dealer's 7 through Ace -- with the majority of instantly stood upon hands having a card count of -2 (hands of two high cards), and a minority of such hands having a count of zero (hands of one high card and one low card).

But, with the dealer's higher up cards, the percentage of hands that represent the minority count total is approximately half of what it is with the dealer's 2 through 6. Whereas the minority count total (-2) amounts to 31 to 35% with the dealer's 2 through 6, that percentage shrinks to 17 or 18% for the minority count total with the dealer's 7 through Ace -- it seems almost

CHART 10-2:

Count Summation of What Cards Players Immediately Stand On

Up Card	-2	-1	0	+1	+2
2	35%	4%	57%	2%	2%
3	36%	4%	58%	0%	2%
4-6	31%	4%	62%	0%	3%
7	70%	9%	17%	4%	0%
8	70%	9%	17%	4%	0%
9	73%	9%	18%	0%	0%
10	73%	9%	18%	0%	0%
Ace	70%	9%	17%	4%	0%

(Figures taken from author's most recent computer research.)

not worth considering. However, that impression disappears when you add up all the percentages of count totals that do not represent the majority count total, and you realize that they amount more than 25% of the immediately stood upon hands you will encounter when facing the dealer's 9 and 10, and nearly 33% of the hands you must consider versus the dealer's 7, 8 and Ace.

So, give some thought as to how you might want to acknowledge this fact.

While developing the methods described in this chapter -- I had at first tried to make things easier by seeing if it were possible to ignore those secondary hand combinations in estimating what the face-down cards were. In other words -- it would have been great if I could have said: when the up card is a 7, 8, 9, 10 or Ace, simply assume the cards immediately stood upon have a card count total of -2, and that they have a count total of zero with the up cards of 2, 3, 4, 5 and 6. That would have provided a simple solution to part of the problem. But that, regrettably, did *not* produce an acceptably *accurate* result. It did not correlate well with reality, when tested and compared with the card runs from my computer research project. So much for the easiest way out.

What The Numbers Are Telling Us

OK, so what have we come up with so far? What the numbers are telling us is not just simply what card count totals I tallied during my research. More importantly: these percentages are telling us a world of information about certain **probabilities**. That is, **they tell you the likelihood of players getting certain types of hands, and then, the likelihood of your finding them on the table when you are facing a particular up card.** Fantastic! That's pretty powerful stuff.

Let's do a quick example, using the chart on the previous page. Let's see if you can answer this question: if the dealer has a 9 or 10 as an up card, what is the *probability* that two-card hands that players immediately stand on versus the dealer's 2 might have a count of +1 or +2?

The answer is: because, as the chart shows, zeros were listed under those counts for the 9 and 10, the *probability* is *zero*. There's no way that could happen. Cards with counts of +1 and +2 would never be found immediately slipped under players' bets. *That's interesting, and quite useful information.*

The Chart Contains The Answers

Continuing along those lines, can you see that the chart holds the clue to our figuring out the identity of the First Category face-down cards?

Remember what I said, on page 219, that these player cards tend to primarily be of one card count total, with a secondary count also appearing in signficant enough numbers that it could not be dismissed?

Let's continue to look at the situations where we're facing either the dealer's 9 or 10, for instance. Referring back to the chart, you can see that the *probability* that the First Category face-down hands would total -2 is 73%. That's the majority total. The rest of the hands immediately stood upon would have an 18% *probability* of being *neutral* hands (a high and a low card), and a 9% *probability* of totalling *-1* (consisting of an Ace and a high card). The neutral hands are the secondary count I talked about earlier. In this case, while there's a count of tertiary importance (the soft hands, with a count of -1), it's small enough that we can safely ignore it in doing our identity estimates.

So...*the numbers are telling you that three in four First Category face-down hands has a count of -2, and roughly one in four is neutral (with a count of zero)*. Therefore, *the trick in including these cards in our card count, and discovering their identity, is to take this reality into account.*

Rotating Count Estimates (RCEs)

How can we implement this idea? With a new concept: the *Rotating Count Estimate*. Here's how Rotating Count Estimates, or RCEs, work:

Let's start with the First Category face-down cards, in cases where the dealer has an up card of 2 through 6. These face-down cards exhibit a count of zero 57% to 62% of the time, depending on the up card. A strong minority of cards -- from between 31% and 36%, depending on the up card -- total a different count, that of -2.

To make these numbers easier to use, we need to round them out a little, and say that the majority count -- the zero counts -- show up in roughly three out five of these hands, and the minority count -- the -2 counts -- account for about two out of five of these hands. That's expressing things in groups of five. Or, we can say it approximates a 66%-33% split. That's expressing things in groups of three. Both approximations are fairly accurate -- and I actually created a method that paid respect to both!

To reflect this reality, I devised a **Rotating Count Estimate system**. Here's how it works:

You will assign a count of **zero** to the *first pair* of First Category face-down cards, a count of **-2** to the *second* such pair, and a count of **zero** to the *third* pair. That ensures that the majority and minority counts are accounted for, in their correct proportions.

So, for the dealer's *low* up cards, that gives us a *Rotating Count Estimate* sequence, or RCE, of **0, -2, 0**. *If more than three players stand upon their first two cards, go to the beginning and start the sequence again.* My tests showed that this RCE performed admirably.

(I tested other similar RCEs, in looking for the one that would give you the most precise results, and this won out. See the charts on pages 224-225 if you're interested in knowing what other RCEs were tested, and what their accuracy rates were. Please note: *the column "Within 2 Points" represents the percentage of times the sequences either were dead-on accurate, or accurate to within 1 or 2 points, in estimating the sum of all First Category face-down hands in a round.*)

We'll need a different RCE for the dealer's *high* up cards, as you can tell from the numbers in Chart 10-2 (page 220). While the First Category face-down cards versus the dealer's 7 through Ace again are primarily of just two different card counts (one *majority* and *one minority* count), in this case, the majority count, *-2*, appears *70% to 73% of the time*, and the minority count, *zero,* appears 17% to 18% of the time. In this case, the majority count accounts for about three of four of the First Category face-down hands and the minority count, one of four. So a *four*-hand RCE would seem to work best here. But the final winner for accuracy, after numerous RCEs were tested for this group, was an RCE that could be expressed in groups of three: **-2, -2, 0**. The wonderful thing about that was that it kept things easy.

By the way, I also tested the method suggested by the emailer I talked about on page 211 -- that of assuming all face-down cards total a count of 0 if the dealer's up card is a 2 through 6, or, -2 if the dealer's up card is 7 through Ace. Notwithstanding the fact that this approach doesn't work at all for other types of face-down cards, you can see from the test results, represented in charts on the prior pages, that this approach performed the *worst*. In fact, in the case of the dealer's low up cards, it flunked miserably.

The Final Results For First Category Face-Down Cards

Now, one of my subsidiary goals in all of this was to make the final result -- the method you would use -- as easy to memorize and apply as possible, so I am especially pleased with these results.

Here are the RCEs you will use to figure out the count of the face-down cards immediately stood upon:

♦ **Use the RCE of 0, -2, 0, when the dealer has an up card of 2 to 6. We will refer to this RCE in the future as RCE #1.**

♦ **Use the RCE of -2, -2, 0, when the dealer has an up card of 7 to Ace. We will refer to this RCE in the future as RCE #2.**

This should be easy for you to remember. These sequences differ only with regard to the first number in the patterns.

To use these, as suggested before, simply assign the count totals to successive face-down hands (those that were immediately stood upon) in this fashion: choose the appropriate RCE listed above, and then assume that the initial First Category face-down hand's count total is the first count in the sequence; if there's a second such face-down hand, assume that hand's count total to be the second count in the sequence; if there's a third such face-down hand, assume that its count total to be the third count in the sequence; if there's a fourth such face-down hand during the same round, go back to

CHART 10-3:

Rotating Count Estimates: Accuracy Test Results

FOR HIGH DEALER UP CARDS:

Rotating Count Estimate Sequence	Within 2 Points	Dead-on Accuracy
-2,0,-2,-2 (Tempting But No)	95%	40%
-2,-2,0 (Our Choice)	93%	55%
-2,-2,-2,0 (Close, But No)	90%	57%
All -2 (Emailer/Other Author)	89%	54%

FOR LOW DEALER UP CARDS:

Rotating Count Estimate Sequence	Within 2 Points	Dead-on Accuracy
0,-2,0 (Our Choice)	80%	34%
0,0,-2 (Close, But No)	79%	29%
0,-2,0,-2,0	69%	28%
0,-2,0,-2,0,-2	67%	28%
All 0 (Emailer/Other Author)	56%	20%

CHART 10-4:

Accuracy Comparisons

THREE METHODS VS. HIGH UP CARDS

Information	-2,-2,0 (Our Choice)	-2,-2,-2,0 (Close But No)	All -2 (Emailer)
Estimates That Are Dead-on Accurate or Within Two Points	93%	90%	89%
Estimates That Are Off	45%	43%	46%
Percentage of Estimates That Are Off, But That Are Within 1 or 2 Points	84%	76%	75%
Estimates That Are Off By More Than 2 Points	7%	10%	11%

THREE METHODS VS. LOW UP CARDS

Information	0,-2,0 (Our Choice)	0,0,-2 (Close But No)	All 0 (Emailer)
Estimates That Are Dead-on Accurate or Within Two Points	80%	79%	56%
Estimates That Are Off	66%	71%	80%
Percentage of Estimates That Are Off, But That Are Within 1 or 2 Points	70%	70%	45%
Estimates That Are Off By More Than 2 Points	20%	21%	44%

the beginning of the RCE again. Of course, with the start of a new round, you'd start the process all over again.

The beauty of these three-number rotating patterns is that, not only do they make things easy for you, but they ingeniously reflect the split between majority and minority counts we discussed before. Here's how:

We agreed that, with the dealer's low up cards, that a three- or five-hand model would work best. With the 0,-2,0 pattern, you have both models covered: with the first three face-down hands you consider, you've assigned 33% of the counts to the minority count of -2 (and 0,-2,0 would have been our choice for a three-hand model); if there are five such hands, your estimate would go thusly: 0,-2,0,0,-2. That assigns 40% of the counts to the minority count of -2 (and, in fact, 0,-2,0,0,-2 would have been the five-hand model we would have used).

With the dealer's high up cards, we agreed that a four-hand model would work best. With the -2,-2,0 pattern we've chosen, we see that, if there were four face-down hands being considered, our estimate would go thusly: -2,-2,0,-2 (which is the four-hand model we would have chosen to use had I not come up with a simpler solution), with a 75%/25% split between majority and minority counts, which closely resembles actuality.

Remember: it is our inclusion of the minority count that makes this method so effective. With minority counts in these situations ranging from 31% to 36%, granted, there is some approximation involved. But, it is the best we can do, and, more important, *it works very well*.

Why Do The Dealer's Low Up Cards Present A Problem?

One word before we move on. I'd like to address the problem presented by the dealer's low up cards -- namely, the factors that cause our accuracy levels to be lower than with the high up cards (see charts on pages 224-225).

There are a number of reasons for this:

1 **The mix of First Category face-down hands is of a greater variety with the dealer's low up cards than with the dealer's high up cards.** With a greater variety, there's a greater number of hand count possibilities. For example, NONE of these hands totals +2 with the dealer's higher up cards, whereas the mix for the dealer's lower up cards covers *all five* possible two-card hand counts! With a greater range of hand count possibilities comes a greater potential for final round counts that are way off from the average, expected count.

2 **Players stand on more of their first two-card hands versus the dealer's low up cards.** This means you have more such hands to estimate. With the dealer's high up cards, players only stand on strong totals; with the low up cards, players often stand on stiffs or underscores. The more hands you need to estimate, the greater potential for a final estimate that might be off by more than two points.

3 **A far greater number of immediately stood upon hands represent just one count, the majority count, versus the dealer's high up cards.** There's less guesswork to do when nearly 75% of the hands you're concerned about total a count of -2. With the low up cards, the majority count percentage is closer to 50%. A 50-50 situation, of course is harder to call.

In spite of all of this, the method is a very sound one.

How To Estimate The Second Category Face-Down Cards

The Second Category of face-down cards we must contend with is that of the cards players place face-down in order to stand AFTER taking hit cards. As you will see, this category has to be handled entirely differently than the first.

The first difference you will notice is that, while the First Category dealt with zeros and negative numbers, this category deals with zeros and positive numbers. In other words, the face-down cards in the category we're about to consider is skewed toward hands containing low cards.

The second difference is that we cannot use a rotating sequence here. Why? Because, here, TWO factors govern what the probable count is: not just the dealer's up card, but also *what total each player draws to*. That total really ferrets out what those cards might be.

Another reason is that this category of face-down cards is more diverse in composition than the first (which would naturally gravitate toward more predictable hands, with strong totals). With the Second Category of face-down cards, most up cards, in fact, generate face-down hands that tend toward *three* different counts, depending on the hit card situation, unlike the First Category of face-down cards, with which we only had to worry about two possible counts.

Yet another interesting phenomenon is the fact that, with the method I have developed for this Second Category, *nearly one third of all errors that result either cancel each other out for the round they're in, or neutralize other in-round errors so that the final round Count Estimate is off just 1 point.* Errors, after all, can either add together, or subtract from each other; it just so happens that, with my method for this category, the happy latter result happens frequently.

Accuracy Rates

Studies reveal that the method I'm about to unveil performs very, very well. Here are some details:

Nearly 90% of individual hand estimates proved to be either dead-on accurate, or accurate to within one point. Approximately 80% were dead-on accurate.

On a complete-round basis, the numbers were equally impressive:

About 65% of the complete-round estimates were dead-on accurate. Of the estimates that were off, nearly 95% were within a very acceptable error limit of 1 or 2 points. Only 6 percent of complete-round estimates were off more than 2 points.

Also -- your accuracy rate overall will actually be better than that. In the course of a round, when combined with the method for the First Category face-down hands, the slight errors of one method tended to cancel out or neutralize the slight errors of the other.

How We Go About This

Early on, in experimenting with various approaches, when I realized that it was *the point total of the hit cards players stood upon* that was the key to demystifying the Second Category of face-down cards, I knew what the next step would be: to look at all the possible hit card totals a player might arrive at without busting, and then figure out what two-card hand combinations might be stood upon in those situations, versus each of the various up cards.

My list went from one-hit-card possibilities, starting with the Ace, to multiple-card scenarios that totalled up to 18 points. Anything above that would bust all possible two-card hands (excluding two Aces, which we know 99.99% of all players would *always* split -- that's a no brainer -- so we won't be worrying about finding those face-down).

The player who stands on one solitary Ace hit card presents us with our most difficult problem, regarding the Second Category of face-down cards. The question you have to wonder about then is: is the player taking that Ace as a 1-point card, or an 11-point card? That changes the whole complexion of what that player's stood upon face-down cards might be.

If the Ace results in a weak total for the player -- in other words, the Ace can't be an 11-pointer, and, as a 1-pointer, it leads to a stiff total, or a weak total of 17 -- the player might verbally, or with body language indicate their disappointment, but stand anyway. That expression of disappointment would obviously solve the riddle for us. But don't hope for that gift too often.

I decided that the safe way to go was to start with a composite picture of all face-down cards that might be stood upon with a solitary Ace. If you look at Illustration 10-5 on the next page, you'll get an idea of what I mean. This is an example of how my research was done. This particular example is for hands that might be stood upon with a solitary Ace, when facing the dealer's 2. (In Chart 10-6, on page 230, you will see the results of my complete analysis of the composite Ace, for all the dealer up cards, in the "Ace overall" row.)

(I later separated out the situations you would encounter if you were able to figure out somehow that the solitary Ace hit card counted as a 1, or an 11; but, most times, without some indication of happiness or disappointment

ILLUSTRATION 10-5:

Composite Ace Vs. 2

Face Down Cards Total	Count	%
Hard 7s	2	3%
Hard 8s	2	3%
Hard 9s	2	3%
Hard 12s neutral count	0	8%
Hard 12s positive	2	1%
Two 6s	2	.4%
Soft17s/7s (A6)	1	1%

-2	-1	0	1	2
0.00%	0.00%	38.74%	7.33%	53.93%

Projected Count After 100:	(54 X 2 Points)+(7 X 1 Point) + (39 X 0 Points) = 115
If We Assume Hands = 0	0 Points X 100 Hands = 0
If We Assume Hands = 1	1 Point X 100 Hands = 100
If We Assume Hands = 2	2 Points X 100 Hands = 200

CHART 10-6:

Counting The Second Category Face-Down Cards

HIT CARD POINT TOTALS	2	3	4-6	7	8	9	9 W/OUT SURR	10	10 W/OUT SURR	ACE	ACE W/OUT SURR
ACE OVERALL	+1	+1	+2	+1	+1	+2	+1	+2	+1	+2	+1
ACE AS 1	+1	+1	X	0	0	X	X	X	X	X	X
ACE AS 11	+1	+1	+2	+2	+2	+2	+1	+2	+1	+2	+1
2	0	0	X	0	0	0	0	0	0	0	0
3	+1*	0	X	0	0	0	0	0	0	0	0
4	+1*	+1*	+2	0	0	0	0	0	0	0	0
5	+1*	+1*	+2	0	0	0	0	0	0	0	0
6	+1*	+1*	+2	0	0	0	0	0	0	0	0
7	+1*	+1*	+2	0	0	0	0	0	0	0	0
8	+1*	+1*	+2	+1*	+1*	+1*	+1*	+1*	+1*	+1*	+1*
9	+1*	+1*	+2	+1*	+1*	+1*	+1*	+1*	+1*	+1*	+1*
10	+2	+2	+2	+2	+2	+2	+2	+2	+2	+2	+2
11	+2	+2	+2	+2	+2	+2	+2	+2	+2	+2	+2
12	+2	+2	+2	+2	+2	+2	+2	+2	+2	+2	+2
13	+2	+2	+2	+2	+2	+2	+2	+2	+2	+2	+2
14	+1	+1	+2	+1	+1	+1	+1	+1	+1	+1	+1
15	+1	+1	+2	+1	+1	+1	+1	+1	+1	+1	+1
16	+1	+1	+2	+1	+1	+1	+1	+1	+1	+1	+1
17	+1	+1	X	+1	+1	+1	+1	+1	+1	+1	+1
18	+1	+1	X	+1	+1	+1	+1	+1	+1	+1	+1

from the player getting the Ace, it might be impossible to tell whether the Ace was a 1 or 11 -- in which case, the composite, or "overall" Ace, works just fine. However, in Chart 10-6 you'll find the recommendations for the Ace as a 1, or the Ace as an 11, for those rare occasions when you know for sure what that Ace is.)

By the way, one note about Aces in the mix of hit cards. If a player takes more hit cards after receiving an Ace, it's best to assume that Ace is a 1-pointer. In that situation, most Aces would be.

OK. So, in Illustration 10-5, look at the top chart. There, I've listed all the two-card hands a player might stand on after receiving just one hit card of an Ace, versus the dealer's 2. The percentages representing the proportions in which each type of two-card combination appears over time come from the chart on page 215.

In the middle chart on page 229, I have summarized the top chart's data, to show the count breakdown for the face-down cards we're examining. While it appears that the +2 count is the majority count, the numbers are actually a bit deceptive. Look at the bottom chart now. In that chart, you see the calculations made from the middle chart, in which I've projected that the actual count for the face-down hands we're investigating would total 115 points over the course of 100 such hands. Now, you can see that, in estimating what these hands might be, we should assume that their individual count total to be +1. Although this means our estimated count will only be dead-on 7% of the time, this compromise is necessary, in order to give us overall greater accuracy.

I think that gives you a good idea of the process behind this research. To complete it, I then continued this type of analysis, for each possible hit card total versus each different type of dealer up card, and arrived at the recommendations you see in Chart 10-6. If you can memorize a Basic Strategy chart, and card counting charts, you certainly can handle this one.

The hit card totals are listed in the leftmost column; the dealer up cards, in the topmost row. In no time at all, you'll notice that there are patterns in blocks that make your job of remembering this chart that much simpler.

In fact, versus the dealer's 4 through 6, you have no job at all! ALL the face-down cards stood upon after player hits can be assumed to total a count of +2. (The Xs in the 4-6 column, by the way, point out situations that would never occur, because all two-card hands would either be doubled upon or split, and would not be found face-down under players' chips.)

One thing that makes learning this easy, right off the bat, is that ALL hit card totals of 10 through 13, no matter what the up card, can be safely estimated to have a count total of +2. Similarly, for most hit cards, except those versus the dealer's monolithic 4-6 up card situations just mentioned, hit card totals of 14 through 18 can always be taken as a pretty good sign that the player hand count is +1. In fact, to backtrack a bit, that's true of hit card point totals of 8 and 9, too.

Notice too, that the columns that offer alternate suggestions if the casino doesn't allow surrender really only pertain to one rare situation, which we've just talked about in part -- that is, when the player stands on a solitary Ace. If you're at a casino that offers surrender (and that's always desirable), you'll assume the player's face-down cards total +2 versus the dealer's strongest up cards -- the 9, 10 and Ace; and, if you're at a casino where surrender is prohibited, you'll assume the player's face-down cards in those situations total +1.

One more note: you'll see that some of the cells that have the number 1 in them are set off with an asterisk, or are white in color. The 1s with the asterisks are cells where you are *approximating* the count, with a +1, to solve the problem of a complex count profile. You will actually come closer to the real count that way. But, it is important to understand that this does *not* indicate there is an Ace in most of these hands. The black 1s *without asterisks* are *cells where Ace combinations (soft hands) predominate. That is important to remember -- the probable presence of an Ace will often give us a clue as to how to handle our hands*. The *white* 1s indicate hands in which *one of the cards is DEFINITELY an Ace -- this is true 100% of the time.* Powerful stuff, if you think about it.

A Quick Way To Make Sense Of This

The shading should help you memorize Chart 10-6. But I have some suggestions to make things even easier.

❶ We'll always assume the Second Category face-down cards have a +2 count when players take 10 through 13 points in hit cards.

❷ With the above in mind, when you're facing the dealer's 2 and 3, attribute a count of +1 to all the *other* hit card point totals (there are just three boxes that conflict with this simplification, in a minor way, and these situations won't come up that often).

❸ Versus the dealer's 4, 5 and 6, all Second Category face-down cards will get a count of +2. So *that's* easy.

❹ When facing the dealer's 7 through Ace, there are primarily four blocks of counts to deal with. The Second Category face-down cards will be estimated to have a count of *0,* when players take hit cards totalling two through seven points; *+1,* with totals of 8 and 9 points; *+2,* with hit cards of 10 to 13 points; and *+1,* with any higher totals. (Recognizing the somewhat logical sequence of *0, +1, +2, +1* in this section should help.)

❺ Finally, we need to account for the hands where players stand after receiving just an Ace. If you're playing at a casino that does *not* allow surrender, this is a piece of cake. We'll count those as +1, except with up cards of 4 to 6, where, as always, we'll count them as +2. In places where surrender *is* allowed, we can use this shorthand method: we'll say these hands count +1, unless you're facing the dealer's 4 through 6, or 9 through Ace. Then, we'll assume their count totals +2.

The few shortcuts suggested above should make your job a lot easier, which makes any minor loss in precision excusable.

Take some time now to familiarize yourself with Chart 10-6. This chart, combined with the Rotating Count Estimate sequences you learned earlier, will provide you with the tools you need to FINALLY (after how many years?) account for those pesky face-down cards that have hindered your card counting for so long.

In the next chapter, we'll actually take this one step further, in unveiling more information about those cards. A card counting approach alone isn't enough.

Now, in a moment, we'll apply what you've just learned to examples of actual situations you will encounter. But, first, let's briefly talk about the final, less troublesome categories of face-down cards you need to know about.

The Third Category Of Face-Down Cards

Let's talk about the problem of figuring out the identity of the cards held, out of view, in the hands of players to your left -- the Third Category face-down cards.

First of all, if you cannot sit in the 3rd Baseman's seat, which would eliminate this difficulty entirely, you can minimize the problem by sitting as close to 3rd Base as possible, so there are only one or two players at most whose hands you'd need to worry about. If that's not possible, create a rapport with the players involved so that they feel comfortable showing you their cards. Tilt your cards in their direction to indicate your willingness to help *them*, and players usually will reciprocate the favor.

That being said, there are inevitably some players who -- out of ignorance -- jealously guard their cards from your view. So here's what you'll do to estimate the counts of the hands they are holding:

Assume these hands to count +1 versus all the up cards -- except the 4 through 6, where you'll estimate them to count +2.

(Note: the +1 count represents a compromise between accuracy and ease of use. It is a count *approximation* and is not meant to signify that all or most of these hands contain Aces. They don't.)

Now, when you're ready to tackle a more precise but involved method, use the approach in the chart on the bottom of the next page. For most players, this might seem daunting, however -- therefore, the reason for the easier system mentioned above.

ILLUSTRATION 10-7:

Counting The Third Category
Face-Down Cards
SIMPLE SOLUTION

Up Card	Your Count Estimate
2	+1
3	+1
4-6	+2
7	+1
8	+1
9	+1
10	+1
Ace	+1

MORE ACCURATE SOLUTION

Up Card	Preferred Estimate	If No Surrender
2	+2, 0, +2	
3	+2, 0, +2	
4-6	+2	
7	0, +2, 0	
8	0, +2, 0	
9	+1	0, +2, 0
10	+1	
Ace	+1	0, +2, 0

The Fourth And Fifth Categories of Face-Down Cards

Finally, let's talk about the last two categories of face-down cards.

You'll be using my Strategic Card Analysis system to tackle the Fourth Category face-down cards, the dealer's hole cards. All of this will be explained in Chapter 12.

The Fifth Category face-down cards -- the extra card players get when doubling -- poses our biggest challenge. Unless fellow players peek at these cards and show you or tell you what they have, you will have a hard time unmasking what they are. Unfortunately, most players don't realize they're allowed to turn up these cards, so you'll only rarely get a glimpse of them. A suggestion: take the initiative, and show the other players the extra cards *you* get when you double down. Just pull it up a bit off the table and give them a look -- I've never been in a casino that prohibits that. If you set the precedent, perhaps the others will follow your lead.

Otherwise, you'll have to use the card flow analysis skills you will learn in Chapter 12 to make an educated guess as to their identity.

OK. Now it's time for some fun! Let's put all of this together, and apply what you've learned, with some quizzes to test your skill, using actual examples culled from my research card runs.

Some Card Examples To Test Your Skill

Let's start by going back to Examples A and B on page 209. Let's make things simple by assuming both of these occurred during the first round following a shuffle, meaning that the count was zero before these cards were dealt.

Take a moment now and use the methods you've just learned to figure out: 1) what the card count is likely to be for both examples, when your turn arrives; and, 2) what you should do with your hand, given the count you've come up with.

How To Count: Example A

In Example A, you're sitting in 2nd Base. What you want to do now is arrive at a *Count Estimate*, using the method you've learned for demystifying the face down cards. You will update your *Count Estimate* continually, as player action unfolds.

OK; in this example, there are three players to your left, who have stood on their first two cards. Since the up card is in the 4-6 category, the Rotating Count Estimate you'll be using for those cards is *RCE #1: 0, -2, 0.* With three players fitting that category, you have a Count Estimate of -2 for their hands.

The dealer's up card being a low card, 4, the Count Estimate is now -1. Since you have two low cards -- 2 and 6 -- your Count Estimate is now +1.

The players to your right now have their turns. The 1st Baseman, turning over his first two cards, doubles. You can't see the extra hit card he received, because, like most players, he didn't know enough to peek at it. His upturned cards, however, 2 and 9, total a count of zero. You still have a Count Estimate of +1.

The next two players also double down on their hands. You don't know what their extra cards are, either, but their face-up cards now give you a Count Estimate of +4, with an Ace count of 1.

I found this example interesting, because it points out that you can indeed make good decisions even if a maximum number of players double down, and you can't make out what their extra cards are.

What should you do? Should you hit your hand of 8 points? Perhaps double?

You have a Count Estimate of +4, with three double down extra cards unknown to you. The overall count might seem to indicate that the dealer's hole card is a high card, which is what you want -- that would bust the dealer's 4 the most. If all of the double down extra cards are high cards (which is unlikely), you'd have a Count Estimate of +1. Then, if the hole card were also a high card, you'd have a neutral count, of course.

But -- ignoring the hole card for now (as is usually done with card counting) -- more than likely, at least one of the double down extra cards is a low card. So, your Count Estimate is likely, in fact, to be +3, or *higher*, if *two* of the three extra cards turned out to be low cards.

With the dealer's hand likely to bust, and a probable favorable positive count, I'd consider *doubling* here. The combination of those two factors makes it tempting.

How did this all play out in actuality?

Doubling down, the hand we said was yours drew a 10, for a total of 18. OK. The dealer's hole card turned out indeed to be a high card, as we had predicted -- a 10. Then, the dealer's hit card was a 9 -- again, no surprise to us. We knew the dealer was likely to bust.

How did our Rotating Count Estimate method of estimating the face-down cards work? The players to your left who stood on their first two cards had a 10-7, 8-10 and 4-10. Using the **0, -2, 0** Rotating Count Estimate, your estimate was dead-on accurate.

Incidentally, the extra cards the players had gotten, from the 1st Baseman on, were 8, 6, 4. So, our assumption that those cards would *not* be all high cards was also correct. The count, at your turn, was actually +5. We had figured it was likely to be +3 or +4, so we were within 1 or 2 points of reality, which is well within acceptable limits. Because this example was highly unusual, having several hands with face-down cards of the Fifth Category (whose count we rarely can surmise), it made this example much more difficult than your typical round of action. But, as you see, you were able to use my method and still make the right choices. *Without* my method, how would you have known what to do?

See how this works?

How To Count: Example B

Example B is a bit more typical of the situations you'll face. At least one player usually busts per round, at a table with 7 players, as you see with this example. That makes your job easier. You get to see their cards. There's a player Blackjack this round, too. No mystery there -- those cards are turned up. That makes things easier for you.

OK. Here's how you should go about deciphering what the cards are telling you:

The first cards you should tackle are the immediately stood upon hands. Because the dealer has an up card of 7, you should be using **RCE #2: -2, -2, 0.** So, you should figure that the two players to your right have hands whose counts are probably -2 each.

The up card of 7 makes the count -3. Your hand, a neutral hand, doesn't affect your Count Estimate.

The second player turned up her blackjack right away, so your Count Estimate now becomes -4, and your Ace count is now 1.

Now, the action begins. The 1st Baseman takes a 4 and stands. Looking at Chart 10-6, page 230, for this Second Category of face-down cards, you see that you should assume those cards to have a neutral count of zero. No change in your estimate because of the face-down cards. But the hit card of 4 makes your Count Estimate -3.

The third player takes a 7 and stands. Again, Chart 10-6 tells you to assume her face-down cards are neutral. No change in your estimate for her face-down cards. But her hit card of 7 now makes your Count Estimate -2.

The fourth player takes a 3 and then a 2, for a total of 5 points, and he then stands. And, once again, Chart 10-6, tells you that his face-down cards are likely neutral. No change in your Count Estimate for the face-down cards, but it does change to *zero* because of the two low hit cards.

It's now your turn. Your Count Estimate is zero. Your Ace count is 1, so you are unlikely to get an Ace with a hit card (you wouldn't want that!). So, should you double on your hand of 11?

Since we usually return to Basic Strategy when the count is zero, the answer is: yes, you should double here.

In fact, the cards ARE telling you something else, which you might not have noticed. And it's time to introduce you to something new: the *hit card count*. Look at the hit cards in this round: 4, 7, 3, 2. See a pattern? *They're all low cards*. If you took the count of the hit cards that came before your turn, you'd see they were *talking* to you, so to speak: their count is +4.

What does that tell you? Well, if you are thinking about doubling down, you want to know that your extra card is likely to be a 10, or, at least, a high card, don't you? The *hit card count* is telling you that this is *very likely to happen*. That's not a guess. It's based upon mathematics.

So, you now have confirmation of what you should do.

OK -- how did this round play out in actuality?

The hand we said was yours indeed drew a 10 as the extra card, which was predicted by the mathematical probabilities indicated by your hit card count. Your hand is sitting pretty with a total of 21, and it looks likely that you are going to win; and, win *twice* your original bet.

The dealer's hole card was a 2. The dealer's hit cards were 5, Ace, 10...the dealer busted! You win, having played wisely.

Of course, a Basic Strategy player would have made the same move, having been playing without regard to how the cards play out. But, we want to play smarter than that. If we make a move, we want to *know* it's the right one. The Basic Strategy player goes only upon the dealer's up card. But, as you know, that's only one important factor in the way a round plays out. You want to be able to react to all of the important factors in making your decision.

OK, now. How good was your Count Estimate, after all? That's what we're especially interested in -- perfecting what you've learned in this chapter. The 1st Baseman's face-down cards were a 9 and a 4. We figured they'd be neutral. The third player had a 6 and a 9. We guessed they'd be neutral, too. The 2nd Baseman had a 3 and a 10. We also guessed those would be neutral. The two players to your right both had pairs of 10s. You had figured that those hands would both have counts of -2. Your estimate was *dead-on accurate*.

This should be no surprise. You are not using tea leaves here. You are basing your estimate on sound mathematical principles.

Let's look at one more example before we move on.

How To Count: Example C

Now, one of the supposed Gospel Truths in blackjack is that you always split Aces, right? ALWAYS. So Example C (on the next page) should be a no-brainer.

This time around, you have a card count, 8 count, 9 count and 10 count that carries over from one prior round. So, as you can see -- with the 8, 9 and 10 counts -- we are now incorporating your Advanced Card Analysis skills into this example.

You're the 3rd Baseman; you have two Aces. (Remember -- this example came straight from my computer research card runs; it's a true card situation, and it's one which you'll eventually find yourself facing.)

1-DECK: WHAT'S THE COUNT AT YOUR TURN?
...SO HOW WOULD YOU PLAY YOUR MOVE?

PRIOR ROUND:
8 COUNT: 2
9 COUNT: 1
10 COUNT: 6
CARD COUNT: +4

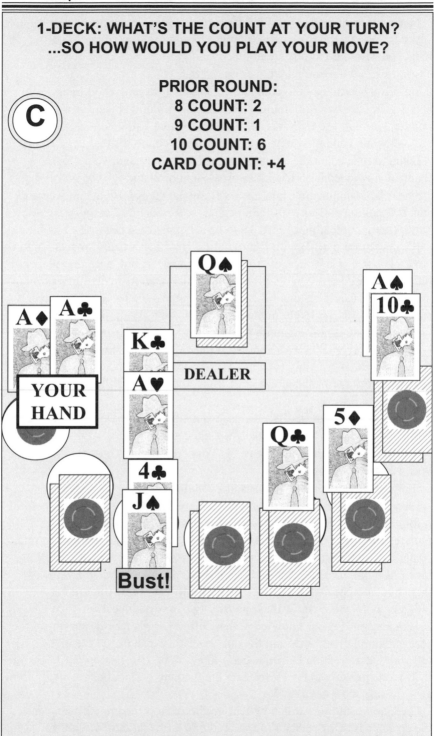

Take a moment now to analyze the cards and decide not only what the card count is, based upon the methods taught to you in this chapter, but also, what you would do in this situation.

OK. Here's what you may have figured out:

First, you should have looked at the cards that players stood upon right away. There are two such hands. Because the dealer's up card is a 10 pointer, you will use RCE #2: -2,-2,0. Your Count Estimate for this round is now -4; when combined with the prior round's count, it's 0.

Taking into account the dealer's up card and your hand, your Count Estimate now becomes -1, with an Ace count of 2, and a 10 count of 7.

Fine. The action begins, and the 1st Baseman takes a 10 and an Ace and stands. Looking at Chart 10-6, on page 230, for Second Category face-down hands (knowing that the Ace HAS to be a 1-point card because of its hit card companion the 10), you figure the 1st Baseman's face-down cards to have a count of +2. Your Count Estimate is now +1, but, with that player's hit cards, it becomes 0, with an Ace count of 3, and a 10 count of 8.

The next player takes one hit card, a 5. Chart 10-6 tells you that player's stood upon cards are likely to have a neutral count. With the hit card, your Count Estimate is now +1, with an Ace count of 3, and a 10 count of 8.

The next player takes a Queen and stands. Chart 10-6 says that player's face-down cards probably total +2, and so -- with the Queen and those cards -- your Count Estimate becomes +2. Your Ace count is still 3, but your 10 count is now 9.

One player busts, as is often the case at a table with 7 players. That makes things easier. That player's cards had a net count of -1.

So, your final Count Estimate is +1. Your Ace count is now full, at 4, and your 10 count is up to 11.

How should you play your cards, do you think?

Take a moment to look at the *hit card count*, which often provides helpful information. With three 10s, two Aces and a 5, it offers a pretty clear picture, doesn't it? The count is -2, indicating that low cards might be due.

But, let's see what your card analysis skills are telling you, too. With the hit cards, your 10 count is now 11 (out of 16 possible 10s); with three of them having appeared in the six cards prior to your turn, you are very unlikely to get what you want -- namely two, or even one 10.

Added to this is your knowledge that, with 11 cards face-down (the players' stood upon cards and the dealer's hole card), the Circle of 13 would tell you that at least three of those are likely to be 10s (raising the 10 count to 14), one is likely to be a 9 (raising the 9 count to 2) and one is likely to be an 8 (raising the 8 count to 3).

There are just three cards now that might make you competitive against the dealer's 10: two outstanding 9s, and one 8 (the latter of which would give you a score below the average score of the dealer's 10). Not very good odds here.

Given all of this, you should have chosen to *hit* your Aces, instead of splitting them. Don't forget -- Basic Strategy recommendations provide you with an averaged out picture of what to do: they provide the forest and not the trees. They cannot and do not account for every card situation in which you will find yourself.

If, as an advanced player, you KNOW you are unlikely to get one good hand out of your split Aces, you'd be a fool to split them. Don't forget -- you are not basing your decision on feelings or hunches. Your decision is based upon *firm mathematics*: an accounting of the availability of cards you need to achieve a score that is likely to beat or push with the dealer.

OK. Here's how the round played out, in actuality:

The virtual player whose hand we said was yours indeed split those Aces, because all such players in my computer research *always* split Aces, to reflect the average player. So, we know what you would have received had you done what this player decided to do: *a 6 and a 2*. Horrible! But you and I *knew* that this was the likely result -- that two bad hands would be created if you had split your Aces.

With one hand now totalling 17 and the other 13, what would you think your prospects would have been versus the dealer's 10? Let's find out!

It's the dealer's turn... The dealer's hole card is...an 8. The player playing your hand loses BOTH split Ace hands, as I had predicted. Even though the dealer drew to a score that was below the average total for the up card of 10, the split Aces were so weak, they could not even beat or push against an 18.

In a later chapter, I'll talk more about splitting and doubling in dicey situations that you need to learn to recognize.

But, more important for now, let's see how accurate your Count Estimate was.

First, you said that the two hands immediately stood upon were likely to have a count of -2. They, indeed, were hands of 10-9 and 9-10. You were right. You were also right, using your card analysis skills, that there were 10s and at least one 9 amongst the face-down cards.

You correctly predicted that the 1st Baseman's face-down cards totalled +2 (they were a pair of 3s); that the next player's cards were of a neutral count (they were 6 and 10); and, that the next player's cards totalled +2 (they were a 2 and a 6).

Your Count Estimate was *dead-on correct*. AND -- more than that -- with the added information you gained by being able to decipher what those 11 face-down cards were, using the method you learned in this chapter, you were able to make a brilliant move: you HIT your Aces, and drew the 6 and 2 (you would not have stood on a soft 18 versus the 10) for a score of 20, beating the dealer. You were up by one bet, rather than splitting unwisely and winding up TWO bets *down*. If you'd split, in fact, you'd have been

THREE bets down from where you wound up, as a winner, by hitting your hand. Your decision to hit your hand was based not on a whim, but upon intelligent mathematical logic. Interestingly enough, too -- you proved that you should NOT always split your pairs of Aces. But, we'll talk more about that later on.

Now -- this bears repeating: will you be dead-on accurate in every round? No, and, in fact, we discussed this issue before. Your Count Estimate *will*, however, be absolutely correct, or within 1-2 points of the actual count, *a great majority of the time* -- if you've forgotten the specifics, you should go back and reread the sections in this chapter that go into great detail regarding the high levels of accuracy you can reasonably expect to achieve.

What Should You Do Now?

Congratulations! You are now amongst the first players in history to know how to account for all the face-down cards that have plagued players for decades at the 1- and 2-deck tables.

It's very important that you spend ample time practicing this method, so it becomes second nature to you *before* using it at the casino. Just like card counting, you need to be able to do this fluidly and without outward signs of strain or effort that might be detected by casino personnel.

You might want to set this book aside for a moment and test your newfound skills!

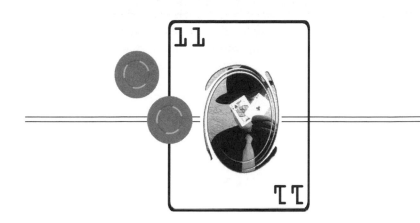

How To Do
Advanced Card Analysis
At 1- & 2-Deck Tables

I am often asked: "Your Advanced Card Analysis* system is great, but, with all the face-down cards, how can I use it at the 1- & 2-deck tables?"

Here's the answer:

While those face-down cards that have been so daunting to players for so many decades seem so mysterious, you can actually unmask their *general* identities because the identities of those cards are *predictable, based on the laws of mathematical probability.* You cannot, of course, pick out the value of each individual card like a magician; you can, though, get a good idea of what each *set* of cards contains, in the way of card values. That usually is all you need to make an intelligent decision about how to play your hand.

You do not need to be a card counter to use the methods contained in this chapter. I am aware that many players do not count cards, so, for those players, this chapter will be especially useful. (Since I will occasionally refer to concepts introduced in the previous chapter, however, you still need to familiarize yourself with them, even if you're a non-card counter.)

The Good Side to the Face-Down Cards

One fascinating thing I noticed is that, in a way, casinos are actually doing players a *favor* by requiring certain cards to be placed face-down on the table -- if you know how to interpret those cards! That's right: the face-down cards often are actually *tipping you off* to certain conditions -- a depletion of high cards, for example -- that will make some card strategy decisions that much easier.

That's because the face-down cards often fall into a particular card category -- skewed toward low cards or high cards, for instance. So, their appearance can actually give us a shorthand summary of what's been played, and what cards are due.

The Questions We Need Answered

Now, of course, you cannot do as accurate an accounting of the dealt cards at a pitch game table as you can at shoe game tables, where all of the cards are face up, and you know *exactly* how many there are of each type of card. However, what's fantastic is that you *can* find answers to the major questions you have regarding those face-down cards, and do a good job of Advanced Card Analysis.

Below, you will find a list of questions you often need answered in order to make smart moves:

♦ **How many of the face-down cards are likely to be 10s?**

♦ **How many are likely to be 8s and 9s?**

♦ **How many are likely to be low cards?**

♦ **How many of the low cards are likely to be 3s, 4s and 5s?**

♦ **How many of the low cards are 4s, 5s and 6s?**

♦ **How many might be Aces?**

The answers to these questions are now obtainable, as you will soon see.

Now -- why do you want more information than you can get from the techniques you read about in the last chapter? Because we can get more *specific* about the details. Card counting gives you the relative division between high and low cards among the cards already played, which is great. But, to play at your best, you need even more information. If you look at Example A on page 246, you'll see what I mean. In this case, knowing the count (using the methods from the prior chapter) isn't enough. You especially need to know: how many 10s and Aces are likely to be among the face down cards, to know whether doubling is smart here. (Take a moment to see if you can figure out the best move in Examples A and B. We'll re-examine them after you've been introduced to some important concepts.)

Don't forget -- it's one thing to count cards at a table where you can see all the cards. It's another thing to do so where many of the cards are a mystery. So, given the handicap of being faced with those hidden cards, here are the times where you especially need answers to your questions:

❶ **When thinking of doubling down.** How can you double down with assurance, if you don't have a clue as to what hit card you are likely to get? If your point total is 10, it would be real helpful to know, for instance, if 10s, and perhaps, Aces, too, have been *depleted*. You would NOT want to double in that case, regardless of what the strategy charts say. To a lesser degree, knowing whether you're likely to get a 9 or an 8 can be valuable information, because a 9 or 8 can certainly turn your hard totals of 10 and 11 and certain soft totals into good scores, when doubling. However, getting an *Ace* when doubling on your 11 would NOT be very good, would it? Nor would it help to get a low card. So, you want to know if the *specific* cards you need for doubling are available, or not!

❷ **When thinking of splitting.** How can you place twice your bet on the line, when you're not sure if you're going to win or lose? What you need in this situation, of course, depends upon what cards you are thinking of splitting. If you have two Aces, for instance, you ideally want to get a 10 upon each Ace; 8s and 9s would make good partners for your Aces, too. If you have two 8s, however, you'd hope NOT to get two 10s. And so on. So, the point is, you want to know if you will get one of the *specific* cards you need, if you take a hit card.

❸ **When thinking of hitting a stiff -- especially your 15s and 16s.** How do you know if hitting your stiff is smart, when you don't know if the cards you need have been played out or not? This is perhaps the most vexing question to most players: should I hit my stiff and risk busting? In this case, you want to know that low cards are due. Wouldn't it be even better if you could know whether the *specific* low cards you need are due? -- 3s through 5s, especially, when you have a hard total of 16? And, if you have a 15, wouldn't you love to know if your hit card is likely to be one of the 4s through 6s? With the information you'll gain in this chapter, you will (finally!) be able to arrive at a likely answer to this most perplexing question.

❹ **When considering the dealer's likelihood of busting.** This is often the crux of the game -- knowing enough to stand when the dealer is likely to bust; but -- how can you do this if you don't know what cards have been played? Sometimes it's wisest to stand on a stiff if you're pretty certain the dealer is going to bust. This is not because of anything you learned from a strategy chart (don't forget -- *no* dealer up card busts a *majority* of the time), but because of the cards that were dealt and the cards that are likely to come. And vice versa -- if *low* cards are due, and the dealer is likely NOT to bust, it might be smart to hit your stiff or soft

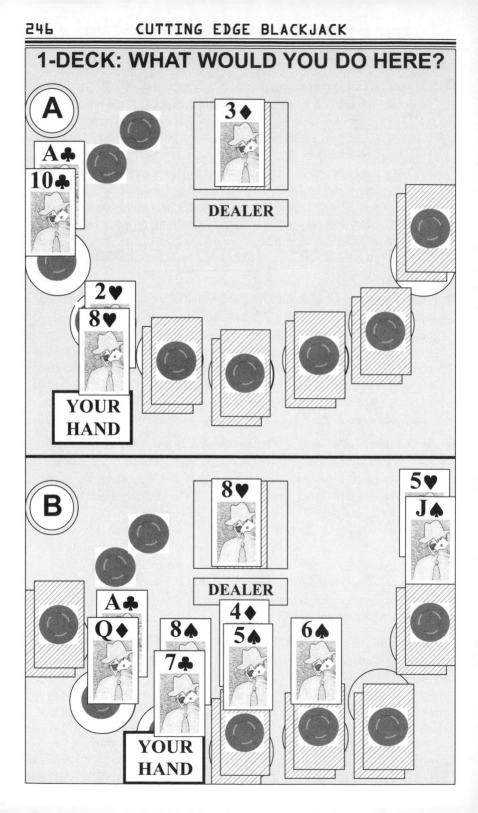

1-DECK: WHAT WOULD YOU DO HERE?

A

3♦

DEALER

A♣
10♣

2♥
8♥

YOUR
HAND

B

8♥

5♥
J♠

DEALER

A♣
Q♦

8♠
7♣

4♦
5♠

6♠

YOUR
HAND

hand, no matter what the charts say. Low cards often make the dealer's hand; high cards often bust the dealer's stiffs. You want to know, therefore, what the dealer's hole card is likely to be, and what any dealer hit cards are likely to be.

The more information you have at your disposal, the more hands you will win.

Now, just a word to the wise -- a quick read-through of this chapter will not be enough. You must become *really* familiar with this material, so you can apply it in the heat of action. This task should be enjoyable, however, if not downright exciting, because of all the discoveries you'll be making -- discoveries that will prove quite powerful when you keep them in mind at the casino.

You'll also need to learn to think on your feet. This method is hand-specific. First, you'll need to *figure out what you need at the moment, specific to each hand*, and *then* you can apply the methods I am about to teach you, to decide, on the fly, how best to play that hand. This concept might be foreign to you now because you've probably been taught that blackjack situations are cut-and-dried, and that *thinking* is necessary. But, once you get into the habit of it, you'll find this process is actually fun!

Taking The K.I.S.S. Approach

Just a word of explanation: my goal in creating the methods you are about to learn was to make them as simple as possible for you. So, instead of overloading you with complicated Rotating Count Estimates (RCEs) and other formulas to squeeze out every ounce of accuracy here, at the expense of usefulness, I am going to give you methods that are relatively *easy* to apply, with very little loss in accuracy.

Reverse Count Techniques

Now, the natural place to start is by using some of the information you can get from the methods you read about in the last chapter. (If you're not a card counter, you may skip to the next section.)

Normally, of course, you are only interested in getting a final total count in card counting. That's because, when card counting was invented, the assumption was you'd be able to see all the cards.

But, much like a reverse phone directory, you can use the methods in the prior chapter NOT only to arrive at a final count, but also to do a *reverse count determination*. That is, to predict what the actual face-down cards are.

To do that, simply pay attention to the *individual-hand count estimates*, or ICEs, which you use in the course of coming up with your total count estimate for each round. That's what will enable you to arrive at the likely card makeup of any hand.

What is an ICE, or individual-hand count estimate? It's the particular count I've told you to assign to each type of face-down hand, depending on what category it falls into, and what the dealer's up card is. So, for example, if the round you're in features an up card of 10, and two players have stood on their first two cards, with another standing after taking 12 points in hit cards, the ICEs for the round are -2,-2 (from RCE#2) and +2 (from Chart 10-6, page 230 of the previous chapter, for Second Category face-down cards).

What you should do at this point is do a *count estimate translation*, or CET. In other words, an ICE of -2 would tell you there are probably two high cards in that hand; an ICE of -1 would tell you the hand likely contains an Ace and a high card; an ICE of 0 would indicate that the hand is probably made up of one low and one high card; an ICE of +1 tells you the hand is likely an Ace and a low card; and, an ICE of +2 reveals that the hand is likely to consist of two low cards.

So, in the case of our example above, the face-down cards likely consist of four high cards and two low. We don't know how many 10s were dealt, or other specifics, however. That's important to know; I'll show you how to obtain that information in a moment.

(By the way -- for some players, it might be smart to master the use of ICEs and CETs before attempting to incorporate the additional information I will give you in this chapter. That would give you a lot of what you need to play a great game and, once you felt comfortable with that, you might then feel ready to move to a higher level of awareness.)

How We'll Go About This

To make things easy, I will divide the face-down cards into the same categories I identified in the previous chapter. This is necessary because, as you should realize by now, each of these categories has a very different card makeup. Our goal in this chapter is to analyze these categories further, to see if we can uncover the likely *identities* of all the face-down cards.

Why Are The Face-Down Cards Predictable?

On page 242, I said that the identities of the face-down cards are *predictable, based on the laws of mathematical probability,* and that this is what would enable us to unmask them. Let's look at this further.

As you saw in the last chapter -- and *as you can see in the charts on pages 250-253 -- you and I know what two-card hands most players stand upon, for every category of face-down cards, versus every dealer up card.* In other words, *we can identify exactly what cards they are simply by listing them, and -- with my computer data -- we know in what proportion they appear.* (The charts on the next two pages demonstrate this to you, for the First Category face-down cards.)

Advanced Card Analysis For First Category Face-Down Hands

Starting with the First Category face-down cards, then, the percentages you see in the charts on pages 250-251 reflect *the mathematical probability* that any one of the two-card hand types listed will be among the face-down cards, vis a vis each type of up card. The charts on pages 252-253 also provide you with probability figures on these hands, for the hand types in which we're most interested.

I don't expect you to memorize these charts. What we are going to do is analyze the results, and pick out the most important, most usable facts from them -- facts that you can apply at the blackjack table. You might want to get out a highlighter and highlight the important points, to make it easier for you to review the material in this chapter later on. Also -- I am not going into painful detail regarding these charts; so, you might want to review them when you have the time, to see if there's something I might have chosen not to mention for brevity's sake that might seem useful to you.

There are clear patterns we can distill from the charts, and they tend to fall into two distinct groups: the patterns that emerge when the dealer has low up cards (2s through 6s); and, the patterns that emerge when the dealer has high up cards (7s through Aces). (Some of these are highlighted in the charts.)

Here are the most important patterns to remember, regarding First Category face-down hands:

❶ **Virtually 100% of these hands contain one or more high cards (8s through 10s).**

❷ **About 75% of these hands contain at least one 10, versus the dealer's low up cards; about 85% contain at least one 10, versus the dealer's high up cards.**

❸ **About 40% of these hands have at least one 8 or 9 versus the dealer's low up cards; nearly *half* have at least one 8 or 9, versus the dealer's high up cards.**

❹ **Roughly half of these hands contain 2s through 6s versus the dealer's low up cards -- and, if you include 7s, more than 60% of these hands contain low cards; when facing the dealer's *high* up cards, however, these numbers go down dramatically -- 0% contain 2s through 6s, and about 20% contain 7s.**

(Continued on page 254.)

First Category Details

Up Card	#	Hands That Are Stood Upon	%
2	1	Hard 13s: Neutral (3s&10s; 4s&9s; 5s&8s)	13%
	2	Hard 13s positive (6s&7s)	2%
	3	Hard 14s (4s&10s; 5s&9s; 6s&8s)	13%
	4	Hard 15s (5s&10s; 6s&9s; 7s&8s)	13%
	5	Hard 16s (6s&10s; 7s&9s)	10%
	6	Hard 17s: Neutral (7s&10s)	8%
	7	Hard 17s: Negative (8s&9s)	2%
	8	Hard 18s (8s&10s)	8%
	9	Hard 19s (9s&10s)	9%
	10	Hard 20s (Two 10s)	16%
	11	Soft 18s (Aces&7s)	2%
	12	Soft 19s (Aces&8s)	2%
	13	Soft 20s (Aces&9s)	2%
3	1	Hard 13s: Neutral (3s&10s; 4s&9s; 5s&8s)	13%
	2	Hard 13s positive (6s&7s)	2%
	3	Hard 14s (4s&10s; 5s&9s; 6s&8s)	13%
	4	Hard 15s (5s&10s; 6s&9s; 7s&8s)	13%
	5	Hard 16s (6s&10s; 7s&9s)	10%
	6	Hard 17s: Neutral (7s&10s)	9%
	7	Hard 17s: Negative (8s&9s)	2%
	8	Hard 18s (8s&10s)	9%
	9	Hard 19s (9s&10s)	9%
	10	Hard 20s (Two 10s)	16%
	11	Soft 19s (Aces&8s)	2%
	12	Soft 20s (Aces&9s)	2%
4-6	1	Hard 12s: Neutral (2s&10s; 3s&9s;4s&8s)	12%
	2	Hard 12s positive (5s&7s)	2%
	3	Hard 13s: Neutral (3s&10s; 4s&9s; 5s&8s)	11%
	4	Hard 13s positive (6s&7s)	2%
	5	Hard 14s (4s&10s; 5s&9s; 6s&8s)	11%
	6	Hard 15s (5s&10s; 6s&9s; 7s&8s)	11%
	7	Hard 16s (6s&10s; 7s&9s)	9%
	8	Hard 17s: Neutral (7s&10s)	8%
	9	Hard 17s: Negative (8s&9s)	2%
	10	Hard 18s (8s&10s)	7%
	11	Hard 19s (9s&10s)	8%
	12	Hard 20s (Two 10s)	14%
	13	Soft 19s (Aces&8s)	2%
	14	Soft 20s (Aces&9s)	2%

Up Card	#	Hands That Are Stood Upon	%
7	1	Hard 17s: Neutral (7s&10s)	17%
	2	Hard 17s: Negative(8s&9s)	4%
	3	Hard 18s (8s&10s)	17%
	4	Pairs of 9s	1%
	5	Hard 19s (9s&10s)	17%
	6	Hard 20s (Two 10s)	32%
	7	Soft 18s (Aces&7s)	4%
	8	Soft 19s (Aces&8s)	5%
	9	Soft 20s (Aces&9s)	4%
8	1	Hard 17s: Neutral (7s&10s)	17%
	2	Hard 17s: Negative(8s&9s)	4%
	3	Hard 18s (8s&10s)	17%
	4	Hard 19s (9s&10s)	17%
	5	Hard 20s (Two 10s)	32%
	6	Soft 18s (Aces&7s)	4%
	7	Soft 19s (Aces&8s)	5%
	8	Soft 20s (Aces&9s)	4%
9	1	Hard 17s: Neutral (7s&10s)	18%
	2	Hard 17s: Negative(8s&9s)	4%
	3	Hard 18s (8s&10s)	18%
	4	Hard 19s (9s&10s)	18%
	5	Hard 20s (Two 10s)	34%
	6	Soft 19s (Aces&8s)	5%
	7	Soft 20s (Aces&9s)	4%
10	1	Hard 17s: Neutral (7s&10s)	18%
	2	Hard 17s: Negative(8s&9s)	4%
	3	Hard 18s (8s&10s)	18%
	4	Pairs of 9s	1%
	5	Hard 19s (9s&10s)	18%
	6	Hard 20s (Two 10s)	33%
	7	Soft 19s (Aces&8s)	5%
	8	Soft 20s (Aces&9s)	4%
Ace	1	Hard 17s: Neutral (7s&10s)	17%
	2	Hard 17s: Negative(8s&9s)	4%
	3	Hard 18s (8s&10s)	17%
	4	Pairs of 9s	1%
	5	Hard 19s (9s&10s)	17%
	6	Hard 20s (Two 10s)	32%
	7	Soft 18s (Aces&7s)	4%
	8	Soft 19s (Aces&8s)	5%
	9	Soft 20s (Aces&9s)	4%

CHART 11-1:

FIRST CATEGORY
FACE-DOWN HANDS
VIS A VIS TWO-CARD TYPES

Up Card	Two 10s	Two High	Two Low	1 High/ 1 Low	1 Ace/ 1 High	1 Ace/ 1 Low	Stiff
2	16%	35%	2%	57%	4%	2%	50%
3	16%	36%	2%	58%	4%	0%	51%
4-6	14%	31%	4%	62%	4%	0%	58%
7	32%	70%	0%	17%	9%	4%	0%
8	32%	70%	0%	17%	9%	4%	0%
9	34%	73%	0%	18%	9%	0%	0%
10	33%	73%	0%	18%	9%	0%	0%
Ace	32%	70%	0%	17%	9%	4%	0%

CHART 11-2:

FIRST CATEGORY
FACE-DOWN HANDS
VIS A VIS CARD COMPOSITION

Up Card	% Hands With 10s	% Hands With 8s-9s	% Hands With 8s-10s	% Hands With Aces-5s	% Hands With 2s-5s	% Hands With 2s-6s	% Hands With 2s-7s
2	74%	39%	96%	38%	31%	46%	61%
3	75%	40%	98%	36%	32%	47%	60%
4-6	73%	39%	96%	45%	41%	54%	65%
7	82%	47%	96%	13%*	0%	0%	21%**
8	83%	47%	96%	13%*	0%	0%	21%**
9	87%	49%	100%	9%*	0%	0%	18%**
10	86%	49%	100%	9%*	0%	0%	18%**
Ace	82%	47%	96%	13%*	0%	0%	21%**

(Asterisks (*) indicate that only the Aces are represented.
Double asterisks (**) indicate that only the 7s are represented.)

⑤ **Versus the dealer's high up cards, about 33% of the First Category hands consist of two 10s. One-third of the hands!**

⑥ **Versus the dealer's high up cards, more than 70% of these hands consist of two high cards (8s through 10s); versus the dealer's low up cards, this figure goes down to about 33%.**

⑦ **Versus the dealer's low up cards, about 60% of these hands consist of one low and one high card.**

Also notice that *50-58% of the First Category face-down cards versus the dealer's 2 through 6 are stiff hands of 12 through 16*. Most of those are neutral hands (consisting of one high card and one low card). *Low cards are to be found in a majority of these hands -- one per hand. No 2s, however, are to be found in these hands versus the dealer's 2 or 3*. That's good to remember if you need a 2, or DON'T, and you're staring at four or more First Category face-down cards when it's your turn. Obviously 2s would be overdue in that case (of course, there would be other cards that were overdue, too).

Note, too, that *soft hands* account for only 4-6% of the First Category face-down hands versus the dealer's 2-6 -- not very many at all. That tells you that *there are not many Aces among the First Category face-down hands, when the dealer shows a low up card.*

Don't forget -- *if cards are under-represented among the face-down cards, they're more likely to come amongst the cards that are about to be dealt, and vice-versa.*

One more thing. Take note of how many *more* types of two-card hands players stand upon versus the dealer's *low* up cards than they do against the dealer's *high* up cards. That's why it's a bit harder to guess what the face-down hands are when you're facing the dealer's low up cards.

Applying The Information To Your Advantage

How would you apply this knowledge?

In the case of pairs of 10s, for instance -- if you see three First Category face-down hands versus the dealer's high up cards, you now know that at least one is likely to be a pair of 10s. If you see six such hands, you know at least two are most likely a pair of 10s. You also know that *a great majority of these hands consist of two high cards*.

Another example: *if you need low cards and you're facing one of the dealer's high up cards, you know you're likely to get one if most or all of the other players stand on their first two cards!* That's because, as noted, *there are no 2s, 3s, 4s, 5s or 6s in any of the First Category face-down hands versus the dealer's high up cards!! The only low card represented amongst those cards is the 7.* This is very valuable information! If you see a significant number of such hands during any one round, those cards should practically be flashing at you! They're telling you something! They're saying: *the high cards have been depleted, and the very lowest cards are way under-represented in that bunch! This is especially useful to know if you have a stiff hand.* For instance, if you have a 15 or 16, and four or five players have stood on their first two cards before you, and the dealer is showing a high up card, you'd be crazy to surrender. *Hit* those hands!

However -- if, for example, you need a high card, and you're in the situation I just described, look out! The cards you need have been taken, and you're less likely now to get what you want. So, if you have two Aces, this is the time you want to think twice about splitting them. If you have totals of 10 or 11, you might not want to double down.

Computer Data For The First Category

OK, now that we've seen the forest, let's look at the trees. We've analyzed the First Category face-down cards, from the standpoint of what types of *pairs* you'll find; now let's take a look at the composition of the *individual cards* that make up those hands.

The charts on pages 256-257 give you a breakdown of how many of each of the individual types of cards you should expect to find amongst the First Category face-down cards, dependent upon what the dealer's up card is. The face-down cards' values -- Ace, 2, 3, etc. -- are listed in the top row of the charts; the dealer's up cards are listed down the column furthest to the left.

A word of explanation about the listing of Aces in the chart. Obviously, these cards have a dual nature -- as both a high or low card. However, I chose to put Aces in the chart listing *low* cards because, if you need a hit card, Aces you draw as hit cards will most often become 1-pointers. Therefore, the chart was done from the standpoint of cards that might help you as hit cards. So, while the Aces *within* the First Category face-down hands will always be 11-pointers, understand that we are more interested in what those Aces mean to you from the standpoint of their usefulness as hit cards. (Granted, if you have a total of 8 or 9 points, or have 10 points and are thinking of doubling, you'd like an Ace as an 11-point card; since the chart simply reflects your probability of getting an Ace, listing the Ace among the low cards doesn't really present a problem.)

Introducing...Over/Under Numbers

The first data that will be immediately useful to you in doing Advanced Card Analysis at pitch game tables is to be found in the Over/Under columns in the charts on the following pages, which I think you will find especially revealing. The numbers in these columns show you which cards,

CHART 11-3:

THE COMPOSITION OF THE FIRST CATEGORY FACE-DOWN CARDS: PART 1

Relative Numbers of High Cards:

Up Card	%10s	10s: Over/Under (31% Norm)	%9s & 8s	9s & 8s: Over/Under (15% Norm)	%HIGH CARDS (8s-10s)	HIGH: Over/Under (46% Norm)
2	45%	+14%	20%	+5%	65%	+19%
3	46%	+15%	21%	+5%	67%	+21%
4-6	43%	+12%	20%	+5%	64%	+18%
7	57%	+26%	26%	+11%	83%	+37%
8	58%	+27%	25%	+10%	83%	+37%
9	60%	+29%	26%	+11%	87%	+40%
10	59%	+29%	27%	+12%	87%	+41%
Ace	57%	+26%	26%	+11%	83%	+37%

Relative Numbers of Low Cards:

Up Card	% Aces	Over/Under (8% Norm)	% 2s	Over/Under (8% Norm)	% 3s	Over/Under (8% Norm)	% 4s	Over/Under (8% Norm)	% 5s	Over/Under (8% Norm)	% 6s	Over/Under (8% Norm)	% 7s	Over/Under (8% Norm)
2	3%	-4%	0%	-8%	4%	-4%	5%	-3%	6%	-1%	7%	0%	9%	+1%
3	2%	-5%	0%	-8%	4%	-4%	5%	-3%	7%	-1%	8%	0%	8%	0%
4-6	2%	-5%	4%	-4%	5%	-3%	6%	-2%	7%	-1%	7%	-1%	8%	0%
7	6%	-1%	0%	-8%	0%	-8%	0%	-8%	0%	-8%	0%	-8%	11%	+3%
8	7%	-1%	0%	-8%	0%	-8%	0%	-8%	0%	-8%	0%	-8%	11%	+3%
9	5%	-3%	0%	-8%	0%	-8%	0%	-8%	0%	-8%	0%	-8%	9%	+1%
10	5%	-3%	0%	-8%	0%	-8%	0%	-8%	0%	-8%	0%	-8%	9%	+1%
Ace	6%	-1%	0%	-8%	0%	-8%	0%	-8%	0%	-8%	0%	-8%	11%	+3%

CHART 11-4:

THE COMPOSITION OF THE FIRST CATEGORY FACE-DOWN CARDS: PART 2

Numbers of Low Cards by Groups:

Up Card	% Aces-5s	Over/Under (Norm 38%)	%2-5s	Over/Under (Norm 31%)	%2s-6s	Over/Under (Norm 38%)	%LOW CARDS (2s-7s)	Over/Under (Norm 46%)
2	19%	-20%	16%	-15%	23%	-16%	31%	-15%
3	18%	-20%	16%	-15%	23%	-15%	31%	-15%
4-6	22%	-16%	21%	-10%	27%	-11%	35%	-11%
7	6%	-32%	0%	-31%	0%	-38%	11%	-36%
8	7%	-32%	0%	-31%	0%	-38%	11%	-36%
9	5%	-34%	0%	-31%	0%	-38%	9%	-37%
10	5%	-34%	0%	-31%	0%	-38%	9%	-37%
Ace	6%	-32%	0%	-31%	0%	-38%	11%	-36%

amongst the First Category face-down cards, are overrepresented and which cards are under-represented in number, based upon their normal proportional representation in the Circle of 13 (the Circle of 13 proportions are referred to in the top row as *Norm* numbers, for short).

Now, here's how Over/Under Numbers work: cards that are *overrepresented* in the mix of face-down cards are indicated by a "+" and the percentage by which they exceed their Circle of 13 proportions; cards that are *under*-represented are indicated by a "-" with the corresponding percentage. Any cards whose proportions are just about what you'd expect based upon their Circle of 13 proportions are indicated by "0%."

(Please note: because the percentages for each card or card group were rounded out to make things easier for you to pick up on all of this quickly, the Over/Under Numbers are NOT to be gotten simply by subtracting those percentages from the Norm numbers. The Over/Under Numbers were arrived at using the actual, most accurate numbers, with decimals to two places; then, they, too, were rounded out, for quick comprehension.)

The reason why Over/Under Numbers are so powerful is that they are indicators of *tendencies to come*, not unlike the numbers used in card counting. *They are based upon the laws of probability and reflect mathematical logic.* Unlike card counting, though, these numbers will not vary in the course of play.

With Over/Under Numbers, a positive number means the card or cards that number refers to have been depleted, or overplayed, to some extent, as indicated by the number next to the + sign, and, therefore, are less likely to be dealt next than others; a negative number indicates the reverse -- that the card or cards referred to are more likely to be dealt than others, because they were under-represented among the face-down cards.

I am not suggesting you *memorize* all the Over/Under Numbers, or other data in the charts on pages 256-257, unless you want to. You can take a much simpler course of action here. What you need to remember are the important general *trends*.

Here's the information that will be of most use to you, regarding the First Category face-down cards:

❶ **Nearly 50% of those cards are 10-pointers, when the dealer has up cards of 2 and 3; more than 40% are 10s when the dealer has a 4 through 6; nearly 60% are 10s when the dealer has up cards of 7 through Ace.** The 10s are overrepresented by 12-14% versus the dealer's low up cards; they're nearly *30%* overrepresented versus the dealer's high up cards.

❷ **About one in five of these face-down cards is an 8 or 9 when facing the dealer's 2 through 6; more than one in *four* is an 8 or 9 when** facing the dealer's 7 through Ace. While slightly overrepresented versus the dealer's low up cards, the 8s and 9s are twice as overplayed amongst the First Category face-down cards versus the dealer's high up cards, so that's more significant information to recall. The Over/Under Numbers versus the high up cards average more than +10%.

❸ Overall, the high cards -- the 8s through 10s -- are about 20% overrepresented in these face-down cards, when the dealer shows a 2 through 6; they're about 40% overrepresented, when the dealer shows a 7 through Ace.

❹ There are no 2s amongst these face-down cards EXCEPT versus the dealer's 4 through 6, and, even then, the 2s are under-represented.

❺ There are no 3s through 6s in the First Category face-down cards, for that matter, when the dealer shows a 7 through Ace. Versus the dealer's 2 through 6, the 5s and 6s are roughly in the right proportion, but 3s and 4s are under-represented.

❻ The 7s are to be found in roughly their Circle of 13 proportions versus the dealer's low up cards, but are very slightly overrepresented versus the dealer's high up cards.

❼ Aces are significantly under-represented versus the dealer's 2 through 6, but are not too far off from their correct proportions versus the dealer's 7 through Ace.

❽ The low cards -- the 2s through 7s -- account for roughly 33% of the First Category face-down cards when facing the dealer's low up cards. However, most of those are 5s through 7s (see ❹ and ❺ above).

❾ When low cards are categorized in groups (see Chart 11-2, p. 253), what stands out is that 2s through 6s are under-represented by nearly 40% in the First Category face-down cards versus the dealer's high up cards. Versus the low up cards, the Aces through 5s are under-represented by about 20%.

How To Apply the Data In These Charts

How do you use this information? *Use the percentages in the bullets above and the added information you gained from the charts on pages 252-253, when applicable, to predict the likely identities of the face-down cards -- in specific numbers. Then, add those probable numbers to the cards you can see, to decide what cards are due and what cards are not, when it's your turn.*

To see how this works, let's take everything you've learned so far and look at an actual example from my computer card runs -- Example A, on page 246.

In this example, you're sitting to the third baseman's right, holding a hand of 8-2, for a total of 10 points. You're obviously intent on doubling. That's what Basic Strategy recommends. But *should* you? Let's see what you can surmise about the First Category face-down cards the first five players stood upon.

First -- ❶ on page 258 tells you that about *50%* of those face-down cards -- that is, *five* -- are likely to be 10s; ❷ tells you that 20% -- *two* of those face-down cards -- are probably 8s and/or 9s; ❸ tells you about 33% of the face-down cards are likely to be low cards (especially 5s through 7s), and so that would account for the remaining *three*. Aces, under-represented in this subcategory of face-down cards, are unlikely to be amongst them.

The next step is: take note of the face-up cards. There's an Ace, a 10, an 8, a 3 and a 2. Also, regarding the overall number of cards: you have counted and determined that there are 16 on the table.

We have a good idea now of what cards are on the table. But there's one more thing we must do. We must use the Circle of 13 to determine which cards are overrepresented (and therefore less likely to come with the next dealt cards) and which ones are under-represented (and therefore more likely to be dealt soon).

Since 16 cards are just a few more than 13, the cards should be closely reflective of their Circle of 13 proportions. Extrapolating what you know about the Circle of 13, you should figure that in 16 cards there should be roughly one Ace and seven or eight low cards, along with seven or eight high cards. If we want to be more particular, there should be about five 10s, two or three 8s and/or 9s, and seven or eight low cards. (See Chart 4-2, page 42 in Chapter 4: The Circle of 13, if you've forgotten how to do this.)

In our estimation of the face-down cards, we predicted there will be five 10s, two 8s and/or 9s, and three low cards. Married with the face-up cards, this would add up to an estimated six 10s, three 8s and/or 9s, one Ace, and five low cards.

So -- you can see that the 10s are probably overrepresented, and, therefore, *not likely to come with the next dealt cards*. The 8s and 9s seem to be in correct proportion, as are the Aces; but, low cards are under-represented, and, *therefore, due.*

You now have your answer. You've unmasked the First Category face-down cards and now realize -- especially since they account for such a high proportion of the dealt cards in this example -- that it's smarter for you to *hit* your total of 10 rather than double, because the cards you especially need in doubling (the 10s and Aces) are the least likely to come next. The mathematical likelihood you've determined is that, if you doubled, *you would probably get a low card*. At that point, with the dealer 3's busting average of 38%, you would have a 62% probability of losing to the dealer (actually, a bit more, because low cards are due and the dealer is less likely to bust than normal). (If you've forgotten how often each dealer up card tends to bust, go back and review Chapter 9 -- that's information you need to remember!)

The virtual player in this example from my computer research card runs, however, was programmed to double in this situation, as most players would. What extra card did that player get? A 3, which fits in with what we expected, based upon the information you've learned in this chapter.

Incidentally -- the dealer's hole card was an Ace. The dealer then drew a 7, to reach a formidable score of 21. The virtual player who played the hand we said was yours therefore lost the hand, and, in so doing, lost TWICE the amount of the player's original bet, because of doubling.

By the way -- what did those face-down cards turn out to be?:

Five 10s, an 8, a 9, and three low cards: a 4, 6 and 7. *Exactly* as we had predicted. *We were dead-on accurate in doing Advanced Card Analysis in this actual pitch game example, even with all of those face-down cards to contend with!*

One more thing -- what would have really happened had the virtual player done what we recommended, and hit that hand instead of doubling? The player would have drawn the 3 and 7, for a total of 20 points. The dealer, with an Ace as the hole card, would have drawn a 10 and a 6, for a total of 20 points. So, the result would have been a push, instead of a loss of twice the bet.

See how much better you would have done than the average player in Example A by using the methods in this chapter?

Advanced Card Analysis For Second Category Face-Down Hands

Let's move on to the specifics my computer research turned up regarding the Second Category face-down hands (the hands players stand on after taking one or more hit cards). As you saw in the last chapter, this category is the reverse of the first, in a way -- it's heavy in low cards. In fact, the first thing you need to remember is: *100% of these hands contain at least one low card.*

Now, we won't be referring to charts for this category. It will be easiest if I just summarize the results for you. (The charts for this category are way too large to present, since they have to take into account not only what the dealer's up card is, but also the point total of the hit cards players stand on. The summary charts for each dealer up card each take up two pages of 8.5"x14" paper, in landscape orientation!)

As you might recall from the prior chapter, Second Category face-down cards offer a bit more of a challenge because you need to take into account a greater variety of possibilities. My goal here will be to take an immense amount of material that would be useless to you in its raw form -- unless you're a genius, with an elephantine memory -- and reduce it to its simplest form, based upon clear patterns that can be identified.

Two Important Facts

There's one generalization that is true, no matter what the dealer up card is, that will help make everything that follows easy to remember: *there are essentially NO high cards (8s through 10s) among the Second Category face-down hands of players who have taken 10 or more points in hit cards.* In fact, these hands are especially heavy in 2s through 5s; and 7s are relatively few in number. ***So, the minute a player takes hit cards totalling 10 or more points, that makes your job of figuring out what their face-down cards are that much easier: they're low cards, perhaps mixed with an Ace or two (except in the case of the dealer's 4 through 6, as you will see in a moment).***

Looking closer at this matter: *for totals of 10-14 points, low cards (primarily 2s through 6s) make up anywhere from 75% to more than 90% of that mix, the percentage of low cards going down with the point total. Once the point total is above 14, Aces make up a minimum of 33% of the mix.*

Another generalization that stands up pretty well versus all the dealer up cards is: ***if a player takes an Ace and then stands, that player's face-down cards are most likely to be two low cards.***

(There is one exception to this rule: when the dealer's up card is 3, these cards are most likely to consist of one high and one low card. However, even in this case, players will have two low cards nearly half of the time. So, you might find it easier to ignore the exception in this case; it won't hurt your accuracy very much to do so.)

Second Category Hands Vis a Vis Low Up Cards

Since there is a noticeable divide between how players approach the dealer's low up cards (2-6) and high up cards (7-Ace), let's divide this project likewise, and start by talking about situations involving the low up cards. Actually, we'll have to further subdivide this group into three sections, since players play against these cards less uniformly than they do with the high up cards.

First -- let's dispose of the simplest subdivision: the dealer's 4 through 6. This is very easy: ***all Second Category face-down hands versus these up cards consist of two low cards. More specifically, they consist entirely of 2s*** *through 6s -- you will find no 7s among them!* This group is especially heavy on 2s through 5s. In rough terms: *the 2s make up about 30% of the cards; 3s account for nearly 25% of the cards; 4s make up more than 20% of the cards; and 5s make up about 20% of the cards!*

This information can be quite useful to you. *If you're at a table where many of the players have taken hit cards versus the dealer's 4, 5 or 6, high cards and Aces are most likely to come with the next cards that are dealt.*

Of course, the hit cards players draw need to be analyzed, too -- if they're also low cards, high cards and Aces are especially due; if they're all high cards and Aces, well, then, things might have balanced out. This information is especially telling if you are thinking of doubling or splitting, and you need a high card. It can also let you know the relative likelihood of the dealer's busting -- don't forget, a flood of high cards is what we hope is coming when the dealer's hand is likely to be a bustable stiff total.

OK. Second -- let's talk about Second Category face-down hands versus the dealer's 2. Let's begin with generalizations: *Aces through 6s are over-represented in these hands; 7s through 10s are under-represented. In fact, 2s through 5s are especially overrepresented; 2s make up more than 20% of the cards, with 3s and 4s close behind!*

For this, and other up cards, it will work best if we divide the hit card totals into subdivisions that reflect patterns we can then remember. This approach will prove to be more uniform with the dealer's high up cards, so understand that the dealer's 2 will require a bit more effort in the way of memorization (the same thing can be said of the dealer's 3, as you will see).

Our first subdivision, for the dealer's 2, will be players' hit card totals of 2 through 7.

For point totals of 2 and 3, always assume the players' face-down cards are one low and one high card. Now, there's one more thing you should know about the high cards that are present: *10s appear twice as often as 8s and 9s (lumped together as a group), among the Second Category hands that might include high cards, versus the dealer's 2.* (Remember: high cards are only present in situations where players' hit card totals are LESS THAN 10 points.) *So, what you should do is estimate the high cards to be 10s for two of every three such hands, and figure the third hand to contain an 8 or 9.*

For hit card point totals of 4 through 7, we need to keep an unusual hybrid result in mind, because there are three types of hands represented, none of which reaches 50% or better representation. *However, it's instructive to remember that more than 50% of the time these Second Category hands will consist of either one low and one high card, OR one low card and one Ace. The high cards outnumber the Aces roughly 2 to 1. So, assume that two out of three appearances, these hands have one low and one high card, and, in the third of three appearances, they have one low card and one Ace.* (Don't forget, with regard to the hands with high cards -- 10s are twice as likely to appear as 8s and 9s, versus the dealer's 2.)

For hit card point totals of 8 through 13, players are most likely to be standing on two low cards.

For hit card point totals of 14 through 18, players are most likely to be standing on one low card and an Ace.

OK. Now, the last low dealer up card we need to tackle is the 3.

For players who stand on hit card point totals of 2 through 4 versus the 3, assume their face-down cards consist of one low and one high card. The high cards are twice as likely to be 10s as the other high cards, because 10s outnumber the 8s and 9s by a margin of 2 to 1, just as they did with the dealer's 2.

For players who stand on hit card point totals of 5 through 9, we have another hybrid situation. Assume their face-down cards consist of one low card and one high card/or Ace. The hands with high cards outnumber the hands with Aces roughly 2 to 1. (And, once again, the 10s outnumber the 8s and 9s by a margin of 2 to 1, just as they did with the dealer's 2.)

For players who stand on totals of 10 through 14: their face-down cards are most likely to be two low cards.

Players who stand on higher point totals most likely have one low card and one Ace.

Second Category Hands Vis a Vis High Up Cards

When the dealer has high up cards, there are a bit fewer low cards among the Second Category face-down hands, but they still predominate, appearing in greater numbers than their Circle of 13 proportions would indicate -- especially regarding the 2s through 6s.

The nice thing here is we can make three major generalizations with regard to ALL the up cards:

❶ **When players stand on hit card totals of 2 to 8 points, the great majority of these hands consist of one low and one high card.** (See the note below regarding the proportion of 10s in the high cards.)

❷ **When players stand on hit card totals of 9 to 13 points, most of these hands consist of two low cards.** (Actually, with 9 points, there's a significant minority of hands -- 49% of them -- that is made up of one low card and one high card. With 10 through 13 points, however, a small minority of hands has one low card and one *Ace*, and NO hands contain one low and one high card.)

❸ **When players stand on hit card totals of 14 and more points, the** majority of these hands consist of one low card and an Ace. (A relatively small minority of these hands consist of two low cards.)

There are some other useful facts you might want to keep in mind:

♣ **Regarding the number of hands that contain 10s:** With the dealer's 7 and 8, well more than 50% of the Second Category hands contain one 10, with player hit card totals of 2 through 7. This number drops to about 25-35% with player hit card totals of 8 and 9. Against the dealer's 9 and Ace, these numbers are about 40% and 20-30%, respectively. When the dealer has a 10, these numbers are about 35% and 20-30%, respectively, with this addition: there are no 10s in hands where the player's hit total is 2 points.

♣ **10s outnumber 8s and 9s by a margin of roughly 2 to 1, with player point totals of 2-6. With point totals of 7-9, the margin is so slim, it would probably be smart to assume half the hands with high cards contain 10s, the other half, 8s and 9s.** The one exception is with the dealer's 7: there, the 2 to 1 ratio stays true throughout the whole range we're talking about here -- totals of 2-9.

♣ **10s are under-represented by roughly 5 to 10 points with player hit totals of 2 through 7, and significantly more (up to 20% and more) with player hit totals of 8 and 9.** The exceptions are versus the dealer's 7 and 9, where, with player hit totals of 2 and 3, the 10s are roughly in the correct proportion.

♣ **8s and 9s are slightly under-represented, with player hit totals of 2 through 9.** The exception is with player totals of 7 through 9, where 8s are frequently slightly overrepresented.

One thing to keep in mind, based on all of the above, is that, if you have stiffs of 14 through 16, and many players at your table take hit cards, you might find that the cards you need for a winning total have been taken. That, of course, depends upon the hit cards the players have drawn, and the types of other cards on the table -- both the face-up cards, and the face-down cards (as you have best identified them).

Conversely, this same situation might bode well for doubling and splitting, depending on what you have, and whether your analysis of all the cards confirms that high cards are due.

Advanced Card Analysis With Third Category Face-Down Hands

The mystery regarding cards held in the hands of players to your left should be minimized in number by applying the suggestions I made in the prior chapter, regarding Third Category face-down hands. However, if any of these players who signal their intent to take hit cards (by holding their initial two cards in one hand) are purposely *hiding* their hand-held cards, no matter. Here's what they are likely to be, based upon the dealer's up card:

With the dealer's 2 and 3: assume half of them to consist of two low cards, and the other half to be one low and one high card. If there's an odd number of hands you're considering, weigh your estimate in favor of the two low card combination.

With the dealer's 4 through 6: here, you *know* 100% of these hands will consist of two low cards.

With the dealer's 7 through Ace: assume half consist of one low and one high card, the other half consisting of two low cards. If there's an odd number of hands you're considering, weigh your estimate in favor of the one low/one high card combination.

This is a simplification of the method I offered in the prior chapter, but one that will work just fine.

Putting It All Together

OK. Let's see how well you've absorbed this material, and have some fun at the same time, by applying what you now know to solving the riddle of Example B, on page 246. You might want to work it out yourself first, and then compare your results with the explanation below.

This one's a bit tricky, for a number of reasons, as you'll find out. But, first, let me give you a head start: the 10 count from the prior round is 6, with 22 cards played. The Ace count is 1. There were 10 low cards. There were two 6s and one 5 played. Two 8s and 9s were played. So, what does that tell you?

Because of what you learned in the chapter on "The Circle of 13," you know from these counts that the 10s were under-represented, as were the Aces. In 22 cards, roughly 7 10s should have appeared, and, perhaps, two Aces. So 10s and Aces are due to come in somewhat greater numbers than the low cards, which were a bit overrepresented.

You're holding a stiff of 15. First see what you can surmise about the face-down cards and, then, see what the face-up cards are telling you.

(Hint: your result will not be perfect, but it will be correct. Very often if we're off a bit on one hand's estimate, that will be corrected by a counter-balancing slight mistake in another hand's estimate. I included a round with this phenomenon to show you that you won't always be dead-on accurate with each hand, but you'll likely be correct or close to it, with your overall prediction for the round's face-down cards.)

Here we go: the 1st Baseman took 15 points in hit cards, versus an up card of 8. You should have estimated the 1st Baseman stood on a hand of one low card and one Ace.

The next player immediately stood on the first two cards. Those you should have assumed were both high cards.

The next player stood on a hit card of 6 points. You know that player's face-down cards are likely to be one low and one high card.

The 2nd Baseman -- the player to your right -- stood on two cards totalling 9 points. You should then have assumed that player's first two cards were both low. (If you were smart, you peeked at this player's cards, but, for argument's sake, we'll say you didn't.)

You know what cards the player to your left has -- they've turned up a Blackjack.

You know what you have: one low and one high card -- a 7 and 8. You also know what you need: a 2 through a 6. Anything else would bust you.

The 3rd Baseman stood immediately upon the first two cards, and those you should have assumed likely to be two high cards, perhaps two 10s, since this is the second such First Category face-down hand.

The dealer's up card is an 8.

So, where does that leave you? Your estimate of the face-down cards is that there are four low cards, five high cards (probably three 10s and an 8 or 9) and one Ace among them.

Counting the cards on the table, you should have noticed there were 21 cards dealt so far this round.

Looking now at the face-up cards and yours, you should have seen you are holding one high card and one low, that the dealer's up card is a high card (an 8 -- you now know there are no 8s left), the Blackjack added a 10 to the mix, and that the hit cards before you were one 10, and four low cards -- one 6 (which you really wanted), two 5s (which would have been your second choice) and one 4. Just from the hit cards alone, your card analysis should tell you your probability of getting what you want is less than hoped for -- especially considering you now know there are no 6s left (from your 6 count from the prior round).

So, the tally this round, so far, for high cards: 9, of 21. That's a bit below expectations, as set by the Circle of 13. Remember -- 10s were already a bit overdue because of the 10 count from the prior round. The 6s are played out, three 5s have been played...four more low cards are probably among the face-down cards...About 18 of 24 low cards have now been dealt.

The evidence says that 10s, and, perhaps Aces and 9s are overdue to come with the next hit cards. I'd say it suggests strongly that you should *surrender* your 15 -- even though Basic Strategy doesn't recommend it here.

This, in fact, is another example that points out Basic Strategy's short-comings, and inability to react to the changing realities based upon what cards were played.

OK -- how did this round play out, in actuality?

The 1st Baseman's face-down cards were two 3s. My estimate was that there would be an Ace and a low card. In actuality, 40% of the face-down hands of players who stand with 15 points in hit cards will indeed be two low cards, but, we were correct in guessing with the majority percentage, the 60% probability that the hand would in fact have one Ace and one low card.

No matter. We know that winning at Blackjack means playing the percentages -- being right most, not all of the time. We played the percentages.

The next player had one Ace and a 9. My estimate was that this player would have two high cards.

The next player had a 2 and a 10 -- this correctly reflected my estimate of this hand being likely to have one low and one high card.

The 2nd Baseman had a 9 and a 2. My estimate that, with 9 points in hit cards, this player would have two low cards. Since, as I pointed out earlier, 9 points of hit cards is a swing point (meaning roughly half the hands are two low cards, and slightly less than half are hands of one low and one high card), this total will throw us off a bit -- but we're still playing the correct percentages in guessing two low cards.

The 3rd Baseman indeed had two 10s, as I had predicted.

Interestingly enough, my overall estimate was correct. I estimated there would be one Ace, five high cards (and probably three of them being 10s), and four low cards. That's exactly what they turned out to be, demonstrating what I have referred to before: that slight mistakes can add together, or subtract from each other. Their equal likelihood of doing either is what makes my method so accurate, in the long-run, as the accuracy figures in the prior chapter prove.

OK, OK -- but what did the player playing your hand do?

In my computer runs, the virtual players were forced to play as most players would, and so, that player hit the hand. They drew a 10 and busted.

The dealer had a 7 in the hole, and then drew...another 10!

But, then...we aren't surprised, are we? We knew that was likely to happen -- based upon the mathematical probabilities, and my method for ferreting out what the face-down cards are.

If the player had surrendered, as we would have done, that player would be up by one bet. Instead, that player took a loss of one bet.

That shows you once again the advantage you will gain by moving toward a more flexible and accurate card strategy, based upon the realities of the moment -- which, coincidentally, is what we'll discuss in the next chapter!

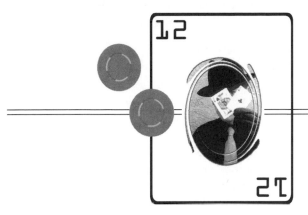

Strategic
Card Analysis
And Your Real-time
Card Strategy

C ard analysis is both a science and an art. To do it justice would require that it be given a book of its own. Even then, it would be a daunting task to try to catalog the enormous number of different card situations you will be confronted with in your blackjack career, and then tell you how handle each situation. (Think of all the possible variations in the *mix* and *order* of the cards, the number of decks in play, the number of players at the table, and so on!) So, rather than doing a tedious encyclopedia that would run into thousands of pages, I decided it would be far better if I give you the *skills* with which you can tackle any challenge that comes your way.

Actually what you'll learn here is a *dynamic*, two-step process. The first step is the performance of a card analysis. So, my *first* aim will be to clue you in on *what you should be looking for*, to make sense of the cards that are dealt. To most players, the playing out of the cards is Greek to them; it sends no message, and they pay no attention to either the *mix*, or the *order* of the cards. But, in fact, you can read the cards almost like a language.

The second step is the execution of a card move, with good *precision*. Therefore, my *second* goal is to show you *how to take all of the dynamite information you'll gain from card analysis, and translate it into a cutting edge card strategy* that will provide you with more wins than you ever imagined, and raise your game to its highest level.

The First Step: Strategic Card Analysis

I have named the first step *Strategic Card Analysis*. Strategic Card Analysis is so named because its goal is to give you the kind of information you need in order to arrive at the smartest *card strategy*. All of the almost infinite number of *card situations* you'll find yourself in cry out for *unique* card strategy *solutions*. Strategic Card Analysis will enable you to recognize each special challenge.

It will alert you to: *fluctuating up card busting and winning rates* you read about earlier -- and whether or not they are working to your benefit, *at a particular moment*; the *repetitive phenomenon* we've explored, and whether or not they are in your favor, *at a particular moment*; and, the mathematical realities presented by the mix of cards that have been dealt, which enable you to make informative *probability assessments* about the cards that are *about* to be dealt, among other things.

Now, we've already discussed how, in blackjack, one *thing tends to lead to another*. This is why *Strategic Card Analysis* requires you to pay attention to the action on *three levels*:

❶ *Intra-round* (within the round)*:* this means analyzing the *mix* as well as the *order* of the cards that have been dealt *in the current round*, for how you should play your hand. You'll be looking for *imbalances* and *card flow indicators* that will clue you in to: **a)** *what the hole card is likely to be;* **b)** *whether the up card can be categorized as either a Duck or a Buck,* as detailed in Chapter 9 (and, hence, enable you to conquer the problem of how to deal with fluctuating dealer busting rates); **c)** *what the dealer's likely outcome will be* (based not only on your Ducks and Bucks analysis, but also on your read on the dealer's likely hit cards); **d)** *what your hit cards will probably be (and whether they will help or hurt your chances)*; and, **e)** *what your probable outcome will be*: will you be competitive against the dealer, or are you in a losing situation that requires you to take the path of lowest losses?

❷ *Inter-round* (from one round to the next): this involves making a mental note of what cards have been dealt in prior rounds (since the last shuffle), to possibly anticipate the strength of the dealer in the next round, but, also, to know the relative supply of each type of card in relation to what you might need to make your hand in the next round, as well as determine what the hole card is.

❸ *Inter-shuffle* (from one shuffle to another): here, you analyze how the cards played out between shuffles, for clues as to what's likely to come after the next shuffle. As you saw in chapters 5 & 6, *what goes around comes around*. Now, Inter-shuffle analysis is a two-level process. On the first level, you must watch the current action closely, to detect any notable patterns (for example, trios or quartets of like cards that are in close proximity) or card flows -- good or bad -- that you can fairly expect to come back in some form after the next shuffle. This includes doing a continuous *spent-card analysis*. This means: keeping track of where each round's cards (including those card patterns, or any *card flows* or groups of cards, good or bad) *go* in the discard pile, and then wind up after being shuffled. This way, you can figure out when the patterns and card flows are likely to return if someone else cuts the cards; and, *where to place the cut card* in case that job goes to you. The second level requires that you *recall* those *after the next shuffle* (taking into account how the cards were rearranged by the casino's shuffling practices), so you can anticipate what's probably going to return -- good or bad -- and *when*. Finally, you must also ask yourself just prior to the next shuffle if there were any *undealt cards* that are worth following, through the next shuffling and card cutting process. You'll want to use the skills you acquired in Chapter 5, to estimate when they might or might not *reappear* after the new shuffle; or, perhaps, if you get the cut card, you might choose to try to bring them into play (for example, you might very well want to bring a closely grouped trio or quartet of Aces to the table in the first round, *if you're good enough to make the cut so that the players and NOT the dealer get those Aces*; this is a skill I've developed, and something I've demonstrated at my seminars -- we talked about this kind of thing in Chapter 6).

Each level of analysis is geared toward getting a handle on your winning potential, with an eye toward adjusting your card strategy and your betting outlays, befitting your current circumstances and probable future events.

This Is Not A Win-All Proposition

Now, before we go any further, please understand that I am not talking about providing you with a magic bullet that will win every hand for you. No such thing exists. I've said this before, but it bears repeating. As you should know by now, you will get your share of hands that fall into the category of losing situations. There will also be hands -- such as hands with hard totals of 18 through 21 -- that require no response other than to stand. And there will be times when your smartest move is the one you were taught in Basic Strategy.

However, you will find there will be a significant number of rounds in which you can put my innovative approach to good use, to make brilliant choices you'd never thought of before, and raise your win rate dramatically. Also -- whether or not the wealth of information you gain from Strategic Card Analysis is immediately actionable, you will usually find it can be put to good use in later rounds.

That being said, *your most important job when first coming to a table, or when new cards are introduced, is assessing the quality of the cards --*

gauging this not only on the Gains Stages parameters you read about in Chapter 7, but, also, on card flow issues. *No amount of skill can make bad cards good* (all things being equal -- that is, if the number of betting spots stays the same).

Anomalous card flows which persist from shuffle to shuffle, for instance, can be devastating. Unusually long strings of low cards will often destroy your doubling efforts and give the dealer a better shot at drawing to a good score. High-low, high-low card patterns will lead to a greater than normal of player stiffs and then, a higher than usual percentage of busted player hands. Like cards that travel around together from one shuffle to the next can make hole card and hit card prediction difficult (this, however, can often be surmounted by anticipating these, once you've detected them).

The point is: this chapter is no panacea. You *will* win more hands than you have before, with the skills you will learn here. But keep in mind that *there will be times when your best option is to leave the table*, and so you must be alert to the factors that we discussed earlier, in this regard. There's no percentage in winning more hands than normal, if the overall picture is bleak.

The Second Step: Your Real-time Card Strategy

The second step is your *Real-time Card Strategy*. If Strategic Card Analysis is indeed like having Delta Force commandos illuminate your target, then your Real-time Card Strategy is akin to a laser-guided missile that takes the target out. *Your Real-time Card Strategy involves the execution of the smartest card move, custom-made for the current-round situation, as indicated by the results of your Strategic Card Analysis. This* is an *active, flexible* card strategy, to deal with the vagaries *of the moment.*

This is when you'll determine how to handle your stiffs; whether to hit, split, double, stand, take Insurance (or Even Money), or surrender. (The power of the Ducks and Bucks will become evident here, because *they give you advice about what your Real-time Card Strategy should be!* Refer back to Chapter 9 for the Ducks and Bucks strategy recommendations.)

Freedom Brings Precision BUT Requires More Thinking

Those who have found comfort in using those dogmatic strategy charts of old may find the transition to a more *free* strategy approach a bit difficult. It is not as simple. But, give it a chance. It will prove much more rewarding.

The idea of a Real-time Card Strategy is not unlike the method used by Bridge players every day. They don't use charts; they analyze the cards mathematically and make moves based upon what they've determined gives them the best probability of success.

I also know that, inevitably, there will be one or two members of the Old Guard who will complain bitterly about this new approach. They are likely to hide behind the cloak of what is "correct" -- that is, what the blackjack researchers of four decades ago *said* was right. But these critics never seem to understand that *even the earliest card counting systems they're so fond of quoting recommended a degree of freedom from Basic Strategy dictates!*

Since the dawn of modern blackjack thinking, theoreticians have said -- for all who have ears to hear -- that *card imbalances create conditions that make Basic Strategy recommendations the wrong way to go.* Go back to your Thorps, Brauns, Reveres, Humble/Coopers, Ustons and Wongs, and take a good look at their indices. Did you realize what those indices were telling you? It was *there* that blackjack's old masters made a stab at dealing with the challenges posed by *fluctuating card balances -- the very source of the fluctuating dealer busting rates, etc., that I've revealed in this book.*

But there are two major problems with their solution. The first way they went wrong was in devising a *binary* system of strategy variations. In other words, they provided just *one* alternate move that differed from the Basic Strategy recommendation *per each chart box.* In choosing to go with a simple "either/or" binary system, everything was presented in black and white, with no recognition that imbalances came in *many forms,* requiring more than just one card move alternative. The second way they went wrong was in trying to simplify things by lumping all the cards into two groups (high and low). This quick-fix type of solution led to a great deal of inaccuracy. The fact is: each of the ten different card types has a different effect on your fate and the dealer's (as you saw especially in the chapters on "The Circle of 13" and "Auxiliary Betting Indicators")

Card counting indices were good for their era (and a card count is still helpful, as an adjunct to card analysis, in knowing *general* trends), but we need to get more specific. There are a tremendous number of card mix variations that come your way, per up card, per each of your hand types, and you need a whole *palette* of move alternatives in order to properly react to them.

We first broached this subject in the chapter on the Circle of 13. Imbalances throw things off; they have their own card *chemistry.* The mix of cards during imbalances numerically *combine* differently than Basic Strategy logic would dictate, producing results unique to each combination, which require you to adjust your strategy appropriately.

For those who still think Basic Strategy is the way to go -- the fact of the matter is that, at any given moment, the cards are uniquely *out of balance.* That's a fact of life in blackjack. There are an *enormous* number of *complex* imbalance *variants* you will encounter. Even if you consider yourself an expert on Basic Strategy, you should remember that those who produced the original idea of a Basic Strategy cautioned that it was correct only under *balanced* card conditions. Such conditions rarely occur.

When I talk about imbalances, I am not talking about them in the card counting sense -- the relative proportion of low to high cards. I'm using the word in a *new* sense -- from the standpoint of *how the proportion of each of the ten types of cards differ from their "normal" Circle of 13 proportions*, in the overall mix. There's a lot of power to be gained from absorbing this concept.

The Principle Of Imbalance & Rebalance

This is the key to a certain kind of blackjack predictability. You see, unless the cards are continuously being shuffled, the cards will not play out randomly, even if they've been shuffled by a machine. While a randomizing shuffling machine can destroy the often bankable shuffle-to-shuffle repetitive patterns that are so useful to you, the cards, nonetheless, once shuffled, still follow certain rules of mathematical logic as they are dealt. I'm talking about *cause-and-effect relationships -- within* rounds and *from one round to the next.*

Another way of saying this is: *imbalances* reveal mathematical *probabilities*. I cannot emphasize this enough: seek them out and cherish them, for *imbalances are like weather vanes pointing out the direction of the future.*

To get this point across, I've created *The Principle of Imbalance & Rebalance*. It says that *in a closed, balanced universe, such as exists in the game of blackjack* (because it's based upon the standard 52-card deck), *imbalances will eventually be followed by opposite imbalances, that trend toward balancing everything out (as the cards run out). In other words, if the pendulum, so to speak, swings to one side, its return to the other side is not only inevitable, but predictable.*

The *imbalances* I am referring to are reflected by the cards that have been *dealt* -- but what you really want to do is to take this evidence and figure out the composition of the cards *that have yet to be dealt. They* are askew, *in the opposite way.* You want to know what cards are coming next, and you know what? *Those are most likely to be the cards that have appeared in numbers below their Circle of 13 proportions* -- these are the cards that were on the short end of the imbalance, so to speak.

FACTOID 12-1:
The Principle of Imbalance & Rebalance says imbalances are like a pendulum swing: they alert you to a swing heading the other way.

Of course, not all cards will be out-of-balance (per their Circle of 13 proportions) at all times. Here's how you should interpret the cards that are *in a balanced state*: they are more likely to be dealt with the upcoming cards than the cards that have been overrepresented, but a bit less so than those that have been under-represented.

(In multi-deck games, be advised that the more decks in the shoe, the longer the swings one way or another can last, and the less of a guarantee that the cards in later rounds will start balancing out before the cards are reshuffled, because of the large number of *undealt* cards in 6- and 8-deck games -- 125 and 166, respectively, on average.)

So, *The Principle of Imbalance & Rebalance* defines your first and foremost job, which is to *be alert to what the imbalances of the moment are, and what those inequities will logically lead to -- in terms of future events.* Knowing how the scales are tipped just before certain key cards are dealt gives you the power of prediction. You can tap into this principle to get a good read on: *your hit cards* to come; the upcoming dealer's *hole card*; the *dealer's hit cards, which clue you in to the dealer's probable outcome*; the cards to come *in the next round*; and so on.

Let me give you an analogy:

Let's say we were to play a game where there are 10 black stones and 10 white stones. The goal of this game is unimportant. All you need to know is that it involves my passing to you one stone after another, until all the stones are in your possession.

Now, what if I've handed you 9 stones, one-by-one, since the game began, and they've all been black? Let's stop and analyze this situation. There's been an *imbalance* here, involving a near depletion of black stones, and, therefore, the *probability* of getting a white one among the next *two* stones is 100%. *This is The Principle of Imbalance & Rebalance in action: one pendulum swing is inevitably followed by a swing toward the opposite direction.* In our closed universe of 20 stones, it all comes down to numbers and simple math, leading to a conclusion about probabilities, which then guides your game strategy.

It's not very different in blackjack. Granted, there are more *types* of "stones," and, as you add more decks to the game, there are even more "stones" to keep track of. Plus, each *type* of stone behaves *differently* than the rest. But mastering the added difficulty is not as hard as it seems.

Anyone of normal intelligence and a desire to master the game can conquer this, with practice and determination. Nothing worthwhile (such as winning at blackjack) comes easy, but this is not rocket science. Let me assure you, however, that while most of the players who have taken my seminars told me they either found card counting too difficult to attempt at the casino (or they tried it but then abandoned it because they felt its results were limited and not worth the effort), the great majority of them found my approach to card analysis not only *easy* to apply, but very *profitable* as well.

In sum, *The Principle of Imbalance & Rebalance* is effective in uncovering underlying trends. Instead of white and black stones, you'll be tracking individual cards. *Those that have appeared in disproportionately high numbers (based on their normal Circle of 13 proportions) are less likely to come next, and those that have not appeared in normal proportions are likely to lead the next imbalance in their favor. Those that are in a state of balance are less likely to be among the next cards dealt than those that have been under-represented in the mix.*

You'll see, in a moment, how we'll put this Principle to good use, in doing Inter- and Intra-Round analyses.

Keeping Track Of The Cards

Now, to use the approach I'm teaching you, you first need to keep track of the specific types of cards that have been dealt since the last shuffle. If you can do this in your head, all the better. If you need to use chips and other mnemonic devices (akin to what I suggested in Chapter 7 regarding WLM units), that's fine, too -- so long as you do it subtly, and don't tip the dealer or casino bosses off to what you're doing. This is the sort of thing Bridge players do, and they keep track of the *suits* of the cards, too -- at least we don't have to do that! Admittedly, they have just one deck to stay on top of, but, sincerely, this can be done rather easily, with practice. Those of you who are card counters (especially those who have used the multilevel count systems, such as the Hi-Opt II, Revere Point Count, Revere Advanced Point Count, and Thorp Ultimate systems) certainly have the skills to pull this off. (Please come up with your own way of doing this, though. There are many ways to skin this cat. I'd rather not prescribe one system for everyone, because, if we all do this the same way, the casinos will get wise and we'll all be busted together!)

Don't forget -- you need to know not only the number played, but the relative *balance*, too (which, of course, also keeps in mind the relative *supply* of each card among the undealt cards). This task will be much easier if you have memorized Chart 4-2, on page 42 in Chapter 4. This tells you the exact number of each particular card you should expect to see each round, based upon the number of betting spots being played, and the Circle of 13 proportions, which reflect balanced conditions.

Here's where you should also integrate your knowledge of how many cards you'll see on average per round, per the number of players at the table (see Chapter 3, on "How The Number Of Players Affects Your Bottom Line"). F*or instance, if you remember that 13 cards, on average, are dealt each round in 4-player situations, you'll know that, after two rounds you've seen about half a deck of cards, and, after four rounds, a whole deck.* This kind of knowledge is power, in determining whether you've seen more or less of a particular card, than you should have; it gives you a neat reference point. If two rounds have gone by in that 4-player situation, and you've seen just one Ace, you will know that there will be a higher concentration of

Aces in the next two rounds than normal (the Circle of 13 tells you that you should see one of each non-10 every 13 cards, if things are balanced; if one card appears in 26 dealt, you've discovered an imbalance on the short side of things). The opposite would be true if you'd seen three Aces.

So...always keep in mind how many rounds it takes to see a deck of cards: roughly 4 rounds with 4 players; about 3 rounds with 5 and 6 players; and approximately 2 rounds with 7 players...and measure the amount of each card you've seen against this measure, to stay on top of what kind of imbalances you're facing.

Intra-Round Analysis

For those of you who absolutely find this task a near-impossibility, don't give up on me. I have a way for you to get your feet wet and still play a better game than you're playing now. What you're going to do is master Intra-Round Analysis, which deals with the cards at hand. Even if you can only remember past round events in general terms, you should find Intra-Round Analysis *easy*. This requires no memory skills at all: the cards are right in front of you, each round. They're telling you worlds of information.

Intra-round analysis is finding a specific solution for a specific problem. It begins with a question, namely: how well will my hand compete with the dealer's, given the mix and order of the cards that have been played?

Your winning potential is based upon the likelihood of your hand's ability to beat the dealer's results -- whether you need hit cards or not. You'll want to consider your full palette of options, with the understanding that some scores are not enough to win (especially considering the fact that the dealer's average score is 19), and conversely, that some stiffs are good enough as is (or with a hit card), especially when facing a Duck. In a losing situation you must choose the path of lowest losses. You might not need a hit card, but, if you know the dealer's score is likely to beat yours, you might not choose to stand and take the full hit (where surrender is an option). We'll cover how to handle your stiffs, as well as splitting, doubling, surrendering and Insurance, in a moment.

Determining What The Hole Card Is

Now, determining what the dealer's got in the hole (and therefore, if the up card is a Duck or Buck) is your top priority, when it comes to Intra-Round analysis. This will give you an excellent read on what the dealer's final outcome will probably be -- will they score high or low, or bust? My method of uncovering the hole card will give you quite a lot of power.

(You've gotten an inkling as to how to uncover the identity of the hole card with the Circle of 13 games; and, if you read *Blackjack The SMART Way*, you've already had an introduction into how to pull off this skill. Here, though, we'll take it a bit further.).

Remember: *imbalances* reveal mathematical *probabilities*. This will enable you to make sense of what the relative proportions of cards on the table are telling you. Specifically: *The Principle of Imbalance & Rebalance tells you that the hole card is not likely one of the types of cards that has appeared in numbers beyond their Circle of 13 proportions.*

I've come up with an introductory *Probability Assessment* method that should be helpful for those who are new to the concept of imbalance. Here's how it works (this works best for tables with 6 or more betting spots in use -- which, of course, is a condition you should strive for):

❶ *If three or more of one type of card (except the 10s) are dealt in one round, consider the card overplayed (at least momentarily, in the case of multi-deck tables), and therefore less likely to appear in the near-future.* In the case of the 10s, six or more just prior to the hole card being dealt, or nine or more by round's end signals this state.

❷ *If NONE of one type of card shows up in one round, this alerts you to the fact that the card is overdue* (this is true to a lesser degree of cards that appear just *once*) -- that is, of course, unless the card is already completely used up, in a later-round situation. With the 10s, this would be the case if three or less appeared with the players' first two cards, or five or less, by the end of the round.

That being said, seeing 2 of one particular card (or 7 of the 10s) in one round is often enough to say that card is unlikely to appear again that round.

Therefore, for example, if there are three 9s on the table, it would be statistically highly unlikely the hole card would be a 9. If, however, let's say this is the first round and there are NO 9s on the table; then, it's one card that might very well be in the hole.

(By the way, the above shorthand or beginner's method, if you will, is also effective in doing a post-round Inter-Round analysis looking ahead to the next round's probabilities.)

One more thing: *card flow analysis* also yields clues as to the identity of the hole card. At most casinos, *the second cards dealt to the players lead directly up to the dealer's hole card, and* the *first player hit cards usually come directly after the hole card.* (Of course, at many casinos outside the States, there is no hole card -- the dealer's *second* card comes after the player's hit cards. We'll talk about how to handle that later.) If you're at a casino where the first player cards are the ones that lead directly up to the hole card (such as the Golden Nugget in Las Vegas, as of this writing), then those are the ones you'll scrutinize. It doesn't matter which row of cards it is. The cards that lead *to* and *from* the hole card are full of clues.

(Now, obviously those who play at the shoe game tables, where all the cards are dealt face-up, have an advantage here. Unfortunately, at most casinos, many of the cards at 1- & 2-deck pitch game tables are dealt face-down, and so analysis of the cards that were dealt immediately before the hole card will not be possible. However, scrutinizing the composition of all cards on the table will provide good clues as to the hole card's identity. So, at pitch-game tables, do an overall card mix analysis using the methods from chapters 10 and 11 to unmask the face-down cards, combining that with your analysis of the player hit cards, if they directly follow the hole card. Figure out which cards are under-represented, and which are overrepresented. The hole card will most likely fall into the group of cards that has not appeared at all, or that has not shown up in the proper proportions.)

Here are some important facts to know, in reading the *card flow*:

❶ *The hole card is very unlikely to be amongst the two or three cards that led up to or from it (except in the case of the 10s).*

❷ *There is a very small chance that the hole card will be the same as the up card (except in the case of the 10s).*

Indeed, one advantage of playing at 1- and 2-deck games is that you can bank on there being *a significantly smaller than normal chance* that the hole card's immediate neighbors will be of the same card variety; *and that goes for the hole card matching the up card as well.*

At 1- and 2-deck tables, for instance, the likelihood that the hole card is NOT of the type represented by the two cards that come before it is approximately 87% (the same is true in reference to the two cards that are dealt immediately after the hole card; each only has a little better than a 6% chance of matching up with the hole card). At multi-deck tables, that figure is roughly 85%. That's a pretty high certainty level. The likelihood that the hole card would NOT be the same as either of the two cards that come before OR after it is nearly 75% at pitch game tables, and about 69% at multi-deck tables. Now, the probability for the hole card to be the same as the card that comes right before it is only about 6% at pitch game tables, and 8% at multi-deck tables (that's true of the card dealt after the hole card, too). If we look at the three cards on each side of the hole card, you have a 67% or 54% certainty, at pitch and shoe game tables respectively, the hole card is not the same as them.

That's stretching the idea a bit thin, though.

Anyway -- a valid assumption to work with is: *the hole card is mathematically unlikely to be the same as the up card, or the two player cards dealt before or after it (in the case of non-10s).*

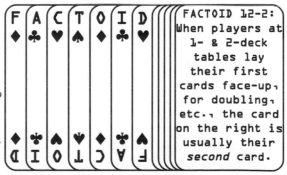

FACTOID 12-2: When players at 1- & 2-deck tables lay their first cards face-up, for doubling, etc., the card on the right is usually their second card.

Card flow, unfortunately, is not helpful with regard to the 10s; for that, you need to analyze the card mix. Because there are four times the number of 10s as other cards, it's not as improbable or surprising to have two or more 10s dealt in a row.

Recognizing Ducks & Bucks

The most important reason to acquire the skill of estimating what the hole card is so that you can identify the up cards that are *Ducks* and *Bucks* (from Chapter 9). This is a very accurate way of predicting the dealer's outcome.

For instance, you will NOT want to surrender with your stiff if you're facing a Duck with a high bust rate. Let's me demonstrate how this works, with Examples A and B, on the following page. These are first-round pitch game examples, where you need to unmask the face-down cards with the knowledge you gained in Chapters 10 and 11. They are also similar in that you hold the same hand, a stiff, consisting of a 5 and a 10. What should your Real-time Card Strategy be?

In A, your first card was the 5. Now, if you were playing according to the most accurate Basic Strategy-type chart, you'd surrender. But let's look at this more closely.

Fortunately, all of the face-down cards are of the First Category, so that makes things simple. What do you know about those, when facing the 10 as the up card? *None are 2s through 6s.* Since the dealer checked for a Black-jack and did not have one, we know the hole card is not an Ace. Nor is it likely to be one of the 10s, which appear to be overrepresented in this mix: you know, from Chapter 11, that 59% of the 10 First Category face-down cards, or 6 in this case, are likely to be 10s. Combined with your 10 and the dealer's 10, that's 8 out of 14 cards on the table -- more than 50% of the mix (and 10s should account for about 31%). It's unlikely the hole card is a 7, 8 or 9, either, since at least one of each of those, as you also know from Chapter 11, are among the face-down cards (that chapter showed that nearly 30% of the First Category cards will be 8s and 9s against the dealer's 10, and nearly 10% should be 7s; of course, one might be an Ace, but at 5% likelihood, that's the least probable). *So, it looks like the hole card is most likely to be a 2, 3, 4 or 6 (since you hold a 5), and the 10 is a Duck.* This is the information you've arrived at through Strategic Card Analysis.

Now, for your Real-time Card Strategy, because the 10 is a Duck, your decision is made that much easier. Simply go to the chart for the 10 Duck, and it tells you that it's smartest to *stand* here, with your 15.

In Example B, too, all of the face-down cards are of one variety, namely, First Category face-down cards. Again, from what you read in Chapter 11 you know there are no 2s through 6s among them. In this case, though, you have some idea of what the card flow was like just before the hole card was dealt (*the cards to the right as the player lays them down are most likely to*

Chart 12-1

Recognize A Duck or Buck?
...And What's Your Best Move?

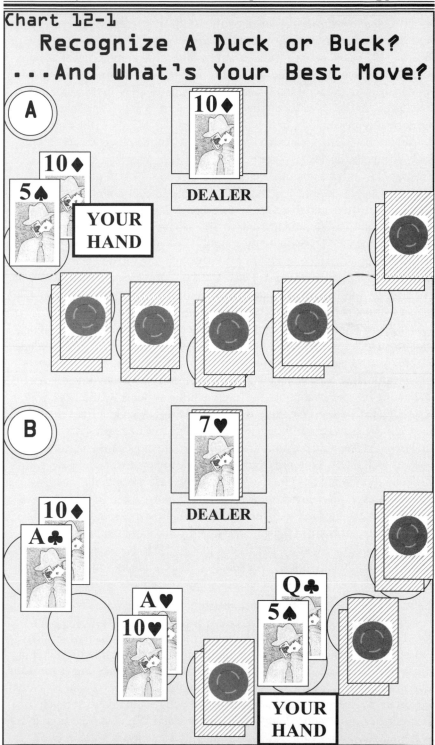

be the second cards they received, by the way). It appears an Ace and a 10 were dealt just prior to the hole card, so *the hole card is not likely to be an Ace (the 10 doesn't help us, in a card flow analysis)*. Your certainty level is actually nearly 94% (see page 279). Boy, is that *great* information! Plus, your analysis of the total likely mix of cards comes up with the same conclusion: of the 14 cards on the table, at least two are Aces. That's twice the normal representation in that amount of cards. So, again, the hole card is unlikely to be an Ace. You also know that 33% of the players' face-down cards versus the dealer's 10 are pairs of 10s (from what you learned in Chapter 11). At least one other face-down card is a 10, and perhaps two (because Chapter 11 told you that 57% of First Category cards versus the dealer's 7 are 10s), and three of the face-up cards are 10s, so at least 6 or 7 of 14 cards are 10s. So, the number of 10s, whose Circle of 13 proportion is a little less than 31%, accounts for roughly 50% of the cards. You've uncovered an imbalance in favor of the 10s. So, with the hole card statistically unlikely to be either an Ace or a 10, the 7 sure looks like a Duck to me. The strategy for this kind of Duck when holding a 15 versus the dealer's 7, as you learned in Chapter 9, is to *stand*.

As these examples should have demonstrated, one of the beautiful things about the Ducks and Bucks is that it speaks directly to the unique imbalance of cards you're facing in a particular round, with regard to how it impacts the up card. Here, you've taken advantage of your newfound knowledge of fluctuating up card busting rates. Card counting systems would have you believe that it's a *negative* thing when high cards (as each defines them -- and each defines them differently) are depleted. Yet Examples A and B point out how mistaken this presumption can be. While most card counting systems would tell you these examples represent negative situations (and most would wrongly tell you to *hit* your 15s), these are actually *positive* opportunities. *It all depends on what hand you have, what cards you need, and whether the up card is a Duck or Buck*. As the Ducks and Bucks tell you, these up cards are at their *weakest*, and you should neither play them according to Basic Strategy, nor from a place of fear. If you know an up card is in a situation where it will dependably bust as much as you've been told 4s through 6s bust (in the 40 percentile range) -- or *more* -- then it makes total sense to play it like a 4-6.

Determining Your Likely Hit Cards & Card Strategy

Analyzing player hit cards has another benefit for you, aside from helping you to uncover what the dealer's hole card might be. *It clues you in on what your probable hit cards will be*. Knowing the likely nature of your hit cards will fine tune decisions as to whether or not you should take Insurance (or Even Money), surrender, double, split, hit or stand. (Of course, if no players took hit cards before your turn, you simply do an analysis of the mix of cards on the tables, as we did in Examples A and B, and that will give you your answer.)

Just as you saw with hole card determination, the *card flow* that immediately leads up to your turn is a tip off as to what you're likely to get. The card or cards you receive are highly unlikely to be the same kind as the two or three cards that came just before your turn (with the exception, once again, of the 10s). We can say with 92-94% certainty (with the highest number representing pitch game levels) that your first hit card is unlikely to be same as the card that was dealt just before your turn (in the case of non-10s). We can say with 84-88% certainty that your first hit card will not be the same as the two cards that led up to it. And we can say with 76-83% certainty that your first hit card is unlikely to be the same as any of the three cards that were dealt just before your turn (except, once again, in the case of the 10s).

This knowledge, and your understanding that imbalances reveal probabilities will power your *hit card analysis* in deciding whether you're likely to get the *exact* card or cards you need to make your hand with any hit card or cards you might take. You're seeking precision: you want to deal with the realities of the moment. In some cases, your hit card analysis will lead you to make more *cautious* moves than you'd ever imagined; in other cases, it will cause you to become much more *aggressive* than usual. *You should go against traditional advice and make a creative move if the hit-card evidence points to its wisdom.*

The question of whether you should or should not take a hit card is a two-level issue, which requires that you not only ask yourself: what's the probability that it will *bust* you; but, also: will it make you *competitive* against the dealer? With regard to the second question -- whether or not you take a hit card is, of course, codependent upon what you've concluded about the dealer's hole card. If you are pretty certain the dealer's Ace has a 10 under it, then taking Insurance (or, asking for Even Money, if you have a Blackjack) is wise, *no matter what hand you hold.*

Here's another example: you have a hard total of 13 versus the dealer's 2, which is a Buck, because the 10s were overrepresented in the cards dealt since the last shuffle. Also, a 9 was dealt to the player immediately to your right, as his only hit card. What should you do? Basic Strategy would say: stand.

But, the only two cards that would bust your 13 are highly unlikely to be amongst your hit cards. That makes statistical sense, because you know that, since a 9 came before your turn, there's a slim chance you'll get one of those cards; and, because there has been a noticeable imbalance regarding there being too many 10s on the table, you won't likely get one of those. Therefore, you should *hit* your 13, because it's highly improbable you will bust. After all, isn't your fear of busting the only reason you might want to stand here??

Now, as I have warned you before, you will sometimes find yourself in losing situations, where you must either choose the path of lowest losses, or go for broke. We are not talking about acting on *hunches* here -- I've given you ample, concrete guidelines based upon sound logic, with which you can make these decisions with intelligence and confidence.

An example of this, on the extreme end of things is: if the probable hole card will give the dealer a score of 20 or 21, you should consider *surrendering* your hard hand totals of 17. That's a case of *knowing* you're going to lose, so why not? OR, instead you might even choose to *hit* your 17 in that situation, in very rare instances where your hit card analysis indicates you're very very likely to get an Ace through a 4. (That's a highly controversial move, however, one to be done with great discretion. If you're being watched closely by casino personnel, don't even think of doing this unless you're a good actor, and can pretend to be either an absolute beginner, or someone who's not very bright -- then you can blame this move on not knowing how to play the game; if it indeed proves to be a brilliant move, you might be labelled a card counter and get barred.)

I'll elaborate on this, in the following sections.

How To Handle Your Stiffs

If you're like most other players, the issue that plagues you the most is how to handle your stiffs, especially of 14 to 16 points, when facing the dealer's 7 through the Ace. My encounters with players around the nation indicate there's a lot of confusion surrounding this issue. However, the great thing is: you're holding the answer in your hands.

My innovation, the Ducks and Bucks, solves this problem, with a level of precision you've never had before. The Ducks and Bucks strategy recommendations in the "What's Your Up Card IQ?" chapter give you explicit advice in this regard. For instance, if a Duck's strategy box says "Play It Like A 4-6," then you should *stand* on your stiffs. Actually, you already saw how this worked in detail, in examples A and B on page 281.

One factor the Ducks and Bucks concept cannot address, however, is how to adjust your strategy to suit the differing results of your hit card analyses, in all the various card situations you will face -- particularly when facing Bucks. Here's what you should do:

If you *know, with a good degree of certainty,* that your hit card will *bust* you, then you have only two choices: to stand or surrender. Your course depends upon whether the up card is a Duck or a Buck. Stand versus the Duck; surrender against the Buck. Conversely, if the probability of getting a *helpful* low card is *good* when holding a stiff against a Buck, it would NOT be smart to surrender. Then, you'd *hit* -- *especially against a high up card.*

*But, in order to reach an educated decision, **you need to especially keep***

*track of the cards that you need the most, when holding the two most
bustable stiffs -- your totals of 15 and 16. The cards I'm referring to are
the 4s through 6s. These cards would give your 15s scores that would have
a good chance of competing with the dealer. The 4s and 5s would give your
16s the highest possible winning totals.*

*If these cards are gone, or greatly lacking in proportion to the other cards,
then hitting your 15s and 16s might not be an option (unless there are some
left, they are way overdue, and you have a high probability of getting one).*

How To Assess Your Chances With Doubling

Now, when it comes to possible *doubling* situations, you will again rely
upon two factors to guide you: the Ducks and Bucks; and, your assessment
of what your likely extra card would be (vis a vis how competitive that will
make your hand versus the dealer's likely outcome). This translates into:
*avoiding traditional doubling moves when the cards you need are lacking,
and/or the dealer will likely achieve a strong score*; and, *pursuing
untraditional doubling moves when the up card is a Duck, and your chances
are great that you'll draw a high score with the extra card you'll get*
(actually, in the case of the dealer's 7 Duck, even an 18 might suffice).

Take a quick peek at Examples C and D on the next page, and see if you
can figure out whether these are good or bad doubling situations, before I
give you the solution... For Example D, I need to tell you that this is a
second round situation, and that in round one, the dealer got a Blackjack,
and you counted *eight* 10s and *two* 9s among the spent first round cards.

(From now on, the examples will have the cards face up, to speed things
along. Also, now that you know how to handle pitch game difficulties, let's
show the shoe game folks how to deal with their realities.)

Let's solve Example C. First: is the 9 a Duck or Buck? It seems to be
leaning toward a Duck -- the 8s have all been played, and the 9s have been
overrepresented. But there still plenty of 10s left. Five 10s are on the table,
but that's normal for 18 cards -- in fact, it's slightly *less* than what might be
expected. So, although the 10s are not *overdue*, they're not *overplayed*,
either, and so it's not improbable that the hole card might be a 10. The 3s, 5s
and 7s have not been dealt at all, so they're *overdue, and might very well be
in the hole.* But that's not necessarily good news. That means *your next hit
card is not unlikely to be one of those cards (which would be devastating if
you doubled).*

What decides the issue for me here is the final question you must ask
yourself: what do you *need*, to make your hand, and is it in good supply?
Without strong evidence the dealer's 9 is a Duck, *you'd want to be assured
your score would be 19 or above before doubling on your 10 here.* Since two
9s were dealt already, getting a 19 is unlikely. Because the 8s are gone, you
cannot achieve an 18. A 7 came in the player hit cards that immediately

Chart 12-2

To Double or Not To Double?

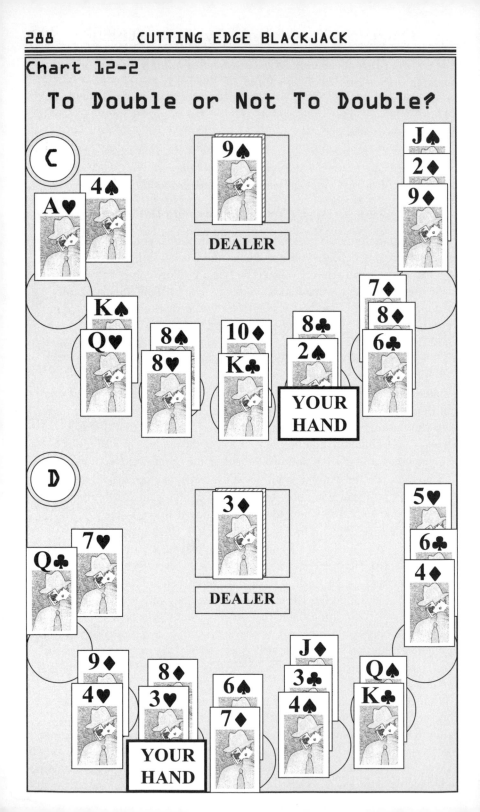

preceded your turn, so you're probably not going to get a 7. And because five 10s are on the table already, they're not overdue and you can't count on getting one. An Ace would be perfect, but one's already on the table; they're not *overdue*, so, while getting one is possible, it's not predictable. I wouldn't double here. *My decision: I'd play conservatively, and just hit this hand.*

And here's the bottom line: if you'd doubled here, you'd indeed have gotten a 3 upon your 10 (which makes sense based upon our assessment of the probabilities), and you would have *lost* (the dealer had a 10 in the hole, an eventuality we also determined was among the good possibilities). However, if you'd *not* doubled, and instead took hit cards, as I'd suggested, you'd have *won* (your second hit card would have been a 7, for a total of 20 -- a card I also predicted was likely to come). So our Strategic Card Analysis assessment was highly effective, and produced a win where we would otherwise have lost (had we followed traditional advice and doubled). I rest my case.

Example D: OK, first, is the up card a Duck or Buck? Well, you know three of four 9s have now been dealt, and twelve 10s, in the 34 cards that came before your turn (and therefore, depleted). The 3 is a *Buck* -- it's likely to score (and -- look back at the Score Profiles of Chapter 9: it tends to score high). Now, ask yourself: "What do I need to have any chance of *winning* against that Buck?" With an 11, you'd need an 8, 9 or 10. Yet, with your holding an 8, getting a second is not likely. The 9s are almost gone; the 10s are low in supply and NOT due. I'd *hit* here, and not risk the extra money in doubling. Anything less than a 6, and you'd be hanging in the wind with a stiff, and there have already been two 6s dealt, just before your turn, and three 7s are gone... No, hit this. In fact...this virtual player, having been programmed to play Basic Strategy, *doubled*, and got an Ace as the extra card, thereby *losing (twice* the player's original bet) to the dealer, who had a 10 in the hole, and then pulled an Ace and a 5, for a 19. With the Cutting Edge method, you would have pulled two Aces AND the 5 (because all the cards that would have busted your 13 -- the 9s and 10s -- were overplayed, and 2s, 5s, 8s and Aces were overdue), for an 18. Now, an 18 is not a high score, but it sure beats hanging in the wind with a stiff that will lose more than win against a Buck -- which is what all of the major card counting systems would have had you do.

If you're curious to know what the outcome would have been had you pulled to the 18, as Real-time Card Strategy would have indicated: the dealer would then have busted, drawing a 10 as the hit card. But, don't let this cloud the issue. In point of fact, the dealer would have drawn to a 19 or greater with the next three cards that were in line to be dealt after that 10 (and with 7 of the 10 cards that were due to be dealt after your turn). But, that should not shock you, since, as I pointed out earlier, the 3 was a Buck. The percentages of it drawing to a good score were in its favor.

The point is, whatever the outcome in this particular instance, pulling to the 18 would have been much smarter than doubling. Yet *all* of the major card counting systems would have told you to double in this situation, and *without* reservation, or warned you about when *not* to. Interestingly enough, their counts would all have registered in the *negative* range at your turn -- from -2 to -16, depending on the system! Just another demonstration of how much more accurate and effective the Real-time Card Strategy method is than the card counting systems of the past.

How To Assess Your Chances With Splitting

Now, if you're in a potential *splitting* situation, and you're thinking of doing that in a daring way, there's something important you should know: *any hands you split will have roughly the same chances of success as any dealer up card of the same value -- so long as you plan on drawing to a 17 or better.* In other words, split two 2s, and they'll bust approximately the same percentage of times as the dealer's 2, and the score profiles will be very similar (when you're pulling to a 17). So, *you can refer back to the Up Card Performance Profiles from the "What's Your Up Card IQ?" chapter, in assessing your own results in splitting any two cards.*

This is a GREAT principle to know!...And yet another way you can make powerfully valid Probability Assessments at the table.

Even better -- *the concept of the Ducks and Bucks can also be applied to your split hands (once again, IF you intend to take hit cards until your score is 17 or better).* THIS is dynamite stuff! *What you should do here, then, is to look for situations in which you believe, based upon your analysis of the composition of the cards that have been dealt, that your split cards will act like Bucks, where their chances of busting are very small.* (If you want to refresh your memory, you might want to refer back to the section where I introduced the Bucks' statistical behavior, starting on page 187.)

I'll give you an example. You've got two 9s, and you know that 3s through 7s have been all but played out. Well, then, instead of *standing* versus the dealer's 7, it's definitely wisest to split in this situation. Your individual 9s will act like Bucks, busting less than 3% of the time!! Your chances of busting here are *virtually negligible, and your score profile would kick serious butt against the dealer's 7! (The Simplified Bucks would work here, too -- i.e., this move makes sense even if only the 5s through 7s are lacking, where your 9s would act like Simplified Buck C's, with a 12.46% bust rate.)*

The flip side of this coin is that *you should not split in cases where your split cards would behave like Ducks, especially versus the dealer's strong up cards.* This means either hitting your pairs of like cards or standing, in situations where you thought splitting should be automatic.

So, continuing the example of your pairs of 9s, if 8s and 10s have been depleted, or 9s, 10s and Aces, you would not want to split versus the dealer's 8 or 9. In that case, your 9s would act like Ducks and bust roughly 40% to 43% of the time, respectively.

Beyond this, your hit card assessment can also determine whether you split or not. If you hold a pair of 8s, and your hit card analysis tells you 10s are coming, while your hole card analysis indicates the dealer's 10 is likely to have a 10 in the hole, then *surrender* those 8s!

Let's also talk about your pairs of Aces. Yes, this often provides a great splitting opportunity. *But...what if you had the power to predict when splitting Aces was wrong...when it would result in worse results than hitting them? Wouldn't it be foolish, then, to split them?* The answer is: of course!

The point I'm trying to get across is: with each hand, in every round, you must ask yourself: a) what do I need?; and, b) is it *available*? It's a supply and demand type of thing. Your Aces will be hanging in the wind if they are dealt two low cards. Don't forget -- split Aces have a handicap other split pairs don't: you get just one card upon each. Versus the dealer's higher up cards, especially, you must know that each Ace will reach a good, high score after splitting. Otherwise, what's the point? Don't tell me you're afraid of what others might say. You've got to be tough-skinned if you're going to be a winner; if you're worried about criticism when you rightly choose *not* to split your Aces in dangerous situations, then you need to adjust your attitude (it's *your* money!). (It really irks me when non-player self-appointed pundits righteously declare you should *always* split Aces! With my system you now have the power to discern when that move is wrong. Ignore the know-it-alls who are not really players, anyway.

Now, here's the real deal. When you split Aces -- especially against the dealer's 7 through Ace, but also against the lower up cards when they are Bucks -- you particularly want to get 8s, 9s or 10s, for two reasons. You want to insure that those hands don't result in underscores, AND that they are *competitive* against the dealer's likely score.

For instance, look at Example E on the next page, taken from my research card runs. First, you know the hole card is not an Ace (the dealer checked for that first). Is the up card a Duck or Buck? A compositional analysis shows the lack of 7s, and 8s, but a slight surplus of 10s having been dealt -- eight, among the 22 cards that came before your turn, but that's really not a bankable imbalance. (It should be easy to get a grip on the total number of cards on the table. It all goes back to the chapter on "How The Number of Players Affects Your Bottom Line." At a 7-player table, 16 cards have been played with the first two cards dealt to one and all. So, just add the number of hit cards to that 16, a constant in every round.) Furthermore, a card flow and compositional analyses lean *against* the 10 being a Duck: a 5 is within the three player hit cards that came after the hole card, and a 4 came three cards before the hole card; plus, there are two 6s, 4s and 3s on the table, and one 2. Here's a case where the up card is neither evidently a Duck or Buck -

Chart 12-3

To Split or Not To Split?

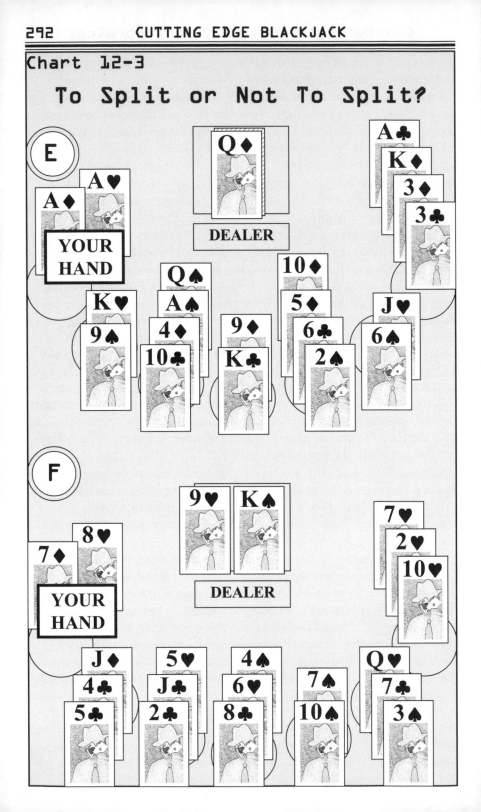

- so it has be treated like the average Weakened 10 (which is, as you know, not very *weak* -- refer back to the "What's Your Up Card IQ?" chapter).

So...how do you play your Aces? A hit card analysis shows that three 10s were dealt in 6 cards, including the one that preceded your move. Facing the 10, you'd want to get at least an 8, and, preferably, a 9 or greater, in order to match up against the dealer. Two 9s are on the table...not likely, therefore, you'll get one of those. No 8s have been played, though, and the 10s have certainly not been played out, so I might split here -- IF this were the end of the story.

Inter-Round Analysis

The truth is, this card situation came in the SECOND round of action. The reason I did things this way was to dramatize the fact that *Inter-Round Analysis* (which involves doing an ongoing accounting of the exact mix of cards that were dealt in prior rounds) *is a necessary adjunct to Intra-Round Analysis.* As you'll see, by taking the first round into account, *a whole different picture emerges.*

The first round is displayed in Example F. An Inter-Round Analysis reveals that the 7s and 8s were used up completely in the first round. In fact, *9s are now all but depleted, as are the 10s* -- 14 have already been dealt!

So...now that you've considered what went on in the prior round, would *you* split those Aces, knowing the cards you need are practically gone? I wouldn't. Your Aces get just one card upon each, whereas the dealer can and will continue to pull to a probable good score. In fact, the virtual player represented in this example did split those Aces (because players in my card runs were programmed to play according to Basic Strategy), and got a 6 on one Ace and a 2 on the other, losing both hands to the dealer, who had an 8 in the hole. I rest my case. If that player had kept those Aces together, they would have pulled to a 20, and won that hand, instead of losing twice the amount of the original bet (you wouldn't stand with a soft 18 versus the 10). That demonstrates the benefits of adopting a *Real-time Card Strategy* -- making a move that fits the occasion -- as opposed to slavishly following advice to "always split Aces" however wrong that might be. You now have the power to know better.

(By the way -- if you think all of this is far out...it appears that one of blackjack's greats, Lawrence Revere, was also moving toward a flexible, Real-time card strategy approach, akin to what I've invented, just before he died. In fact, *he even suggested that you should split your pairs of 10s under certain circumstances* -- see page 149 of his *Playing Blackjack As A Business!*)

So, we've established that analyzing just the current round's action can be very misleading -- you need to do a constant reckoning of the imbalances that have been created and the relative supply of each card, through Inter-

Round Analysis, or your card strategy will be off.

One last thing about Inter-Round Analysis. Aside from using it to direct your Real-time Card Strategy, you should, of course, also use it to help guide your betting strategy (with regard to what you learned in Chapter 8, on "Auxiliary Betting Indicators"). There's no reason to repeat all of that here. Just make sure that your Inter-Round Analysis includes an assessment of how the mix of cards played out since the last shuffle might work to your advantage or against it, in predicting future round results, so that your betting strategy adjusts to the reality you're facing.

Inter-Shuffle Analysis

Inter-*Shuffle* Analysis is the detection of all the repeating phenomenon you've read about in *Cutting Edge Blackjack*, and then, capitalizing on the predictability that comes with repeating events. (As you read before, this process includes utilizing the skills you gained in Chapter 5, to follow the cards through the shuffling process -- and taking advantage of your knowledge if you get to cut the cards.) It is also making a mental note of any important *groups of like cards* that were either spent during the rounds, or left undealt at the shuffle, in case they're worth tracking (or worthy of bringing back through your placement of the cut card, when it's your turn).

Unless you join a table when new cards are being introduced, some of these repeating events have been ongoing and may or may not be at their end. So your job will be twofold: first, spot the already-existing patterns; and second, be watchful for any new ones being made as the cards play out.

The new ones will be created in one of two ways: either through the *dealing* of cards during a round (we'll call these *Hand-Dealt Patterns*), or in the *discarding* of player cards (we'll call these *Hand-Discarded Groupings*). I use the modifier "hand-dealt," because these events would have no significance if produced by a computer or a randomizing shuffler (both of which generate random results, which will not repeat).

Hand-Dealt Patterns (HDPs) are many. They might be consecutive *strings* of like cards (of two or more) that end up next to each other within one player's hand during the dealing of a round, which are likely to repeat either together or close together after a certain number of future shuffles. Hand-Dealt Patterns also include: situations where two or more like cards wind up close together (these are the *proximate cards* you read about in Chapter 6, which can be within one player's hand, or within several nearby players' hands, which we refer to either as duets, trios, quartets, quintets, depending on how many lie close together); *orbiting associations* -- groups of different kinds of cards dealt in one round, many of which will keep returning together from shuffle to shuffle (which are especially good when the mix causes the dealer to bust more than normal, or provides dependable repeating player blackjacks); as well as the creation of other repeating phenomenon, including *dealer up card and hole card repetition* (which, with regard to the formation of dealer Blackjacks, could have disastrous consequences), and *repeating player splitting opportunities* (where cards that players often split keep coming back together in player hands from shuffle to shuffle).

See how many possible Hand-Dealt Patterns you can find in Examples G and H on the next page. We'll discuss them in a minute. (Hint: don't forget that some hands will be discarded when they bust, which changes the whole picture!)

One reminder: the cards in these examples are pictured in a way that was easiest to display, but, as I warned you before, is a bit deceptive. The cards that lie above the players' lower cards are actually on TOP of them, and are not slid below them. This is key to your understanding their order, after the dealer later removes them from the table.

Now, *Hand-Discarded Groupings (HDGs)* are made because of the three types of player hands that are collected by the dealer before the round is over: hands that bust; hands that are surrendered; and player Blackjacks. Interesting things can happen when these hands -- which might have been relatively far apart before -- become neighbors in the discard rack. For example, when two or more players have Blackjacks, the Aces in those hands now become proximate cards that tend to repeat together. To a lesser degree, hand discarded groupings worth following can result from the placing of one round's spent cards on top of the last. The first players' hands from the last completed round are placed on top of the dealer's hand from the prior round (which is, in turn, on top of the last players' hands from the prior round). So, for instance, if the dealer had a Blackjack in the prior round, and the first few players in the most recent round drew Aces, a large grouping of Aces would result in the discarding process. Once again, look at Examples G and H and see how many possible Hand-Discarded Groupings you can suggest.

Done? Let's compare notes on our Inter-Shuffle Analyses of Examples G and H.

First, here are the *strings* I found: in G, the second baseman has a string of three Aces (a *trio*), which becomes a quartet of Aces in a hand-discarded grouping, when the dealer collects the hand of 8♥-A♥, to the second baseman's right (the A♥ being a proximate neighbor of the other Aces until then). There's also a string of 6s in the third baseman's hand, which becomes a trio of 6s when the dealer's 6, a proximate card, joins up with them, when the dealer clears the cards at the end of the round. In H, there's a string of two 3s (a hand-dealt pattern), and two strings made by Hand-Discarded Groupings: the proximate Aces will become neighbors when the two player Blackjacks are collected, and the proximate 7s will also become neighbors when the dealer takes all cards left at the end of the round. Any strings are worthy of note, because many will come back relatively intact after later

Chart 12-4
How Many Possible Newly-Created HDPs & HDGs Can You Find?

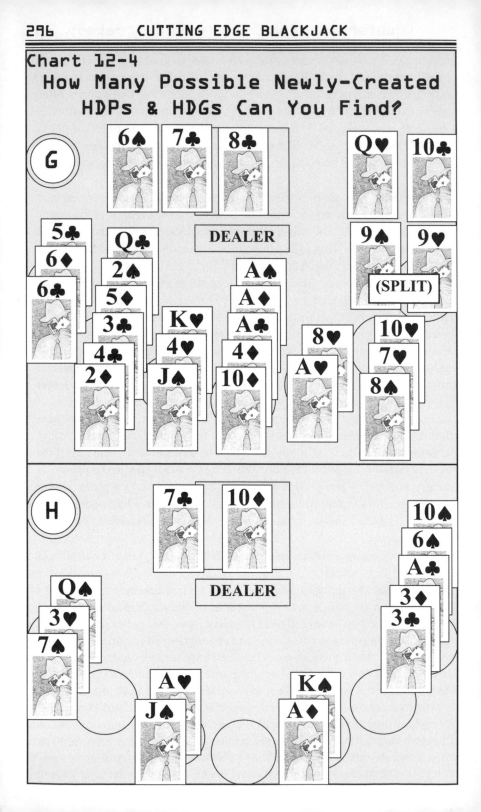

shuffles, and will signal you to the other's imminent return. Any strings of Aces have great potential in returning together in the next half-dozen or so shuffles (at least), either helping you or the dealer, so you'll want to monitor their progress through the shuffle carefully. For instance, if, after a shuffle, the first of these particular Aces is dealt two or three cards before the hole card, and the dealer has a 10 showing, look out! I'd play that round cautiously, because the dealer might very well have a Blackjack -- unless, of course, the other Aces in the string were dealt to the players.

(By the way -- they're not demonstrated here, but relatively long strings of 10s sometimes form too. You should pay attention to these, too: they can help or hurt you later on. If you're aware they exist, and you make note of the start of their return in following shuffles, you can use them to your advantage, in predicting probable events, and take appropriate action.)

There were other proximate cards, as well: note the two 8s and 9s in G, and three 9s in II. More importantly, there's a proximate A♣ in the busted first baseman's hand in H which, having been taken immediately before or after the two player Blackjacks (depending on whether the casino takes the Blackjacks immediately, or when each player's turn arrives), becomes a near-neighbor of the other two Aces -- a very fortuitous hand-discarded grouping, indeed. I'd want to follow these Aces through the shuffle, either to bring them back in the first round if I got the cut card (cutting, perhaps, in the midst of them, to avoid giving the dealer an Ace), or in anticipation of their return (seeing one of the three would indicate the other two are likely to come in short order -- this might help in your decision whether to double on a 10-point hand, or, perhaps, in estimating what the dealer has in the hole).

Orbiting associations? Depending on how the cards are cut after the next shuffle, I wouldn't be surprised to find most of the cards in G and H returning together in later rounds, because of how close the defining clusters of cards are in the discard tray. One especially interesting thing to note about the possible orbiting association created in H: all of the 10-point cards from the spades is represented -- I'd look to this as a possible tip off after later shuffles in figuring out what the dealer's hole card might be, as well as your hit cards (if they're coming around together, as is likely, the first one of these that appears is a signal that the others are probably due!) -- in other words, the minute the first of these appears, it is reasonable to expect to see at least one or two, if not all of the others, closely following. This kind of thing (the appearance of all the 10s in one suit in one round, in close proximity to one another, or perhaps all four Queens, etc.) becomes a great Inter-Shuffle Analysis aid in predicting future events. The quartet of Aces in Example G and the trio of Aces in Example H are likely to provide players with a higher-than-normal number of Blackjacks after future shuffles, if the cutting of the cards doesn't destroy their value...HOWEVER, if you notice these Aces winding up part of a repeating dealer up card or hole card phenomenon, as is possible, beware! Once you've noticed such trios and quartets, bet a bit more cautiously upon seeing them result in one or two dealer Blackjacks. You saw in Chapter 6 how dealer up cards and hole cards tend to repeat.

Are there any possible repeating split cards in Examples G and H? In this case, the only cards split were the 9s in G, and, because 9s provide fairly good results in splitting, their return would be a favorable event, and not entirely unexpected, as things go. Anticipating and capitalizing on repeating split cards, however, is difficult. It should simply register, in this case, as a possible favorable factor, with regard to the personality of these cards.

One last thing -- Example G offers a classic instance of showing how Inter-Round Analysis should motivate your betting strategy. If this were a first-round example, seeing this mix of cards would be like a flashing green light to me. The 4s and 6s (crucial score-maker cards) are nearly spent, and *the Aces are completely played out!* I'd raise my bet in the next round (see Chapter 8, for the reasons why). With this type of imbalance, the dealer would have a high probability of busting in the next round, and zero probability of getting a Blackjack; plus, the players would have a strong likelihood of winning. The interesting thing about this example is that most card counting systems would miss the boat here. One would say the count is -3, two would tell you the count is -2, two would say, no, it's actually neutral (0), and one would register +2. What a mixed bag of results! Only *one* identified this correctly as a *positive* situation!

Don't Forget The Undealt Cards

Before wrapping things up, let's look at Examples I and J on the next page. They show you the cards as they played out in the first and second rounds of action at a 1-deck table just before the shuffle. Do a quick Inter-Shuffle Analysis. Where might you want to place the cut card following the shuffle?

Did you pick up on the fact that no Aces were dealt? There is an abundance of 10s among the undealt cards, too. So you'd have a good shot at getting a Blackjack if you brought this bunch back into play in the first round following the shuffle, by careful placement of your cut card.

If you chose to attempt that, you would place the reshuffle card *just* above where your analysis of the shuffling procedure told you the Aces probably wound up. Or, even smarter, you might try to put the cut card in the *midst* of the Aces and 10s from the last round, in the hope that you would get one of the Aces, yet lessen the dealer's chances of getting one.

However, because you now know that, when Aces are *gone*, your probability of winning is even better (see Chapter 8, on Auxiliary Betting Indicators), you might instead choose to cut the cards so that the undealt Aces are *unlikely* to appear after the next shuffle. Then, you can start off with an

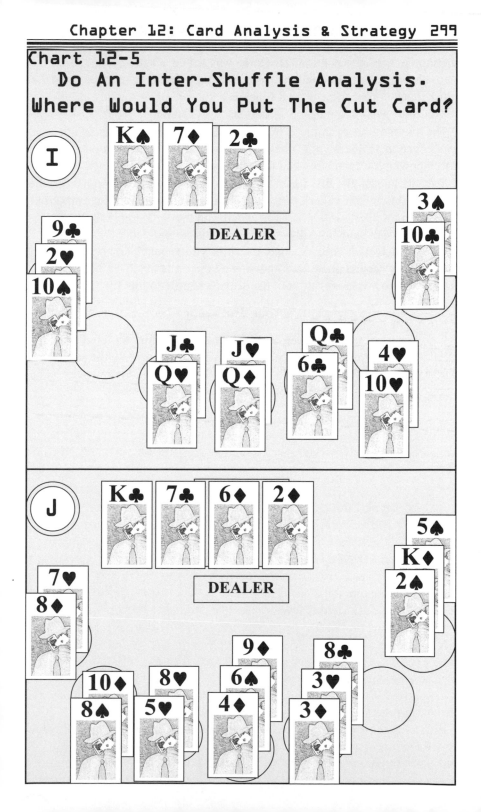

Chart 12-5
Do An Inter-Shuffle Analysis.
Where Would You Put The Cut Card?

appropriately bigger bet, too. That's the way I'd go. That way you *know* your chances of winning will be better than they would be had you gone the other route, hoping to be dealt a Blackjack. (Catching an Ace at a multi-player table even in the best of situations is no certainty.)

The moral of this example is twofold: one, don't forget to size up the *undealt* cards in doing your Inter-Shuffle Analyses; and, two: look at how much power you're given when the dealer places the cut card in your hand!

Two final notes, the first for multi-deck players: if you've been handed the cut card, this is your chance to try and change your fortune if the cards from the last shuffle period were not very good. Cut the cards to put the large stack of undealt cards into play. If the action is still no good, it might be time to find another table. Second, the skills you've just learned are powerful, but they depend upon your knowing all the cards that have been played; so, it would be wise to wait until the dealer's shuffle to join the table.

It's Time To Practice

OK! You've gotten your feet wet, and it's now time for you to take out a deck or two and practice your Strategic Card Analysis and Real-time Card Strategy! Make sure you shuffle the cards with a casino-style precision. The cards won't play out as they would at the casino unless you do.

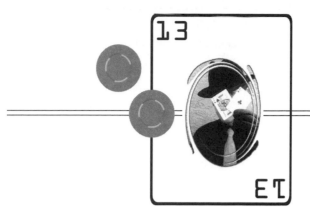

Practice, Practice, Practice

I can't emphasize this enough: it's time to practice what you've learned.

All new techniques and skills you've acquired need to be refined so you can pull them off smoothly at the casino. If you don't attend to this important part of the process, you'll make mistakes, and, if you're sloppy in your attempt to use them at the casino, you're likely to get unwanted scrutiny from casino employees, and, perhaps, get barred.

Re-read this book, as well. The first go-through might not sink in completely. Take notes to make things more clear.

That being said, if you find the wealth of information you've gained somewhat daunting, it makes sense to divide it up into bite-sized chunks, if you will, and conquer each, one at a time. Take on what seems most useful to you first. It's a lot to digest all at once!

This book took a lot longer to write than I had thought, but it was primarily due to the great rewards I was getting from my research. I chose to expand and extend my computer studies, and so I missed my original publishing deadlines, but I'm glad I did.

I'm very proud of this book. I hope you have found its contents to be as helpful to you as they have been to me, in my career as a player.

...Maybe I'll see you at the casino!

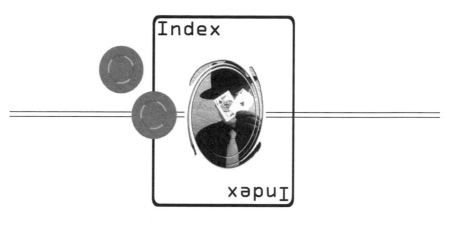

Index

Symbols

A

B

Glossary of Terms
(Note: Terms starting with numbers are listed under the letter
that starts the alpha-numeric spelling of those numbers.)

All-Inclusive Counting System: The *Blackjack The SMART Way* card counting system which takes into account every one of the 13 possible cards. Low cards are defined as the 2s through 7s; high cards, the 8s through 10 pointers.

Auxiliary Betting Indicators: Determinants in raising or lowering your bets. Mr. Harvey's research has revealed that a players' likelihood of winning or losing in the next round can be predicted with good accuracy by assessing the card imbalances of the moment. For instance, if the 9s have all been played, you are more likely to lose than win in the next round, all things being equal. For details (in actual percentages, for each card, see Chapter 8).

Basic Bet: The name I give to the minimum bet you want to play, whatever Level you're at. If you're at Level 0 or 1, the Basic Bet is 1 Unit. If you're at Level 2, the Basic Bet is 2 Units. If you're at Level 3, the Basic Bet is 3 Units. At no point during play at any Level will you place a bet that's lower than the Basic Bet.

Basic Strategy: A beginners' strategy for deciding how to play their hands. It's dictated by Basic Strategy charts. More advanced players, however, will use this as a reference point, in pulling off some of Mr. Harvey's more precise strategies (such as his innovative Ducks and Bucks method).

Basic Strategy Charts: Diagrams or spreadsheets which tell players how to play their hands in every card situation, when the cards are neutral,or balanced. Beginners use these charts exclusively. These diagrams contain only one suggested move per situation.

Betting Spot: The place on the table, in front of your seat, denoted by a circle or square usually, where you must place your betting chips. There are typically seven spots per table, although some casinos have been going to 6 player tables (and, recently, some casinos have even been experimenting with 5 player tables, which reduce players' likelihood of winning; for details on how the number of players at the table affects your winning rate, see Chapter 3).

Blackjack: When your first two cards contain an Ace and a 10-point card, for

21 points. It typically pays 1-1/2 times your bet (unless you tie with the dealer, in which case you win nothing unless you've chosen to take Even Money or Insurance; if you've chosen one of those options, you're paid an amount equal to your bet). In some casinos, Blackjacks at 1-deck tables are paying just 6 to 5.

Bounceback Factor: The author's term for a player's likelihood of returning to even or positive territory once the player has dipped into negative territory. This can be predicted with good accuracy, based upon what a player's WLM is (see Win/Loss Margin Unit for definition).

Boxing: A shuffling practice where roughly the top half of the cards is moved to the bottom.

Brutal Up Card or Buck: The author's term for situations where the likely hole card makes the up card extremely strong for the dealer, and hard to beat for the player.

Burning A Card: The dealer's discarding of the top card into the discard rack after the shuffle. Some casinos burn as many cards as there are players, before the dealer starts dealing from the newly shuffled stack.

Bust: To go over the maximum allowed point total of 21 when drawing a card. Whomever busts — the player or the dealer — loses instantly.

Card Counting: The practice in which cards are divided into two groups (one called "low cards," the other, "high cards"), the low cards then assigned a positive number (usually +1), the high cards a negative number (usually -1). The cards so labelled are then "counted" as they are played, according to their assigned card count number, in order to keep track of the proportion of low and high cards played. One reason for doing so is in an attempt to predict what cards might be dealt next.

Card Imbalances: When certain cards have been over-played or under-played, based upon their normal proportion in the Circle of 13 (or, the undealt deck).

Casino Countermeasures: Moves made by casino bosses and dealers to win back the money won by players. Often unfair, these moves include, among other things, shuffling up, speeding up the action, and changing out the dealer. (For details, see Chapter 11 of *Blackjack The SMART Way*.)

Cashing out: Taking your chips to the cashier's window (found off to the side somewhere in the casino) in exchange for their cash value.

CET: (See Count Estimate Translation.)

Charts: Diagrams or spreadsheets in which suggested moves in particular card situations are displayed.

Chips: The colored "coins" you use instead of money to place your bet. Although the colors of the various denominations — $5, $25, $100 and $1,000 – are usually the same from casino to casino (red, green, black and pink), the graphics and writing on each coin is peculiar to each casino, and always contains the name of that casino.

Circle of 13: A learning device introduced in *Cutting Edge Blackjack*, the audio book *Preparing YOU To WIN,* and seminar material. It's used to help determine what the mathematical probabilities are, to make smart moves.

"Color me in": What you say to the dealer to exchange your lower denomination chips for easier-to-carry higher denomination chips. Low stakes table players -- who play with red, $5 chips -- will be exchanging those chips for green, $25 chips, or black, $100 chips. How to do this: Wait for the dealer to finish collecting the cards from the last round, or finish shuffling the cards, and then place your chips on the table, just beyond the Insurance circle, and say "color me in, please." The dealer will then make the exchange. The dealer decides which of the higher denomination chips to give you. The reason this is done is that the casino does not want the dealer to run out of the more commonly used red or green chips.

Count Estimate Translation (or CET): Looking at the All-Inclusive Card Count count of the moment, and looking at it in reverse, for use in applying the author's method of figuring out the identity of players' facedown cards. For instance: if that method tells you a player's cards has a likely count of -2, that means the hand would probably contain two high cards (because high cards are assigned a value of -1 apiece).

Cutting the Cards: After the cards are shuffled, the dealer offers the shuffle marker to a player, who then pushes that marker into the cards wherever they choose, thereby cutting the cards in two. The cards above where the player places the marker go to the bottom of the stack; the card directly below the marker   becomes the top of the stack, to be the first card played (and that card is "burned," or discarded by the dealer; the card below it usually then becomes the first card dealt).

Doubling Down or Doubling: Placing an amount of chips equal to your bet (doubling the amount of money you have on the table), in exchange for just one more card dealt upon your hand. You may do this only immediately after having been dealt your first two cards (except at rare casinos, who might let you do this after you've received three cards). You only want to do this when you have a point total that won't bust with the taking of an extra card. You usually do this when you think the dealer will bust, and/or you'll achieve a great score with the next hit card due.

Diminished Up Card (or Duck): The author's term for situations where the likely hole card makes the up card extremely weak for the dealer, and much easier to beat for the player.

Even Money: When a player who has a Blackjack asks the dealer to be paid off right away, in even money (chips equal to the players bet, instead of the normal 1-1/2 times bet winnings), after the dealer's up card turns out to be an Ace. This option prevents the player from being "robbed" of a win if the player, using Mr. Harvey's method of determing the identity of the hole card, knows the dealer is likely to have a Blackjack. To avail yourself of this option, you say "Even money" when the dealer asks "Insurance?" (Not allowed at all casinos.)

Eye In The Sky: The cameras that are focused on your table, whose pictures are being viewed by casino employees in a surveillance room in an effort primarily to identify cheats, card counters and winning players. It's also occasionally used to resolve betting disputes, and monitor junket players.

Face Card: A Jack, Queen or King.

First Baseman: The player whose turn comes first in every round (who sits next to the dealer's left hand).

Flow of the Cards: the order in which the cards were dealt, vis a vis what that tells you when employing the author's card analysis methods.

Gains Stages: Introduced in Cutting Edge Blackjack, these are ranges of Win/ Loss Margin Units that precisely identify how good a betting spot is for a player. Categorized as "Horrible," "Bad," "Neutral," "Good" and "Great" periods, these provide a guide the player as to how to bet as well as when to leave a table.

Get-Out Points: WLM numbers that indicate it's time for a player to leave. (See Win/Loss Margin Units for WLM definition.)

Hand: Your, or the dealer's, first two cards. Secondary meaning: how your cards played out during any one round of action.

Hand-Dealt Patterns: Card patterns created in the dealing of the cards.

Hand-Discarded Groupings: Card patterns created in the dealer's collection of the cards.

Hard Hand: A hand of two cards that does not contain an Ace.

Hard Total: A total number of points in a hand without an Ace, or where the Ace counts as 1 point.

Hit: To take another card.

Hole card: The card dealers deal to themselves *face down*. The "mystery" card you won't see until you've played out your hand. In some locations around the world, such as in Europe and Canada, the dealer only gets an up card and takes no further cards until all players have finished their turns. The author's Ducks and Bucks method can be used in those locations to determine the dealer's relative strength. (Also see Page 185.)

House: Another way of saying "the casino."

Individual Hand-Count Estimate (or ICE): That's the card count you arrive at for a particular player's hand, when using the author's method of identifying the players' facedown cards.

Insurance: A separate bet you're allowed to make, paying 2-to-1, when the dealer's up card is an Ace. If you place chips amounting to half your bet in the Insurance circle, you're paid an amount equal to twice your Insurance bet if the dealer indeed has a Blackjack. You lose that bet if the dealer does NOT have a Blackjack. It's essentially a way to break even if the dealer has a Blackjack.

Intra-Round Card Analysis: Looking at the mix and the order of the cards dealt in a particular round for indications as to how well the dealer might do; also gives you indications as to how likely you are to get whatever hit cards you might need.

Inter-Round Card Analysis: Taking an accounting of the cards that have been dealt so far in predicting your likelihood of winning in the next round. Also means keeping track of cards dealt in prior rounds in order to make accurate predictions in the *current* round of action, vis a vis the dealer's likelihood of scoring or busting, and your probability of doing well.

Inter-Shuffle Analysis: Analyzing how the cards played out between shuffles for clues as to what's likely to come in the rounds following the next shuffle.

Lead Cards: With regard to the betting spot card repetition phenomenon, the cards that *repeat* the most.

Low Up Card Stiffs Effect: A phenomenon discovered by Richard Harvey, whereby the card move choices typically made by players against the dealer's up cards of 2 through 6 actually increase the odds of the dealer busting -- the more players in the mix, the greater the effect (in fact, there is veritably no such effect with less than 4 players).

Money Management: How you handle your bets. Secondary meaning: how you manage your money in coming out a winner or loser.

Multi-deck Games: Games in which more than two decks are used. Also known as Shoe Games (because the cards are typically held in a shoe, a plastic card storage device).

No-Shows: With regard to the betting spot card repetition phenomenon, the cards that are NOT dealt to a particular betting spot over a protracted number of shuffles.

Negative Count: When the card count tells you that more high cards have been played than low cards. If this number gets high enough, you should low cards are overdue to appear.

Orbiting Associations: Groups of cards dealt in one particular round involved in a repeating phenomenon whereby most of them return together in a round following the next shuffle(s).

Penetration: The percentage of cards that the dealer marks off with the re-shuffle card after a player cuts the cards. The percentage of cards ABOVE the re-shuffle card is the penetration you will get. In other words, if that represents 60% of the cards in the dealer's hand, or in the shoe, the penetration is said to be 60%. An important concept, because, the more cards you see, the easier it is to take advantage of the game's inherent predictability.

Performance Profiles: The author's term for the complete set of numbers that describe how well each of the dealer's up cards perform with regard to busting and/or reaching each of the five winning scores (17, 18, 19, 20 and 21). Includes Tell Numbers, Score Profiles, and Rankings (vis a vis wins and losses).

Personality of the Cards: The author's term for the peculiar characteristics of the particular set of cards being used at the table, which tend to repeat from shuffle to shuffle. Included in this concept is your determination of whether the cards are "Great," "Good," "Neutral," "Bad," or "Horrible," as well your identification of any patterns that repeat from shuffle to shuffle. (See *Blackjack The SMART Way*, Chapter 9.)

Personality of the Dealer Up Cards: The author's term for the behavior of each of the up cards, each of which has its peculiar tendencies in leading the dealer toward a particular winning total, or toward busting.

Pips: The cards that say "10," which differentiates these from their 10-point bretheren, the face cards.

Pit Boss: The casino manager who's in charge of a certain number of dealers and lower casino bosses (floormen) who directly supervise the tables in a "pit" (an enclosure encircled by Blackjack tables).

Pitch Game: A 1- or 2-deck blackjack game, where the dealer holds the cards in his or her left hand and PITCHES them to each player, face down. The players then must pick up their cards (in one hand only) to play out their hands.

Pivot Points: A WLM number that indicates you've entered a new Gains Stage (which, in turn, indicates your likelihood either of doing better or worse).

Placing a Bet: Putting the amount of chips you're wagering on the next round in your betting spot.

Player Card Gravity: The author's term for the effect he's discovered that players have on the dealer's likelihood of busting, based upon their card move decisions.

Player Progress Pattern (or PPP): Introduced in *Cutting Edge Blackjack*, this is the author's term for the graphical representation of your Win/Loss Margin Unit pattern over the course of many rounds of action (showing how you've fared). It looks very much a like a stock chart.

Point Of No Return: WLM number that indicates that your likelihood of returning to zero (or even) is nil.

Positive Count: When the card count tells you that more low cards have been played than high cards. The higher the number, the greater the likelihood that high cards will be dealt, rather than low.

Post-Marker-Dealing Phenomenon: Author's term for the fact that, in most cases, more cards must be dealt after the reshuffle card has been reached, in order to play out the final round. Mr. Harvey has discovered that, the more betting spots in play, the more cards that are necessary, in general, to finish out the round.

Principle of Imbalance & Rebalance: Author's invention, which states that, in a closed, balanced universe such as represented by a deck of cards, a imbalances will eventually tend to be followed by opposite imbalances.

Proximate Cards: Cards lying close together on the table in one round, which repeat, either in the same hand or nearby hands, in following rounds.

Push: When you tie with the dealer, neither winning nor losing any chips. You keep your bet. (The dealer typically knocks lightly on the table to indicate that you've achieved a tie.)

Real-time Card Strategy: The new, highly accurate approach to card strategy introduced in *Cutting Edge Blackjack*, which utilizes Strategic Card Analysis in order to make the most precise and appropriate move.

Repeating Phenomena: Discovered by Richard Harvey, these are the existence of repeating patterns due to the non-random nature of standardized dealer shuffling. They include groups of cards that are dealt to the same betting spot from shuffle to shuffle, up cards the dealer gets repeatedly over many shuffles, as well as whole groups of cards that tend to stay together from shuffle to shuffle (orbiting associations).

Riffle: The type of shuffle most people know and use when playing most card games.

Rotating Count Estimates (or RCEs): Used in the author's method to identify players' facedown cards, it's the use of a repeating count sequence or pattern to determine the likely count.

Round: The period of play from the first card dealt to the First Baseman to the last card dealt to the dealer.

Running Count: A card count you get by simply adding each card's card count value as it appears in the course of the game. This is what you use with the *Blackjack The SMART Way* **All-Inclusive Count**after a dozen or less hands upon first arriving at a table or with the arrival of a new dealer. Whether the result of rogue dealer cheating or simply a downturn in the card cycle, it's time for you to leave the table. This indicates a loss rate of 75% or greater. Invoke this twice in any one session and you should probably leave the casino.

Score Profile: The author's invention; a term describing the unique percentage of times a particular dealer up card reaches scores of 17, 18, 19, 20 and 21. Also includes the dealer's probability of drawing to a Blackjack, in the case of the 10s and Ace.

Soft Hand: A hand of two cards that contains an Ace.

Soft 17: When a score of 17 is made with the aid of an Ace, where the score might otherwise be considered to be 7 if the player or dealer choses to count the Ace as a 1-point card. In some casinos, the dealers must continue to draw cards if their 17 was achieved this way.

Soft Total: A point total in a hand that contains an Ace, where the Ace is being counted as 11 points.

Splitting: When you are dealt two like cards, say, two 2s, you are allowed (in most casinos) to divide those cards (after putting down an extra bet equal to your original bet) and start new hands with them. You tell the dealer "split" when it's your turn, while you put down the extra chips to cover the new hand. The dealer then plays each card as a new hand, giving you as many cards as you'd like on each card — with the exception of Aces; if you split those, you get just one extra card placed upon each Ace.

Stand: To "stand pat," not take any more cards, after receiving your first two cards.

Stiff: A hard total of 12 to 16 points, which is in danger of busting with an extra card.

Strategic Card Analysis: A new, three-tiered method introduced in *Cutting Edge Blackjack*, in order to accurately read what the cards are telling you regarding what your best card move is, and how you should bet. It involves Inter-Round, Intra-Round, and Intra-Shuffle analyses.

Stripping: A shuffling practice where small clumps of cards are (most commonly) moved from the top of the deck or decks held in the dealer's left hand, to the table, effectively moving the top cards to the bottom and vice versa.

Surrender: Where the player decides his or her hand is so very poor and the dealer's hand so very strong that he or she wants "out" of a round of action. Upon saying "surrender" (as soon as it's the player's turn) – without making any signals – the dealer takes half of the player's bet (leaving the other half to the player), and discards the player's cards. (Not allowed at all casinos.)

Table Winning Percentage: The author's term for the approximate number of hands you win, in percent. You can do it through exact mathematics — dividing the actual number of times you've won, by the total number of hands you've faced, and then multiplying the result by 100. Or, an approximation is often just as useful. (See *Blackjack The SMART Way*, Chapter 9.)

Tell Numbers: The author's invention; denoted either by a "+" or a "B." Numbers denoted by a "+" indicate how often a dealer's up card achieves the winning score denoted, or higher winning scores (for example, an 18+ would give you the percentage of times a particular up card reaches scores of 18, 19, 20 AND 21). Numbers denoted by a "B" indicate how often a dealer's up card achieves the score denoted, lower winning scores, and busts (for example, an 18B would give you the percentage of times a particular up card reaches scores of 18, 17 AND busts).

Ten-pointers or 10s: The cards that say "10" and the face cards, which all count for 10 points.

Third Baseman: The player who sits in the seat dealt to last by the dealer, immediately to the dealer's right.

3-Level, Notch-Up, Notch-Down, Bet Management System: A 3-tiered betting system developed by the author.

Tip: Chips or money you give to the dealer, as in tipping a waitress. Also known as a "toke." For strategic tipping, see *Blackjack The SMART Way*.

Tip Slot: The slot where the dealer deposits any tips. Dealers typically tap the tips (usually chips) loudly on the table before depositing them in the slot, to alert the floor managers (which is a safeguard against dealers stealing chips).

Toke: A tip for the dealer.

Tray: Where the dealers keep the house's chips (the chips they use to pay off winners, or collect losing bets).

True Count: A card count you arrive at by taking the running count, and dividing it bythe number of decks of cards that have not yet been dealt. (With some systems, the running count is actually divided by fractions of decks.)

True Penetration: The author's term for the exact number of cards that are dealt between shuffles. Introduced in *Cutting Edge Blackjack*, this is highly dependent on the number of betting spots being played.

Unit: The absolute lowest bet you will play. Usually, it coincides with the minimum at the table. If you're at a $5 minimum bet table, a $5 chip will be your "unit." At a $10 table, two $5 chips will be your basic "unit." They don't give you $10 chips, or we'd say here "a $10 chip" would be your unit.) And so on. It's a way of simplifying how you think of your bets, and how you want to raise and lower them.

Up Card: Of the dealer's first two cards, the one that's face up.

Washing: A shuffling procedure when new decks of cards are introduced, whereby the dealer spreads the cards facedown, on the table, and swirls them around, in an attempt to randomize them somewhat.

Weakened Ace (or Aᵂ): The author's term for how the dealer's up card of an

Ace behaves when the dealer does not have a Blackjack. This is the Ace you actually play against, and its stats are considerably weaker vis a vis dealer strength than the overall Ace (where dealer Blackjacks are included).

Weakened 10 (or 10ʷ): The author's term for how the dealer's 10-point up cards behave when the dealer does not have a Blackjack. These are the 10s you actually play against, but, unlike the Weakened Ace, the Weakened 10 is not so much weaker than the overall 10 so as to allow the player to take much advantage of it.

Win/Loss Margin Unit (or WLM): Richard Harvey's term for the number you get when you subtract your losses from your wins (introduced in *Cutting Edge Blackjack*). This has proven to be a very good indicator of your future success. You'll use this number to determine: what Gains Stage you're in; how to bet; and when to leave.

WHAT CRITICS AND READERS
HAVE TO SAY ABOUT
Cutting Edge Blackjack:

"Richard Harvey's as brilliant as Ken Uston was!" – George S., a reader

"Richard Harvey has my *respect*." – Jack S., a reader

"The new book is really fantastic. Lots and lots of info and analysis. I am completely amazed by your facedown card analysis. It makes complete sense and is easy to understand. The Circle of 13 is tops. Ducks & Bucks are really great. Also, WLM is another thing I have not heard anyone else talk about. This book is so complete it feels like no other information on Blackjack Strategy is necessary. Great Job!!!!!" – Wayne H., a reader

"This is the only new book in 40 years that changes *everything*." – Albert D., a reader

"Most other books are just spin offs of Thorp and Braun. You guys have a fresh approach." – Frank L., a reader

"I have both [of Richard Harvey's] books and your tape. I think they are the absolute best on the market ever." – Jim D., a reader

"I will be buying your book as gifts for my friends. The material included in your books is second to none." – Clarence R., a reader

"*Cutting Edge Blackjack* is probably the most informative blackjack book I've ever read!" – Mark C., a reader

"*Cutting Edge Blackjack*...breaks new ground and gives players great new ways to win. [In it you will] learn about his newest discoveries and methods of winning at blackjack, which enable you to make card moves and bets with a precision never before thought possible...Richard Harvey is recognized worldwide as one of the foremost innovators in the field..." – The Learning Exchange

"I've got friends who want to get their hands on my copy [of *Cutting Edge Blackjack*], but they'd better go get their own! I'd never get mine back!" – "At The Casino" columnist Bill Previtti

"In this book [Richard Harvey] disputes most of what is taken for granted by today's blackjack community. He believes that because most of the current material presented for beating the game is based upon a single body of investigation from the 1960s, it doesn't work for the new century – and that the work is actually flawed!...In 12 chunky chapters, he tells you why he believes actual card studies are superior to computer-generated studies; why penetration is such an   important factor; how the number of players affects a player's ability to win; and the impact of shuffling on a player's game. He also explains the   phenomenon he calls the low up-card stiffs effect...His section on how to count at one- and two-deck tables and his establishment of the various categories of face-down cards should make the [player] who loves to explore new possibilities and theories all that more optimistic. *Cutting Edge Blackjack* is loaded with charts and graphs and has a 12-page index at the book's end, which should make isolating specific theories, angles and concepts a bit easier for those who have specific needs." – Midwest Gaming & Travel

"The best source of study [of blackjack], you ask? Richard Harvey's *Cutting Edge Blackjack.* Harvey's newest book is the result of three years of computer research that completely disproves the effectiveness of "basic strategy" and "card counting," two "winning" methods that have been popular since the late '50s." – The Santa Fe Reporter

"[This book] by blackjack guru Richard Harvey offers the first new way of winning at blackjack in more than 40 years...Although [his] research is based upon complicated theoretical mathematics, you don't have to be a math wizard to apply the results to the blackjack table...Most people...can understand the concepts in less than three hours." – The Herald News

"National blackjack expert Harvey...developed a playing system, outlined in his books, that...is beyond the antiquated method of card counting."
– The Arvada Sentinel

"I really like the way you organize and present your data. It is very interesting, and very compelling! There is a TON of material there to digest!" – Brian H., a reader

"It's way ahead of the other books!" – James P., a reader

"I like the fact that Richard Harvey bases his system on his own research. A lot of other authors take what (innovators of the 1960s) said as being handed down in stone – that's Stone Age blackjack!" – George S., a reader

Coming Soon!

Stay in touch with Mystic Ridge Books for exciting upcoming books and products by Richard Harvey!

Here's what's in the works for late 2003 and early 2004:

♦ A new CD version of the popular audio book *Preparing YOU To Win,* called *Richard Harvey's Blackjack PowerPrep.* Previously only available through our web site, **www.blackjacktoday.com**, this will now be on the bookshelves of your favorite neighborhood bookstores! (And if it's not, have your bookstore call us and order it!) This will be out by the summer of 2003.

♦ Practice makes perfect, and that's what Richard Harvey's new blackjack board game, as yet untitled, is all about. Designed to train you how to implement methods discussed in this book, in *Blackjack The SMART Way,* and at Richard Harvey's seminars, this contains some great new learning tools which will really speed along your development as a player. After making good use of this board game, you'll be surprised at how much better you'll do the next time you're at the blackjack table!

♦ Richard Harvey's DVD/Video, not yet named, will cover the full gamut of things you need to know to become a consistent winner, with an emphasis on clear explanations of the many innovative concepts and methods exclusive to the Richard Harvey system that make it so uniquely successful. As many players who've taken Mr. Harvey's seminars have found, some aspects of blackjack are best taught visually, in tabletop demonstrations. This DVD/Video won't disappoint!

♦ Richard Harvey's *third* book. This will contain new material from the author's ongoing computer research as well as a unified, simplified approach that players of all levels can easily understand and apply.

Now, if you're like most loyal Richard Harvey fans, you'll want to be notified the *minute* these books and products are released! So, drop us a line and give us your name, address and phone number and you'll be among the first to find out when they're available! *Write* us, at **Mystic Ridge Books, P.O. Box 66930, Albuquerque, NM 87193**. (Be sure to let us know exactly what future books and products in which you're interested!)

Meanwhile, don't forget to visit our web site for free monthly blackjack tips and other updated information regarding Richard Harvey's books, seminars and products! It's easy to remember: **www.blackjacktoday.com**.

About The Author

Richard Harvey began his blackjack career in Atlantic City after being a victim of corporate layoffs. The system he used, which he'd developed in the two years beforehand, sprang from a love of cards (he was a member of a New York City Bridge club at the time) and math (he'd minored in theoretical math and statistics in college).

His decision to create his own blackjack system was born out of frustration at his lack of success using others' methods, in computer tests. Although his approach has been greatly refined over the years, even his early experiences at the blackjack table were highly profitable. He went on an immediate tear in AC, and hasn't looked back since.

The spark for his first book, *Blackjack The SMART Way* (now a bestseller in its Revised Third Edition and acclaimed worldwide) was a request from his friends that he write an instructional manual for them. (They'd witnessed how often he won at blackjack.) The rest is history.

His latest monumental computer research studies (spanning more than two years) resulted in many incredible historic breakthroughs, as well as the book you now hold in your hand. The end result was his creation of the first entirely new (and better) way of playing the game in more than 42 years. (He then updated *Blackjack The SMART Way* to refresh that book, given the many discoveries he'd made in his most recent research project.)

Since 1999, Mr. Harvey has been on 100+ talk shows in the USA and elsewhere, and he's has been written up in countless favorable newspaper and magazine write-ups.

He continues to play blackjack, do blackjack research, work on future projects (see page 328), and give seminars (see page 330).

He says he is especially proud of the fact that so many readers have gone on to great success using his unique approach to the game.

Take A Seminar!

Mystic Ridge Books is a proud sponsor of Richard Harvey's nationally-acclaimed seminars, held from coast-to-coast. Many players have flown *hundreds of miles* to attend one!

(Get on our mailing list so we can let you know when these events are scheduled! Send your name, address and phone number to: Mystic Ridge Books, P.O. Box 66930, Albuquerque, NM 87193.)

Richard Harvey's newly-updated *Table-Intensive* Blackjack Seminar Experience focuses on Mr. Harvey's *new* research breakthroughs, such as:

1. His leading edge, more precise *Real-time Card Strategy*
2. *New Scientific Standards for Knowing When To Leave*
3. A *State-of-the-Art Betting System*
4. *Strategic Card Analysis*
5. *How Shuffling Affects the Cards and Your Ability to Win* (includes *Shuffle-Tracking)*
6. *How to Determine What The Dealer's HOLE CARD is*
7. *Newly-Discovered Dealer Up Card Vulnerabilities*
8. *His Methods to Take Advantage of the Game's Predictability*
9. *Repeating Phenomena* (from which you can profit)
10. *How the Number of Players Affects Your Probability of Winning*
11. *How to Identify the Facedown Cards at 1– & 2-Deck Tables*

Every *serious* blackjack player owes it to him or herself to attend Richard Harvey's *Table-Intensive* Blackjack Seminar Experience.

Here's just some of the great feedback past seminar-goers have sent us:

♦ "Thanks for the seminar! I thoroughly enjoyed it! There is no doubt in my mind that you understand the game far better than most so-called experts. The material on shuffle tracking was great. I do believe you are on to something (big)." — Ken H.

♦ "I flew (to New Mexico) from California to attend this seminar. Given the quality of instruction and the material, I would not hesitate to repeat the process." — Mark L.

♦ "Went to the tables after the seminar, relieved them of $600...Fantastic!" — Dr. Bob B.

♦ "Since attending your outstanding seminar, I realized just what a novice I was. Now I have been winning *consistently!"* — Jim S.

♦ "Truly a must for all players! It has given me many insights and inside information on the game, dealers and casinos. Thanks!" — Melissa R.

Blackjack is like any other subject for which you have taken courses — it requires *training*. Richard Harvey's *Table-Intensive* Blackjack Seminar Experience demystifies the game, so you'll never ever leave the casino again in frustration. If you've been unhappy with the methods of the past and you're not winning consistently, these events are for *you!*

For more information, visit **www.blackjacktoday.com.**